My Name Is
Caroline

◆

Caroline
Adams Miller

gürze books

My Name is Caroline

Gürze Books
P.O. Box 2238
Carlsbad, CA 92018
(619)434-7533

Cover design by Abacus Graphics, Carlsbad, CA
Cover photo by Linda Rosenthal

The story of my slide into seven years of bulimia and my recovery is true. To protect the anonymity and privacy of others, however, some names, identifying characteristics, and situations have been changed.

NOTE: The author and publisher of this book intend for this publication to provide accurate information. It is sold with the understanding that it is meant to complement, not substitute for, professional medical and/or psychological services.

Library of Congress Cataloging-in-Publication Data
Miller, Caroline Adams, 1961-
    My name is Caroline / by Caroline Adams Miller.
    p. cm.
    ISBN 0-936077-07-7
    1. Miller, Caroline Adams, 1961—Health. 2. Bulimia—Patients—
    United States—Biography. I. Title.
    RC552.B84M55 1988 87-19852
    616.85'2—dc 19
    [B]

2 4 6 8 0 9 7 5 3 1

TO HAYWOOD,
*without whose love and support
this book never would have been possible
and*
TO MY HIGHER POWER,
without Whom nothing would be possible

ACKNOWLEDGMENTS

I AM INDEBTED TO a number of people for their encouragement and advice in deciding to tell the story of my seven-year battle with bulimia and my subsequent recovery.

Nancy Allison, Anne Carey Boucher, Toby Rice Drews, Judy Friedman, and Barbara Kulp helped crystallize my direction at various points in the writing. Denise O'Connell was also an early supporter of my decision to go public.

The vicissitudes of word processing were eased immensely by the patient coaching of Bruce Goldberger, who helped me out of more bungled software and printing snafus than I care to remember.

Others, too numerous to mention, shared their recovery from compulsive overeating and bulimia with me daily, prompting me to include long-forgotten or buried memories of my own in the book. Chief among them are Linda R., Arlene G., Jackie S., Ann G., Linda K., and Diane W. You know who you are.

A major part of my recovery has been my spiritual awakening—a gradual process that William James would call "the educational variety." Pat Reese of Cookeville, Tennessee, has been largely responsible for many of the changes in me, and her foresight and love are greatly appreciated.

A huge thank-you goes to Charlotte Sheedy, who took a chance on an unknown writer, and to Vicky Bijur, my agent, who was an indefatigable cheerleader and advisor throughout the months.

My editor, David Gernert, and his assistant, Lucy Herring, were not just careful readers with astute observations; their good humor and professionalism were invaluable.

Finally, I'd like to thank my family—my parents, Bill and Millicent Adams, my grandmother, Dorothy Roberts Benner, and my sister and brother, Elizabeth and Billy—for their love and support in this venture.

My husband's family—Jane and Hoyle Miller, Ann Elise and Andy Bouchard, Elise and the late Hoyle Miller, and Ron and Ann Swinford—were similarly supportive and enthusiastic throughout.

My husband, Haywood, deserves the biggest round of applause and gratitude. Although it isn't easy to have a wife writing at three A.M., especially when the computer breaks down, he managed to comfort, proofread, and encourage when doubts assailed me. Most of all, he wholeheartedly agreed with my decision to publicize some of the most intimate parts of our marriage in the hopes that others will identify with my story and seek help for their bulimia before it's too late.

INTRODUCTION

When MY NAME IS CAROLINE was first published three years ago, I hoped that my story would inspire others with eating disorders to seek help before their secrecy and denial irreparably harmed their physical and emotional health. Although, I didn't know what kind of response to expect to my book, I was flabbergasted by the avalanche of phone calls and letters that began to stream into my home, and that still arrive daily. To date I have heard from people in thirteen countries varying in age from eight to seventy-four, and ranging from barely literate, poor people to affluent professionals, Olympic medalists, models and housewives. Altogether I've received approximately 10,000 letters and hundreds of phone calls, each of which I have answered personally.

The letters are often heart-breaking. Frequently, they are from parents who are desperate to help their children, but more often they are from men and women who are suffering with anorexia and bulimia, yet are afraid to actively seek nearby help for their problem — either out of shame, embarrassment or fear of the consequences. Many of the letters are ten or more handwritten pages long and include pictures of the writer and his or her family. It's common for the pictures to show beautiful cheerleaders or homecoming queens, whose outward appearances belie their inner turmoil and sadness. Only a trained observer would take note of the subtle signs of an eating disorder, such as a swollen face or awkwardly distended stomach.

I've also received letters from people who have suffered severe consequences as a result of their eating disorder. Among them are prostitution and embezzlement to support a bulimic habit, repeated miscarriages, infertility, jaw displacement, pancreatitis, epilepsy, serious dental erosions, heart abnormalities, colitis and osteoporosis. Often an eating disorder can strain a marriage to the point of divorce.

I also hear from a great number of recovering alcoholics and drug addicts who say that food has suddenly become an overwhelming, unbreakable addiction for them. One of the biggest obstacles they face by not having addressed the food problem is persistent low self-esteem, a devaluing of their progress in beating other addictions, and finally, relapse.

I'm struck by the widely differing attitudes of the individuals who contact me. Most of them are willing to do whatever it takes to recover, they just need a push in the right direction and encouragement from someone who has "been there" to start taking steps. Others, however, are deeply divided about whether they want to get well or not. One call that particularly saddened me came from a 24-year-old bulimic, who was hospitalized for the eighth time. She said that she suffered from facial bruises, such severe joint problems that she required a wheelchair, a torn esophagus that necessitated tube feeding, and brain wave abnormalities. After she detailed her various problems, she asked in a plaintive voice how I had finally "hit bottom" and decided to seek help. Despite the side-effects she had experienced, she said she still wasn't willing to give up her eating disorder, but hoped I would have words that would inspire her. Although we talked for a long time, I was depressed when I hung up because I felt I hadn't really reached her. This type of frustrating conversation, however, is counterbalanced by other grateful calls and letters I receive from people who get into treatment and begin to reclaim their lives a year or two after they have read my book or talked to me.

The extraordinary response to MY NAME IS CAROLINE changed the course of my life. Instead of returning to my former profession, I decided to start a non-profit foundation called F.E.E.D. (The Foundation for Education about Eating Disorders) to assist those who need information about eating disorders, treatment options, and other available help. Sometimes all people want is a friendly voice on the end of the line that will listen non-judgmentally to their despair and pain. What started on a shoestring has blossomed into a nationally-recognized resource that publishes a bi-monthly newsletter, VITALITY!, and that has been featured on numerous radio and television shows.

My professional life is not the only thing that has changed. When I reread MY NAME IS CAROLINE to write this introduction, I was struck by how much I've continued to mature and metamorphose since it was published. The more I've practiced the principles of my self-help group and sought to address some of the behaviors that led me into bulimia, the more confident, joyous and compassionate I've become. I've also weathered some very difficult and emotionally trying times without turning to food, which has given me reserves of strength and confidence that I didn't possess before.

As happy as I have been with the book's reception, I must admit that it has brought some discomfort, too. I frequently find the food I eat being commented on or scrutinized. Sometimes I long to get away from the phone, which at times has rung continuously all day and throughout the night. I've even fended off charges of anorexia, as my body has settled into a lean frame — just like my parents'. At one time these pressures and criticisms would have sent me headlong back into bulimia, but fortunately, the process of recovery brings with it a strong sense of self-love!

The biggest change in my life, however, has been the birth of my son, H. Haywood Miller, IV who joined us on May 7, 1989. Like many women who have had eating disorders, becoming pregnant was not easy for me because of the damage I had inflicted on my body. It took my husband and me two years to conceive. In hindsight, I'm glad I had almost four years of recovery behind me when I did become pregnant because I feared that the weight gain, food cravings and fatigue would disrupt my life and cause a relapse, as I had seen with others. I'm happy to say that with the support of many friends, I survived this experience with a minimum of anxiety and turbulence. In fact, I'm hoping another little Miller will join us before too long.

I'm fond of an Ernest Hemingway quote, "The world breaks everyone and afterward many are strong at the broken places." I like to think that the breaks I've had have enriched and strengthened me, not destroyed me. If you are feeling hurt and broken, this is the ideal time to start healing and using your experiences to build a better, wiser you. Let's unite to provide strength and encouragement to each other.

Please feel free to write me and I'll do what I can to address your concerns. Happily, there are so many more new treatment centers, books, qualified therapists and research studies every year that finding the approach that works best for you isn't a dream anymore, it's a reality.

Caroline Adams Miller

To contact me, please write to:
F.E.E.D.
P.O. Box 799
Middletown, MD 21769

Please enclose a self-addressed, large envelope with enough postage for two ounces of mail. I try to give each letter careful attention, so it may take several weeks to hear from me. . . but you will.

ONE

I WANTED TO EAT. I wanted to eat ice cream. I wanted it immediately.

My brain, crammed moments before with facts for a history paper, clicked off. Nothing mattered now except getting my fix.

I pushed away notes and papers and looked outside. It was starting to snow. It was always snowing or getting ready to snow in Cambridge, Massachusetts, during the endless, gray winters. Harvard's founders had probably delighted in this grim atmosphere, I often thought to myself during my four years there. With such unappealing weather seven months of the year, compounded by a bone-chilling wind that whipped off the Charles River and ruined even mild days, there was often no choice but to hunker down and study.

But tonight's bleak skies and blizzard forecasts could do little to alter my plans. As I shut my books and filed the note-cards away, I mentally rehearsed my now familiar routine. On the way to Harvard Square I would stop at the ice cream shop that had recently opened. There I would get several scoops of some exotic flavor with Oreo cookies crushed in it. That would be step one on this evening's self-destructive journey.

First, though, I had to escape from my roommates without attracting attention. Shrugging on my coat, I casually walked into the living room where three of my four suite-mates were listening to the stereo and studying.

The scene was a cozy one: our spacious quarters at the top of Kirkland House's ivy-covered B entry included a view of the Charles River, where we could see the crew teams bending to their oars as they sliced through the water. A more endearing portrait of collegiate life could not be imagined, I thought as I looked around.

"I'm going up to Lamont Library to check out a book. Does anyone need anything?" I lied, praying no one did.

Lynn, a wiry, intense young woman, looked up with interest. Despite her gaunt appearance she was always looking for ways to burn off extra calories. During our freshman year she had even written out some rules to herself about eating. On weeknights there was to be no eating after six P.M., and on Friday nights she could indulge a bit, but only on protein. I had been impressed by her slimness and ability to stick with such rigid restrictions, but had been unable to duplicate her willpower.

I blanched at the thought of Lynn joining me. I wasn't going to the library; I was going to binge and I had to be alone. The fact that I was bulimic, and had been for more than six years, was my deepest, darkest secret. To the outside world I had it all: good looks, good family, good grades, and athletic abilities. But I also had a side that no one knew about. Almost daily I ate vast quantities of food and got rid of it through vomiting, laxatives, diuretics, syrup of ipecac, or compulsive exercising. And as much as I wanted to stop, I couldn't.

"Well," I faltered, "I'm actually not going straight to the

library. I have to drop an article off at the *Crimson* and check out the sports page layout, and you wouldn't be interested in that."

Lynn sank back into the beanbag chair with that news, disappointed that she wouldn't be able to walk the cold mile. My other two roommates glanced up at me and muttered something about the impending snowstorm, and how I was crazy to be going out in such awful weather.

My abrupt disappearances, ostensibly to get books or go to the *Crimson*, the campus newspaper, were not unusual to them anymore, though. And I could always explain away my suspiciously frequent library excursions with my obsession to make good grades, or with the honors history thesis I was rushing to complete.

Satisfied that I was going to escape from the confines of our suite without anyone tagging along, I slung my backpack over my shoulder and headed for the door. "See you all soon," I gaily cried out as I clattered down the stairs.

Outside I shivered. It was colder and more slippery than I had anticipated. Underneath my blue parka I wore only an old sweatsuit, and my worn-out Nikes were a poor match for the rapidly forming ice base coating the streets. I had also forgotten to bring my gloves, but none of this should have surprised me. When I decided to binge, all unrelated thoughts were shunted to the back of my mind.

Within two minutes I was standing in line at Steve's Ice Cream, scanning the choices I had already memorized. Coconut-cream, banana-mocha, fudge-swirl and butterscotch-marble ice creams all beckoned. I wanted everything but knew I'd attract attention if I ordered four scoops. So I settled on a sedate coconut-chocolate combination with crushed Oreo cookies and took a seat in the corner.

As I sunk my spoon into the ice cream, I thought about how I had learned to practice this crazy behavior. I had been fifteen, enrolled in a top girl's prep school in Washington, D.C. One afternoon I had been eating lunch in the school cafeteria with two friends, Cheryl and Gina, when I noticed they were both eating an extraordinary amount of food. Cheryl had just finished her third bacon, lettuce, and tomato sandwich loaded with mayonnaise and catsup and was prepar-

3

ing to down a stack of ice cream sandwiches that were piled next to her plate.

Eyeing her slender figure, I enviously asked how she managed to stay so slim while eating foods I had only dreamed of since I had begun one of my countless diets in eighth grade.

At my question, Cheryl glanced at Gina and laughed knowingly. She chose not to answer, however, so I just continued to watch them march through several more plates of food, interspersed with ice cream bar breaks.

There was nothing the two girls omitted from their meals. Both ate several bowls of cottage cheese, a few apples and oranges apiece, mountains of mashed potatoes swimming in butter, and stewed tomatoes. The school's dining room style was buffet, so they just made several trips back and forth to the serving tables, weighting down their plates every time.

My own tray forgotten, I kept my eyes riveted on my companions, fascinated by their eating. Cheryl and I were competitive year-round swimmers, but I knew that activity couldn't begin to burn off the gargantuan number of calories she was ingesting. Unlike me, though, she had a slim, muscular body that cut through the water quickly in workouts, so if she had some kind of training secret, I wanted to know what it was.

After what seemed an endless orgy, the two girls groaned and patted their protruding stomachs. "Are you ready?" Cheryl asked Gina. Gina, whose normally flat stomach was straining the buttons of her green seersucker uniform, smiled and nodded.

I followed the two as they dumped their empty plates in the kitchen and headed for the building's front door. They detoured, however, as we neared the exit, instead walking upstairs to the deserted second floor. I followed. "Where are you going?" I pestered.

"Don't tell anyone," Cheryl said conspiratorially as we mounted the stairs, "but we're going to throw up now."

My mouth dropped open in shock. So that's why they had been eating so much! I vaguely recalled hearing about this kind of thing from a classmate several years previously who had commented that her older sister and college friends put

4

feathers down their throats after meals to get rid of their food and stay thin. I had been surprised, but it hadn't had much of an impact on me. Later I had read articles about how bulimia —the binge/purge syndrome—was sweeping the country, but I had never knowingly met anyone who actually indulged in the practice.

I stood outside the bathroom and listened to Cheryl and Gina lose their lunches. I began to feel queasy as I heard them heaving and gasping for several minutes. A few times they called out to each other, either urging the other one on or laughing about what had just come up. "It's great how the ice cream comes up so easily," I heard Cheryl say gleefully.

I was glad the second-floor hall was empty. I would have been appalled if anyone had come to use the bathroom. I could just see me explaining that my two friends had the flu.

Finally Cheryl and Gina emerged, their faces red and puffy, eyes watering. Despite their traumatized physical conditions they both appeared happy, even jubilant. "Do you both do this a lot?" I asked in wonderment.

They nodded, looking at each other and giggling. "Don't tell anyone," Cheryl warned. "If my parents knew, they'd kill me. Besides, my mother is happy if I can just be thin and swim well. She doesn't need to know how."

I promised not to divulge their secret.

"How did you learn to do it?" I pressed Cheryl, a little hurt that she had never confided in me about it. She and I had traded diet secrets for years, going so far as to police each other, especially during the intense summer swimming season.

Cheryl jerked her thumb toward Gina. "Her mom told her how," she said. Gina's mother was a beautiful former model, married to a prominent senator.

Gina chimed in, "My mom says all models do it. It's the only way to be as thin as the agencies want them to be. She doesn't mind me doing it. Sometimes we even do it together!" she laughed.

She and her mother binged and purged together? I couldn't imagine that. My mother wanted me to be thin, too, but not that badly. She just wanted me to eat like her: three meals a day, moderate portions, and no snacks. That was impossible for me, though. I was always going from one crazy diet to the next, convinced that if I just lost a few more pounds with the latest fad, then I would be happy.

I walked back across the street to school with Gina and Cheryl, my mind whirling with what I had just witnessed. Maybe vomiting wasn't such a terrible way to keep weight off. In fact, it sounded like nirvana. If I could eat all my favorite foods—as much as I wanted—and not gain an ounce, then it wouldn't hurt to try it, I reasoned. So as the two girls merrily discussed what they were going to binge on for dinner that night, I decided to give this new "diet" a shot.

Little did I know how much that one afternoon would alter the next six years, wiping almost all joy, enthusiasm, and happiness from my life. Almost overnight I became addicted to binging on huge amounts of food and then purging through a variety of methods. I also became an expert at manipulating, lying, and stealing to support my increasingly expensive habit. I also blamed society for my bulimia, angry that expectations for success included being bright, beautiful, and witty, as well as model-slim. It was just too much pressure for me, and binging and purging was my silent rebellion.

While I had been a weight-conscious, calorie-counting teenager before being introduced to bulimia, my food obsession became all-encompassing as the disease took a firm hold on my mind and body. I became an avid coupon clipper and recipe reader, shopping and cooking with a vengeance and talking endlessly about diets and weight. If I noticed someone with an eating disorder—be it anorexia, bulimia, or spitting chewed-on food out in a napkin—I made fun of the person, belittling him or her to my friends. My own weakness was never admitted; the denial was too strong.

I thought about all these things as I finished my sundae at Steve's. While I worried about my "problem," as I euphemistically called it, I had no overwhelming desire to stop binging. Food was my anaesthetic. If anything bothered me, I usually felt a fleeting sense of relief while eating over it. Just as children are given cookies and other sweets when they feel bad, I faced uncomfortable situations or problems with mountains of coffee cake and other snacks. I never felt any better about myself or my problems when I was through binging, though.

6

In fact, I invariably felt worse—angry, depressed, and frantic. But as much as I hated it, I couldn't break the vicious eating cycle as my coping mechanism.

I looked around Steve's. No one from Kirkland was in sight. Good. If anyone saw me they'd probably figure out what I was doing. I knew, though, that no one would ever say anything to me if they suspected I was bulimic because most people stayed far away from me. My intense shyness and imposing five-ten height gave me an aura of aloofness that most men and women found intimidating. I hated the loneliness, but was grateful that my image afforded me the privacy to continue practicing the eating disorder undetected.

I was aware that some people considered me beautiful. But just as I had been initially surprised at learning that people found me unapproachable, I had been taken aback the first time someone had said I was attractive.

True, I was tall, blond, and had a "California" look, but I had never translated those features into beauty. In fact, during my high school years I had never had a single date. Although popular with my girlfriends, boys had always run the other direction. I had endured countless humiliations of being one of the only girls among my friends not asked out to something, being left standing on dance sidelines, and usually being the one to listen to my friends' trials and tribulations with boyfriends.

I was convinced that my seeming unbecomingness was because I was—at least in my mind—fat and ugly. Usually I would say that to myself in the mirror with great conviction, over and over again, before beginning my purges. Bloated and filled with self-loathing, I would survey my bulging stomach and tormented face and say angrily, "You're nothing but a failure. You are fat and ugly and you will always be fat and ugly!"

The same self-hatred began to fill me as I pushed my sundae glass away and prepared to leave Steve's. Just that day I had been surveying my body in the mirror, vowing that I would drop at least one dress size by the time of my graduation in several months. I had written down instructions to myself about what to eat and what not to eat, ordering myself not to binge. Well, that resolve had clearly disintegrated within a few hours. "You really are a loser if food has got such a grip on you," I thought to myself as I stepped back into the chilly night to continue on my way.

Before I hit the next ice cream parlor, I had to swing by the drugstore to get another tool I used in my endless quest to be thin—laxatives. Although I was planning to find a bathroom to throw up the thousands of calories I was in the process of ingesting, the massive dose of laxatives I would take afterward would scour out any remaining culprit calories.

I wasn't planning to buy the laxatives, though. I was going to steal them, a habit I had fallen into early in my bulimic career because I hadn't wanted the drugstore clerks to suspect that I had an eating disorder. Stealing had also become a form of denial that I was abusing my body: if I wasn't actually buying the laxatives, I wasn't really engaging in the destructive habit, my twisted mind reasoned.

I walked into the CVS Pharmacy and headed for the medications aisle. Reaching for the familiar pink box of pills that I knew from experience would act like Drāno on my intestines, I was about to slip it into my pocket when I noticed a security guard sauntering down the aisle.

My heart started to pound. I was going to be arrested. "Wouldn't that be something?" I thought to myself. Just as I was preparing to exit college in a *magna cum laude* blaze of glory, I would destroy it all with an embarrassing shoplifting charge.

My parents would be stunned. "You have the money to buy things," I could hear them say. "What were you thinking of? What did you need laxatives for?" And then I would have to tell them about the bulimia, which I couldn't do. No one could know that I was anything less than perfect, especially my parents. I needed approval too badly.

I feigned disinterest in the security guard. I would have to try to dispel his suspicions. I quickly loaded my arms with things I didn't need: toothpaste, cotton balls, Tampax, and sugarless gum. Maybe now I would just look like another student taking a break from studying. I bustled toward the counter with my buys, hoping the ruse was a success.

The bored girl at the cash register looked familiar. Was she in one of my classes? Now I definitely couldn't pay for the

8

Correctol. I would just have to manage to steal it without getting caught. I slipped the box into my pocket with a practiced move, praying that all my other purchases would keep the clerk too occupied to notice my actions.

"Hurry, hurry," I mentally urged her as she rung up the purchases. Not only was I eager to get out of the store, but the sundae had whetted my appetite for more food. I knew my mind wouldn't be stilled until I had eaten as much food as I could possibly hold, but I also had to work fast during these binges because the longer the food stayed in my stomach, the less chance I had of getting it back up. If that happened I would have to deal with the thought of gaining weight—a tormenting prospect. The food always had to come up at any cost.

I got outside without a question, half expecting to hear theft-detection alarms clanging or the firm grasp of the guard on my shoulder. But I was safe again. "One of these days," I chided myself, "you are going to get caught." The possible future consequences of my actions didn't interest me much, though. Instant gratification was the name of the game. My thoughts quickly turned to my next stop.

I wound my way through the narrow Cambridge streets to a popular soda shop where I had become wonderful friends with the thick milkshakes that this famous old saloon had been dishing out for decades. Just seeing the ads for the quaint store with its offers of free sundaes at certain hours of the day made me start to think binge thoughts.

Once inside, I gave my order for a double-thick vanilla frappe, as they called it in New England. I gazed at the rows of toppings lining the polished, marble counter and listened to the whirring blender. Colorful jimmies, peanuts, chocolate chips, coconut, and other ice cream accoutrements beckoned. I wanted to ask the woman to toss some jimmies and chocolate chips into my shake, but I knew that normal people didn't do that kind of thing. And I was striving to look and act normal even though I was feeling crazier and crazier by the minute.

I paid for the drink and headed back into the cold night, pulling deeply on the straw and enjoying the icy sweetness. Just as I was letting myself surrender to the numbness this

9

behavior always brought on, I noticed some people I knew coming toward me on the street.

Panicking, I ducked into the Harvard Square newsstand and buried myself in the corner. I didn't look or feel out of place there. On my left were some beefy Italian men ogling spreads in the porn magazines lining the shelves. On my right were two young women wearing long, saffron-colored robes and white turbans, intently discussing "the path." Harvard Square had a reputation for attracting a diversity of people and activities. Buddhists, drug dealers, magicians, and musical performers were part of the changing scenery; among this mélange I just felt like one more weirdo.

Once again certain that the danger of detection had passed, I pressed on to my next destination, David's Cookies. The sugar I had eaten was racing through my body, giving my cravings an even keener edge. My robot personality took over.

David's was redolent of melted butter and chocolate. I quickly picked out two pounds of cookies, which were rolling out of the big Dutch ovens as I watched. They all looked divine, but I settled on a combination of chunky fudge, peanut butterscotch, coconut macaroons, and pecan shortbread. I crammed a few cookies in my mouth while I paid, put the rest in my deep coat pockets, and kept going.

Baskin-Robbins was next. My eyes were glazing over, and my head felt as if a wad of cotton had been inserted where my brain ought to be. Impatient with any delay that prevented me from completing my rounds, I became belligerent, striding down the bumpy sidewalks and making my displeasure known to anyone who impeded my progress.

As I walked into Baskin-Robbins, I felt tears starting in my eyes. I was out of control and nauseated from the richness of the food, but I couldn't stop. I wanted to be back in my room going to sleep. I wanted to be normal.

I glanced at a couple next to me, each buying a single-dip cone of vanilla ice cream. I was angry that they looked happy. I was also angry that they could order a single dip. I could no more order a single dip than an alcoholic could content himself with half a glass of wine. I needed that final gallon of ice cream to quench my sugar craving and to make me sick enough so that all the food would come up easily.

I ordered a mixture of Pralines 'N' Cream and Jamoca Almond Fudge. I also asked for four spoons so the clerk might think I was going to share my gallon with others. No such luck, though. With the cookies in my pockets, I was going to make a huge crunchy mess and finish it all myself.

I paid for my ice cream and headed for the history department's building, where I knew I would find an unoccupied bathroom. It was late and there would not be many people there.

A few minutes later I locked myself into a musty bathroom on the bottom floor of the ancient building. This place was ideal: There was only one toilet; therefore I had utter privacy.

I sat on the floor, coat buttoned, and rested against the wall. I crammed the remaining cookies into the ice cream, sprinkling crumbs everywhere. Discarding all sense of propriety, I began to scoop the mixture into my mouth with two fingers, barely tasting what I was eating.

Faster and faster I worked. I felt as if I was about to give birth to a basketball, and the sweetness of the food was cloying. I no longer wanted it, but there was no turning back. I leaned on my elbow, hoping this position would ease the cramps and fullness I felt.

Scenes of ancient Roman feasts floated through my foggy mind. I remembered reading in history books about lives of indulgence where wealthy men and women would enjoy multicourse meals, punctuated by trips to the vomitorium. In all the illustrations the Romans leaned on their elbows, the position I now found myself in.

I licked the remnants of my ice cream from the carton and looked at my watch. I had left my room less than an hour ago, so my absence wouldn't look suspicious yet. I also had not let much time elapse since the start of my binge, so I probably would be successful in getting it all up.

I threw my coat into the corner of the bathroom and looked at myself in the mirror with disgust. My face looked pudgy. I saw plain features and no cheekbones. I was breaking out, too. There wasn't much good to see. My outside reflected how I felt inside—terrible.

Even in my misery I recognized the ridiculousness of my predicament. I knew a lot of people would have loved to be in my shoes. I was from an upstanding, affluent family in Bethesda, Maryland, and had enjoyed many of life's finest pleasures. I had had awards and laurels heaped upon me from an early age for academic and athletic pursuits, and now I was at a school that many considered the finest in the world.

I was even going to get married in a few months to a wonderful man who had distinguished himself—at least in my eyes—as one of the very few members of the opposite sex who had taken an interest in me at college. We had begun dating in the waning months of my sophomore year and his senior year, but within two weeks I had announced to him that we were going to get married. While I had definitely felt I was in love, I had also had an overwhelming fear that no one else would ever have me. Luckily, he was rather attached to me as well, so I was thrilled when he gave me a beautiful engagement ring.

I had everything to live for. So why was I here again, angry, lonely, and depressed, standing in a bathroom with a grossly distended stomach and wishing I were dead? I stared dully at my reflection.

Enough thinking: it was time to start my purging ritual. Putting the seat of the toilet up, I leaned over the antiseptic-smelling basin and held my hair back with my left hand. I jammed two fingers down my throat and felt the familiar bile rising. Harder and harder I thrust, gouging the back of my throat in the process.

All of a sudden the food came up in gushes, splattering all over the toilet seat, the floor, and my clothes. Disgusted yet elated at my success, I kept probing, trying to make sure I was getting everything up. To make the food come up faster, I balled my hand into a fist and punched my stomach hard, repeating it with a vengeance. I would have black and blue marks there tomorrow.

For several minutes this torturous activity continued. The vomit became tinged with red streaks of blood from my raked throat. Finally I had nothing more to give and was heaving drily, my stomach screaming in pain from the blows and repeated contractions.

Exhausted, filthy, and despondent, I slumped on the floor and began to cry. The back of my hand throbbed where my teeth had scraped away the skin, and my throat was so swollen and sore that it hurt to swallow. "When will this all stop?" I wondered in despair as I lay my cheek against the cold floor and let the sobs overtake my body.

No one who knew me would have recognized this emotional mess on the dirty bathroom floor. I felt like a closet junkie, slowly killing myself with food instead of heroin. While the choice of drugs was different, the obsession and misery were the same. Feeling utterly alone, I stood up and began to clean myself and the bathroom so I could return to my room.

I was bone-tired. Scared, too. For while I hated these binges, hated the powerlessness and misery they stirred up in me, I knew that the degradation and pain would probably not prevent me from returning here tomorrow night to do the same thing again.

TWO

ONE YEAR LATER, AFTER MY WEDDING and move to Baltimore, a small announcement in *The Sun* caught my eye. "Meetings of compulsive overeaters, including bulimics and anorexics, are held daily in various locations in the city," it read. "No dues, no fees, and no scales—just a supportive atmosphere for recovery." A number for a local hotline was included.

I stared at the item, wondering if I had the courage to pick up the phone and find out when and where the next meeting was. Last year I had naively hoped that marriage would release me from the food prison with its freedom from the pressures of school and a commuting relationship, but it hadn't. In fact, my bulimia was getting worse—not better—and I could see how the strain of maintaining the facade of normalcy could cost me my sanity and my marriage.

Haywood, my husband, had no idea that I was in such desperate straits, although I had tried to talk to him about the bulimia within two months of getting married after one particularly rough day of nonstop binging and purging. While he had been surprised and concerned about my tearful confession that night, he had also been emphatic that my problem was merely one of willpower, and that I just needed to be sterner with myself when the food beckoned.

I had immediately regretted opening up to him. He clearly didn't understand what I was going through because willpower had nothing to do with my crazy food obsession. Yes, my competitiveness and determination had helped with grades, swimming, and other activities over the years, but the bulimia had consistently defied all of my best intentions and firm resolve; I knew that recovery would involve more than just promising myself I wouldn't binge or purge. I wasn't sure what that "something" was, though, so I had tried to throw Haywood off by reassuring him that I could probably conquer the bulimia on my own, and that I shouldn't have even mentioned it to him.

Although the months after my confession had been filled with renewed efforts to arrest the bulimia through various fad diets and yet another failed round at Weight Watchers, nothing had changed except for Haywood's new watchfulness of me around food. He even took it upon himself to follow me into the bathroom—especially after meals—to see if I was purging. The net result was to make me indignant and angry that he didn't trust me, and more devious in the ways I plotted and carried out my binges outside of our apartment. While I felt relieved every time I "got away" with it, the increasing strain of keeping up my destructive double life of lies, missing food, and plunging self-esteem was taking a toll on my physical and emotional well-being. In addition, my body was showing the ravages of the disease: my teeth were crumbling, my heartbeat was irregular, I was frequently dizzy, and I never had my period. I knew that death was a possible next step, and that frightened me.

Part of me just wanted to get caught red-handed by friends or relatives so that I could admit the jig was up and that I desperately needed the help I couldn't ask for. But no one ever said anything; my excuses for frequent bathroom forays—menstrual difficulties, indigestion, or contact lens problems—continued to be accepted without anyone batting an eye. I even got sympathy for my "flu" if I happened to emerge from the bathroom with watery eyes, a scratchy throat, or vomit stains on my clothes. And my compulsive exercising was the envy of my more sedentary friends, who thought it was so admirable that I could make myself run nine miles in subzero temperatures after meals.

But while I was able to continue hiding my eating disorder from Haywood and others, I couldn't conceal from him one of its most obvious symptoms: an obsession with my weight and my body. It worried him that my mood could change so quickly from elation to despair if a pair of pants didn't fit right or if I thought my arms looked heavy in a sleeveless dress. And he dreaded the mornings I weighed myself because I was usually miserable afterward, lashing out at him for no good reason and saying things I didn't mean. Once he even made the mistake of telling me that I looked like I had gained a little weight; I had cried for hours and given him the silent treatment when he tried to make up for it. I could tell he was wondering if he had married a Dr. Jekyll and Mr. Hyde character, but I felt powerless to stop myself from being so nasty.

My unhappy reminiscences crowded my mind and caused my eyes to fill with tears. I put down the newspaper and gazed out the window, thinking about the insanity of my life. I didn't like the fact that my food obsession had changed my personality and thinking so dramatically over the years. I couldn't remember a time anymore when I hadn't stared enviously at thin women on the street, hating them for their slender bodies. The same went for models; all it took was a bathing suit or lingerie ad to make my jealousy and self-hatred start to churn.

As I looked at the happy children frolicking in the fountain outside, I thought about the months leading up to our wedding when my concern with my weight and appearance had reached a zenith. Although it should have been one of the happiest periods of my life, it had been one of the worst, primarily because I had tortured myself with images of how I ought to look in my wedding gown.

Foremost in my mind had been the idea that I had to be as slender as possible, and that Haywood ought to be able to put his hands around my waist. I had gotten this latter idea from the "Little House on the Prairie" books by Laura Ingalls Wilder, in which the heroine had been praised because her husband had been able to span her wasp-like waist with his hands on their wedding day. No matter how much air I sucked in, I never got my own hands anywhere even close to touching each other.

Another woman whose body I unsuccessfully tried to emulate for the wedding was Scarlett O'Hara. Although her nineteen-inch waistline was the talk of the *Gone with the Wind* crowd when she married Rhett Butler, my tape measure never went below twenty-four inches even at my thinnest. When I added these two obsessions to the fact that every bridal magazine I studied had page after page of wolfhound-slim women, I felt overwhelming pressure to be as skinny as possible on the big day.

So, in addition to worrying about classes and my senior honors thesis, I tried to run a lot farther than usual and to be extra scrupulous about the food I ate in the last few months before the wedding. I also made a concerted effort not to purge because of the subsequent abdominal bloating which prevented me from wearing any piece of clothing that clung to my body, naturally making gown fittings sheer agony. Vanity also played a part in my resolve not to vomit; I had developed the telltale "chipmunk cheeks" and puffy face most bulimics get from irritated and swollen salivary glands. With bridal pictures fast approaching I knew I had to be more careful.

Not vomiting, however, had simply led me into an increased reliance on laxatives. Whenever I deviated from my planned meals by as much as a bite, or felt the slightest bit too full, I simply downed a handful of laxatives and waited for them to clean me out. What the resultant emptiness usually triggered, however, was the desire to eat again. I reasoned that I hadn't retained any of the calories so I could afford to eat again. It was an ugly catch-22 situation out of which I couldn't find my way.

One drab May afternoon in the middle of my final exams, right before the wedding, I had a distressing conversation with my mother that brought my concern with weight to a head. Our relationship, already strained by years of fighting and bitterness over my food obsession, had reached a breaking point over this issue, and when she brought up the subject of my body that afternoon, it was the equivalent of stepping on a land mine.

"Mrs. Magill told me that you had to let the waist out on your wedding dress the last time you had a fitting," she remarked. "Is there some problem?"

I bristled and felt my defenses start to rise. "Mother, my weight is fine and I look fine," I lied. "Are you criticizing me?"

"No, dear," she remarked placidly. "I just thought that you might want to lose a bit of weight. You were looking heavier than I remember seeing you when you were home, and you even look like you're getting a bit of a double chin. Do you eat desserts?"

Weight again. We could never escape the topic. At least she and my father didn't make me stand on the scale in front of them anymore. Once my father had commented on the tight fit of my jeans and had asked me to weigh myself in front of him so that he and my mother would know what the terrible numbers were. I had felt exposed and vulnerable as I had watched the needle soar upward. My mortification—and rage—at the intrusion into my privacy had been intense.

"Mother, I really have nothing more to say," I answered in a cold voice. "I have to go study now. In case you had forgotten, I am in the middle of exams, and I think that my performance on them is a little more important than how much I weigh, don't you?"

My words were hard and sharp, each one driving a larger wedge between us.

"Caroline, you don't need to get so upset, do you?" my mother said in an exasperated voice. "Why can't we ever have a civilized conversation anymore?"

I felt the tears starting in my eyes. I didn't want to talk to her. I wanted some comfort, not a discussion about my waist size. I steered the conversation to a close and managed to hang up just before the storm of sobs overtook me.

I walked into my bedroom and sat down, looking around forlornly at the green shag rug, single bed, scarred desk, bookcase, and bureau. On my bulletin board was a calendar. Only a month until the wedding. I was going to go crazy.

I stood up, walked over to the mirror, and stared into it. My mother was right; I was too fat. I hopped onto the bed to get a better look at myself. And still no wasp waist. As I turned sideways, peering at my body from every angle and poking the offending bulges, I felt slightly ridiculous. I prayed that none of my roommates would return to the suite unexpectedly.

I continued to survey my misshapen figure for several minutes, finally deciding to try on some clothes to get a better sense of whether or not I had lost any weight.

First I pulled on a pair of jeans. Uh-oh. They felt too tight. "Were they this tight last week?" I thought frantically, starting to panic. I tugged a bit on them to make them looser. But there was no question. They were tighter, and I hadn't washed them and made them shrink, either.

The tears started to flow anew. I was fat and I was going to be a fat bride! No one would think I was pretty at my wedding. Everyone would probably think that it was so surprising that a pudgy girl like me could marry a handsome man like Haywood.

Despairing, I went into the living room and grabbed the phone. Pulling the cord behind me, I carried it into my room and shut the door. I had to do something fast about this situation.

I flipped open the phone book to the "Diet and Weight Management" page. I had tried Weight Watchers a number of times and had fared miserably, so that was out. For some reason, all the lists of food and regulations had made me even more obsessed with my meals, if that was possible. I had also always eaten liberally from the "free foods" list, downing pounds of carrots, asparagus, lettuce, and cucumbers every day. It was no wonder my weight never budged, except to go up.

I quickly dismissed the other weight-control organizations as possible solutions. I needed someone to help me with this bulimia thing first. Maybe that would enable me to get thinner, too. Although I had originally tried binging and purging as a way to lose weight, the method had backfired on me over the years, and now the pounds were adding up because of my inability to completely purge the large quantities of food I was regularly consuming.

My finger ran down the page and stopped at the number of a local hotline for anorexics and bulimics. That looked interesting. I picked up the phone and dialed the number.

A pleasant-sounding woman answered the phone. "This is Esther, may I help you?" Esther sounded so nice and motherly that I just wanted to crawl into her lap and cry on what I was sure was a broad shoulder and ample bosom.

I began apologetically, "I hope you can help me. I think I have bulimia, and I feel like I want to eat right now—actually binge. I'm in the middle of my final exams and I'm getting married next month and the whole world seems to be falling down around me. Sometimes I even want to kill myself to escape from this food obsession," I added in a rush.

"My daughter has bulimia and I know what you are going through," she responded sympathetically. "Just remember that you don't have to eat every time you feel pain. Can you do anything to release stress in a nondestructive way, like walking or writing in a journal?"

"Actually, I run a lot. I try to run every day, but even that doesn't give me any pleasure anymore. I feel guilty if I don't run, and I feel especially guilty if I don't keep increasing my mileage every week."

"That's very common among women like you," Esther chuckled. "You are probably what is called 'pathorexic'—addicted to exercise. Can you stop running so much and find another way to exercise that might be more pleasurable?"

I thought for a minute. Running burned the most calories the quickest. After a binge, there was nothing like a long run to make me feel that I wasn't going to retain any calories. And when I added that to my other weight-control methods, sometimes I was able to escape from my binges with little or no weight gain.

"I'm not sure if I'd enjoy another sport as much," I lied. "What I really want to do, however, is stop binging. Can you help me with that?"

Esther talked for a few minutes, giving me the names of therapists in the Cambridge area who specialized in eating disorders, as well as names of local hospitals that had outpatient eating disorder clinics.

I thanked her for her time and hung up feeling marginally better. While she had certainly been able to relate to my pain, I had silently despaired at the notion of seeing either a therapist or starting counseling at a hospital just as I was graduating. For one thing, I didn't want my parents to know that I was seeing a professional, which would certainly show up in the tuition bills under insurance costs. They would want to know what I needed support for, and in a family that prized willpower and winners, that wouldn't go over very well.

Also, I didn't like the idea of going to a hospital for help. Only real sickies went to hospitals. Feeling more boxed in and hopeless than ever, I simply decided to redouble my efforts to stop binging and purging alone.

In the succeeding weeks and throughout graduation festivities and last-minute wedding preparations, I managed to curtail my eating significantly, genuinely losing my appetite several times in fear of forgetting my vows, tripping in front of the wedding guests, or of not being able to handle the pressures of the big day. A few nights before the wedding, however, disaster struck.

"Caroline, why don't you come over and have dinner with us and just forget about everything for a while?" one of my parents' best friends called to ask three days before the ceremony.

I accepted gratefully. I couldn't wait until the wedding was over. I was especially glad it would be an Episcopal service because the entire ceremony would only last about fifteen minutes. That only left the reception before Haywood and I would be able to escape to the pristine beaches and Planter's Punches of Jamaica to do nothing for a week.

"I can't wait to come," I thanked her.

I arrived at the Nances' house in a new clinging jersey

dress that had a belt. I usually avoided belts like the plague because they emphasized my protruding stomach, but I had managed to diminish the bloat and lose enough weight that I didn't think I looked so bad.

"You look so thin!" Maura, one of the daughters, exclaimed loudly as she greeted me at the door. I preened a bit. The words were like music to my ears. There was not a sweeter phrase in the English language to a bulimic.

Dinner was rather uneventful until the plates were cleared for dessert. A cake appeared that was partly in my honor and partly in honor of Maura's birthday. I blanched. I couldn't possibly eat a piece. If I did, I would never get into my wedding gown. My hands started to sweat. In my mind, one piece of cake could do a tremendous amount of damage. But I couldn't think of a polite way to say I didn't want any.

"Thank you," I murmured as the slim piece of chocolate cake was set down in front of me. It looked tempting. This was one of my favorite binge foods: golden cake with creamy chocolate frosting. Maybe just a few bites wouldn't hurt.

I tuned out the conversations around me and concentrated on the food before me. It was delicious. I tried to savor every morsel, but once I started to eat, I also had to finish the slice quickly. It was like a switch had been tripped in my head. "More!" my mind screamed.

I looked around me. One of the girls had turned the cake down. She was dieting and had lost almost all the weight she had gained at college. She looked great, and I was jealous of her willpower. One of the other daughters was absolutely breathtaking in the perfection of her body, and she was eating her cake with great relish, putting her fork down between bites to laugh about the conversation she was engaged in with her brother. I couldn't dream of putting my fork down between bites. She even looked like she was going to leave part of her cake uneaten.

I stared at her incredulously. How could anyone leave cake on their plate? Maybe that's why she looked so wonderful. I resolved to try that trick as I thought of ways I could maneuver her leftovers to my plate, but finally decided against it when I realized it would draw too much attention to me. Besides, I had to decide whether or not I was going to keep the cake down. My mind was made up as I bid the Nances farewell and journeyed home.

On the way, I stopped at a supermarket and went inside. As I headed for the laxatives, I tried to talk myself out of the impending overdose.

"It was only one piece of cake—that's not so bad," I reasoned with myself. But then I thought of the rest of the dinner. I had eaten a helping of steak, corn on the cob, and some tomato slices. Too much, I decided. Steak was fattening. I would have to go through with the purge.

I bought the box of laxatives and a diet soda to wash down the pills, and went out to my car. My stomach started to churn as I unwrapped the bright pink pills. The extreme nausea and malaise that always accompanied a laxative overdose was so intense that even looking at the shiny pills made me feel sick. My college psychology courses had explained in great detail why I had developed an unpleasant physical association with these pills. But even an intellectual understanding of how awful I would feel the next morning had no power to stop me from starting to swallow.

I took a swig of the soda and gulped eight of the pills. Ugh. They slid easily down my throat as I drank again, hoping the artificial soda taste could mask the acrid taste of the pills. I gulped eight more. The package only had twenty-four tablets. "Maybe I'd better take them all," I told myself. "The thinner the better."

I took the remaining pills and tossed the carton into the street. No evidence now of my actions, except for the bile starting to rise in my throat. It was going to be a long night, I thought grimly as I sped home.

In the two days preceding my wedding I spent most of the time in the bathroom. Nausea and fright, I pleaded, as my parents looked at me questioningly every time I disappeared looking slightly green. I wasn't able to keep much real food down either. And I was so drained from the overdose that I slept for hours and hours at a stretch, grateful that every time I woke up the wedding was that much closer.

June 18, 1983, dawned sunny and muggy. It was going to be one of those dreadful days so common to Washington, D.C., in the summer. I still felt queasy from the laxatives, and the heat wasn't making me feel any better. Besides that, my dress weighed a good ten pounds and I dreaded the thought of donning the massive white petticoat and being laced into the yards of taffeta and silk.

Finally, it was time to leave for the church's 2 P.M. ceremony. My curls were already wilting and I was much weaker than I had anticipated. I sank gratefully into the back seat of the limousine that waited in our driveway, wishing only that the ride to the church was longer than the ten minutes it took to get there.

My father and sister complimented me. "You look beautiful, dear," my dad said approvingly. And my older sister, Elizabeth, chimed in, "You look great in that dress. You look so thin!" I was thankful for their words. Maybe all the pain was worth it if I could be slender on this important day.

Washington's National Cathedral is a national treasure, so tourists are never barred from the church. Nevertheless it was disconcerting to have Japanese men and women giggling and snapping pictures of me as I lined up with my father in the main aisle, preparing for the long walk up to the enclosed Great Choir.

"Jesu, Joy of Man's Desiring" started on the organ. That was our cue to start marching. The deep chords resonated in the marble floors. I felt as if I was in the center of the universe.

All of a sudden we were up the steps and in the Great Choir. The alabaster, larger-than-life-size statue of Jesus on the High Altar stared down at us. I dimly saw Haywood ahead, his six-three form clearly outlined by the dark colors of his morning suit. I saw his father, his co-best man, poke him, as if to say, "Here she comes!"

On both sides of me I saw nothing but rows upon rows of people. "Should I look to the left or the right?" I wondered. I decided to concentrate on my friends and I smiled what I hoped was a broad smile at the people to my left.

I saw my college roommates and high school friends up in front. They were crying. All of a sudden the day took on significance. I was getting married! It had certainly not sunk in before. I had just kept moving toward the wedding, not stopping to think. In fact, I had occasionally felt like an actress playing a part in an absurd drama. Me, get married? It had never seemed possible, so I had never stopped to dwell on it.

Then I saw my mother and beside her, my grandmother, Donny. Both were beautiful in their silver-gray outfits. My mother was achingly thin. I tried to smile at her when I noticed, to my great surprise, that she and Donny had tears glistening in their eyes, too. This day was certainly getting heavy. I stifled an urge to laugh, my usual way of dealing with nervousness.

My father and I finally reached the front of the church, where I mustered a smile at Haywood. He looked thin and tired, too, and dark circles rimmed his brown eyes. I knew he couldn't wait until everything was over and we could finally be alone together. Our two-year engagement had been punctuated by dozens of weeks apart, and we were both eager to end that lonely cycle.

Before I knew it, we were kissing happily as man and wife, turning to face the crowds. "Let's walk slowly," I whispered, determined to make eye contact with some of the hundreds of people who had come. "The idea is to walk briskly," Haywood responded, hustling us out of the cathedral before I could protest.

My main memory of the reception in the Gothic building next door is the giant carrot wedding cake I had specially requested. Starving after not having eaten much for days, I hungrily devoured several pieces, partly because I knew I would never have to diet to get into my wedding dress again. I partook of the elaborate buffet, too. Greedily munching on kiwi fruit and rare roast beef between greeting people, I didn't stop to think that it probably wasn't seemly behavior for a bride at her own reception.

Several hot hours later, Haywood and I made our way upstairs to one of the small rooms visiting preachers and other church visitors usually stayed in. Our going-away clothes were laid out on the bed with a magnum of iced champagne glistening in a bucket on the bureau. "To marriage!" we giggled as we quickly shed our clothes and headed for the shower, only to discover that priests only take baths.

It was not long afterward that we departed through a

hailstorm of rice for the Ritz-Carlton Hotel, where we were lodged in a palatial three-room suite with extras ranging from Godiva chocolates and brandy, to heated robes and telephones in the bathrooms. I started our marriage in true form by binging on all the chocolates and a magnificent fruit and cheese basket while Haywood polished off the brandy and a bottle of chilled wine.

I paused in my reverie to observe the happy children out my window. When was the last time I had been that spontaneous and carefree? I couldn't remember. Suddenly, I was hit hard with the full realization of what my food obsession had robbed from my life. I also knew that while I had started my marriage with a binge, I didn't want to end it with one. I reached for the phone and dialed the hotline number.

Two nights later I sat in front of a solid brownstone church, dubiously watching a procession of men and women stream into a side door through lightly falling snow. Doubts assailed me. Was I really sick enough to need help? Maybe if I just tried a little harder not to binge, or ate a little differently, I could curtail the bulimia on my own.

But even as I tried to talk myself into leaving, I knew that I had reached the end of the road. I hadn't been able to stop binging or purging on my own for good for seven years, and none of the diets or behavior modification tactics I had tried had helped. It was this or a hospital clinic. At least this was free, so I had nothing to lose. Just then there was a knock on my car window.

"Are you going into the meeting?" a pretty girl queried as I rolled the window down. "You just looked kind of lost and I thought you might need to know where to go," she continued in a friendly voice.

There was no turning back now. I was committed to going to the meeting. Maybe if I sat in the back and didn't open my mouth, no one else would notice me. The girl—her name was Janice—walked inside with me and said she would be happy to talk to me afterward if there was anything I didn't understand. I thanked her and settled into a folding chair in the corner of the room, arms crossed defensively across my chest.

I wasn't prepared for what followed. After a short explanation of how the group functioned—no obligations, no fees, and no diets, only a willingness to stop eating compulsively and help others stop, too—several people shared briefly about the "tools" of the program. As I heard writing, phone calls, literature, service, abstinence, sponsorship, and meetings outlined as helpful aids to recovery from compulsive overeating, I started to relax. I liked to write; if that would help me stop binging somehow, I wanted to hear what these people had to say. The meeting was then turned over to the main speaker.

"Hi, I'm Bill, a recovering compulsive overeater," one man began.

"Hi, Bill," the group chorused.

Bill then talked about his obsession with food and how he had never felt good enough about himself to buy new clothes or go on dates. I was surprised. I didn't know men suffered as much as women about weight and food issues. I thought it was only a woman's obsession. He continued on for several minutes, describing how he was married to a former bulimic and that he had not only bought her binge foods for her at one time, but that he had held the grocery bag for her to vomit into.

I shifted in my seat to get a better look at him. He didn't look too unusual. In fact, he looked like a nice man. And from what he was saying, it sounded as if he still loved his wife despite her bulimia, and that she had a supportive circle of friends in the program who were helping her recover.

I was thunderstruck at the notion that it might be possible for people to be understanding of my problem and not run away in horror at the mention of it. Outside of Haywood, no one knew about my bulimia because I was afraid I would be treated like a leper if I confided in anyone. And I hadn't even let Haywood in on the more sordid details of my past because I was sure he would be horrified. Here, to my great surprise, bulimia was being discussed almost nonchalantly.

Several people raised their hands when Bill finished and talked about themselves and issues they were currently wrestling with without turning to food for solace. The situations they described ranged from dealing with troublesome co-workers to not binging during pregnancy. The shared thread in their dialogues was that they were experiencing and deal-

27

ing with things that made them angry and uncomfortable, but weren't reacting to these pressures by eating.

My mind was a jumble during the hour-long meeting. These men and women were giving me a lot to think about. Every single person said something that struck a responsive chord within me. And the honesty of their statements took me aback. Many were baring their souls to this group of fifty or so people without embarrassment, and some were even crying. I was intrigued.

The meeting ended with the group standing and grasping each other's hands. I tried to think of an unobtrusive way to avoid this. I didn't hold anyone's hand, not even Haywood's. Touching or expressing any kind of emotion was *verboten* to me.

Too late. The women on either side of me grabbed my hands and smiled as they bowed their heads. In unison the group intoned the Lord's Prayer.

"Wait a minute," I thought. "This isn't for me at all." I kept my lips closed during the prayer and eagerly shook myself free of the offending hands when it was over.

Then everyone started to hug. I had had enough. I escaped from the embraces and backed toward the door, but not before Janice reappeared and guided me to a table filled with literature.

"Would you like to go out for some coffee and talk?" she asked.

"No, thank you," I responded. "I must get home. My husband doesn't know where I am."

"Please keep coming back," she said. "Is there anything that was said that you didn't understand?" I hesitated; she looked so friendly and open that I thought she might be understanding of my pain.

"I think I'm bulimic," I surprised myself by saying. "Can I keep coming back if that's my only problem? I don't think I have to lose a whole lot of weight."

Janice's kindness had caught me off guard, as had my sudden admission of my own problem.

"I was bulimic for years," she laughed. "I read every book I could find about eating and diets, but nothing ever helped me. Doctors, psychiatrists, the whole nine yards—I did it all.

But it wasn't until I found a group of people willing to talk honestly about their obsession with food, and who could tell me how they had begun to live without binging as a crutch, that I got well.

"While what you heard today may not seem like a very effective kind of program at first," she continued, "I promise you that if you keep coming back and listening, and are willing to follow the steps of the program, you'll be able to stop binging, too."

I looked at Janice in amazement. Not only was she pretty, but she was slim, her features were well-defined, and her skin was clear. I thought unhappily of my blemishes and puffy face. Maybe she knew something that could be helpful. I promised to give the program a try.

"Here are the places where we meet," she said, handing me a piece of paper with more than fifty meetings listed in all corners of the city. "We advise that people go to at least six before making up their minds whether this program will work for them. But I can promise you that if it got me well, it can get you well, too."

With that, she scribbled her phone number on the sheet and left, urging me to call her if I wanted to talk further.

I filled my hands with literature, eagerly taking pamphlets which addressed all aspects of eating and compulsive behavior. My mind had absorbed enough so I headed for my car.

Although snow was a rarity in the mild Baltimore climate, enough had fallen during the meeting that the world outside resembled a fairyland. A huge Scotch pine near the church's front door was frosted with the white powder, making me think of the gingerbread cookies I had thickly iced and eaten as a child. The streets and telephone lines were likewise blanketed with snow, and the only sound breaking the silence was the tolling of the church bells.

I started to feel lighter, even happy. There was something good about this organization, and I knew that I would have to come back to another meeting. I had heard too much that spoke to my gut-level emotions not to come back. At the very least, the stories that had spilled from people's lips were fascinating. I had always heard that truth was stranger than fiction, and the tales I had just listened to were better than any soap opera I had ever watched.

I unlocked my car door and slid into the driver's seat, watching the departing people stop to congregate in animated clusters. They looked as if they were all friends. Maybe if I kept coming back, I would have them as friends too. I knew no one in Baltimore outside of my work colleagues, and the thought of having at least one or two new people to talk to outside my job was welcome. If for no other reason than to meet people, I would come back next Friday, I promised myself.

I started my car and felt inexplicable joy. "You are going to get well" suddenly flashed through my brain. "You are going to stop the binging, Caroline," I heard distinctly inside my head.

I didn't question my inner voice. I knew that I had reached the end of a long, painful road and that my recovery had just begun.

THREE

I CRACKED MY NEW NOTEBOOK open to the first page. The fresh smell of unused paper reminded me of the thrill I used to receive when buying my school supplies every September. I thought the world and my abilities were limitless when I had blank paper and ballpoint pens. Anything was possible with these two items.

I dated the page April 7, 1984. This was the salutation to my journal. I had kept diaries before, but I had never put any of my deepest thoughts in them. Somehow they had all begun and ended with diets and lists of food and calories. The despair of looking at my body had usually triggered some kind of introspection, with the opening line of any diary usually running something like: "This time I'm really going to do it. I'm really going to lose enough weight to become the person I hope to be."

This journal was going to be different. In the meetings I had been attending in recent weeks I had heard repeatedly that writing one's thoughts, fears, resentments, and other feelings was one of the keys to stopping compulsive overeating. I enjoyed writing, and this "tool" seemed easy enough, so I decided to give it a try. I wasn't sure just how it was going to help me, but I had bought the lime green Spiral notebook anyway and was now prepared for the catharsis.

"Why don't you write about your first memories of abusing food?" one woman suggested to me after a meeting. "Just let your mind go. Free-associate. And don't write for perfection. Just write whatever comes to you. It'll help, I promise you."

Abusing food. I had lots of memories of abusing food. In fact, I had to stop and think carefully for several minutes about when I had ever had a "normal" relationship with food. It seemed that starting very early I had made decisions about "good" and "bad" foods—substances that would either render me willowy or relegate me forever to the ranks of the forbidden fat, society's outcasts.

In college I had certainly abused food. I had often been the first one at meals and the last to leave, finding comfort in great quantities of the mass-produced food. When I was on a binge, I often went alone from one dining hall to the next, furtively eating in a corner, hoping no one would notice me. I had also stolen food, squirreling away raisin bread, peanut butter, and carrots in my room to eat whenever the urge struck.

I had also abused food throughout high school, raiding candy machines and fast-food places, eating in stairwells, bathrooms, and cars. I had hidden food under my bed, in my desk, and in my bookbag, and the pockets of my clothes were always filled with crumbs and Sweet 'N Low packages. My high school classmates had even recognized my obsession with sweets by giving me the "Sweet 'N Low Award" in our yearbook. But how early had this obsession with food and weight started?

My languid train of thought stopped abruptly on a nearly forgotten scene in a Howard Johnson's dining room. I saw myself as a young girl of about eight, surrounded by my family at a lunch table. I loved eating at Howard Johnson's. I could get all kinds of delicious items there that we never had at home, like french fries drenched in ketchup. The nine words that changed the way I felt about food for the next fourteen years were uttered in this happy atmosphere.

"And the vanilla milkshake goes to the heavy one," my father said playfully to the waitress.

My mind snapped to attention. Was he talking about me? A new, uneasy feeling crept into my being. I had just heard an adjective used to describe me that was totally unfamiliar. I was used to hearing people call me bright, funny, tall, big, athletic, and helpful. But heavy?

My father smiled indulgently at me. "She's not heavy," the waitress protested with a laugh. She had probably felt the same humiliation at another time, I now thought as I jotted down the scene and my hurt, probing my mind for details. The only image that filled my head, though, was of an eight-year-old girl with pain in her eyes, hearing the word "heavy" sounding again and again in her head.

Heavy, heavy, heavy. I am heavy. Does that mean I have to diet?, the eight-year old girl wondered. Only grown ladies and obese children go on diets! They were the ones who bought those diet chocolate milkshakes called "Metrecal" in the supermarket, and who were featured in magazine and television ads touting the virtues of weight loss through the latest, greatest diet system—Ayds, Figurines, Diet Workshop, or whatever. I didn't want to do any of that, but if I was heavy I would perhaps have to submit to a similar kind of unappealing regimen. I would have to give up things like Howard Johnson's milkshakes. The thought was abhorrent.

Normally a cutup, I remember being strangely subdued during the rest of the meal, looking over at my father for some sort of confirmation that he still loved me. My whole world had just turned upside-down. I was one of the thoughtless ones at school who made fun of the fat girls in my class and now I felt like one of them. Would people taunt me, too?

I thought of poor Leslie, a hefty girl in my third grade class who always had the drabbest lunches of anyone. While the rest of us had mothers who packed us mayonnaise and bologna sandwiches and macaroon cookies, Leslie always just had a few crackers with a smidgen of cheese, two stalks of celery, and an orange. Her doctor had put her on a special diet to lose fifteen pounds, she told us. She always responded to our cruel comments somewhat sheepishly as she turned a bright shade of pink, embarrassed by the negative attention.

I knew I wasn't as fat as Leslie, but maybe I was heading in that direction, I rationalized to myself. My father couldn't possibly mean to hurt my feelings; he was probably just trying to save me from becoming miserable like Leslie. But clearly, I now saw, I would have to be more vigilant in the future about what I ate and didn't eat.

When the milkshake arrived I drank it, but my pleasure was tainted. From that day on, guilt was my silent partner every time I ate anything that wasn't "healthy" or low-calorie.

I finished describing this scene in my journal with satisfaction that I had identified the genesis of my preoccupation with food. But my quietude was quickly replaced with hot, recriminating anger toward my father. How could he have laid that kind of guilt trip on me at such an early age? Did he have any idea what he had unleashed in me as a result of that one, unthinking comment?

For a moment I sat paralyzed at my desk, too emotional to think clearly. Waves of rage washed over me—toward my parents, toward people who had commented over the years about my large size and strange eating habits, and toward society for giving half the country a skinny ideal to meet that was unhealthy and all but impossible to reach and maintain.

This simple act of writing had unlocked an anger so fierce that I couldn't move. Obviously I was the victim of other people's cruelty. At least I could now direct all the venom I had formerly reserved for myself toward others—in meetings, in my journal, or in punitive actions. Was recovery this easy? Were we supposed to just identify all the people who had hurt our feelings and despise them? I stared out the window at the chattering birds and riotous mixture of azalea bushes and tulips in our apartment's courtyard, confused.

As I pondered this question, I thought of something I had heard the previous night at a meeting. An older woman, Jane, had spoken about her lifelong obsession with food, and her

34

mother's unrelenting emphasis on everyone in the family, particularly her daughters, being slim.

"Eat lightly, dear," her mother would call after her as she went out on a date. "Boys don't like to dance with fat girls!" In a blind rage at this comment, Jane would then eat everything in sight for the rest of the week, thinking she was getting back at her mother. After attending meetings, though, she had realized that she was only hurting herself.

"For a long time after coming into the program, I blamed my food obsession on my parents because they always commented on my weight, monitored my meals, and made me feel inadequate," she explained. "It was a nice change from blaming myself for my 'lack of willpower,' or whatever else I thought was wrong with me. So I spent my whole first year in the program being angry at them, and then wondering why I wasn't feeling any better about myself or losing any weight.

"Then one day after a meeting, someone gently said to me, 'Why don't you take a look at the fact that whenever you point a finger, three more are pointing back at you?' That one comment forced me to look hard at myself and see that no one had ever held me down and made me eat, and that I alone was responsible for my eating problem. Once I faced that, my real recovery began."

Jane's words struck a resonant chord within me now. Was I just pointing fingers? Was I responsible for my eating disorder? I didn't want to pursue this train of thought, though. First things first. I had identified my earliest memory of feeling insecure about my eating, and that was enough work for one day. Deep inside, I also knew that I couldn't shoulder responsibility for the bulimia yet. For years I had excoriated myself for my bizarre eating habits and had developed a healthy case of low self-esteem. The last thing I needed to do right now was face the fact that I couldn't blame anyone else for it.

I picked up my pen to start writing again, deciding to spend some time describing the athletic and academic pressures I had lived with since childhood. I could just be factual about this, and I knew that it connected somehow with my abuse of food. Perhaps putting it on paper would help clarify the tie-in.

"The competition to get into the 'right' schools and to get onto the 'right' track leading to the 'right' Ivy League school begins around the age of three in Washington," I wrote neatly. "Very few children of intelligent and aspiring parents are immune to this intense pressure to be bright and successful. It did a number on me and a lot of the boys and girls I grew up with."

This statement was true, documented every year in The Washington *Post*'s "Style" section, which annually runs a hilarious article on preschool mania. It focuses on the great lengths to which prominent parents go to to see that their precious Bobby or cute Sarah gets into one of the area's elite nursery schools. The idea is to get your child into the right place early so that prestigious schools and high-paying professions will follow as naturally as the domino effect.

Otherwise honorable and self-assured men and women have been known to offer vast sums of money and other inducements to school directors to admit their children, and some of the city's most well-known businessmen, television anchors, and politicians are often reduced to tears and gelatinous masses of insecurity when their children are refused admission. "Janie will be stunted for life," they tearfully cry to friends. "She'll never be a doctor now!"

When I was three I was admitted to the Concord School —one of the "right" places—a tiny nursery school nestled in the basement of a church on the National Cathedral's grounds. I remember nothing of the competition that surely preceded my entry there. In fact, my memories of the two years I spent there are mostly of our daily drills from the phonetics chart. In unison, my class—a small group of boys and girls—faced a huge, colorful chart and recited, "*F* is for Fan, *Wh* is for Wheel, *P* is for Pig," accentuating the sounds of the first letters.

Buried in my parents' basement is my one souvenir from this school, a rudimentary glitter-coated calendar I assembled. The glitter must have been my ingenious contribution to the effort. A smiling snapshot of me is affixed to the top, surrounded by masses of dolls and blocks. The most prominent feature of the picture is a big, black tooth next to my two front teeth that I had created earlier that year in a blind rage.

Liz, my older sister by barely fourteen months, had committed the unforgivable sin of beating me to the newspaper lying outside our house one morning. By doing this, she had usurped my role as the obedient, pleasing child who needed constant positive strokes to feel worthwhile. In frustration and anger, I had thrown my face against a stone wall in the front yard, striking my tooth forcefully on the ledge and killing the roots. The tooth had turned a dirty brown soon afterward and we had all waited patiently for nature to take its course and cause it to fall out, removing our constant reminder of my willfulness.

Kindergarten was the next step after the Concord School. Unless you wanted to send your child to one of the local public schools, which had decent if not great reputations, a battery of tests had to be undergone by the child in question to determine his or her I.Q. and ability to do advanced work in the private schools. Liz had begun attending a public school in our neighborhood and seeing the lack of rigor in her school day, my parents had decided to try to send me the other route.

One brittle winter day, my father drove me to a church in Bethesda, where an outstanding kindergarten through third grade school had been founded several years previously. The graduates of Norwood Parish School were rumored to all be bound for some of the area's best prep schools afterward: Sidwell Friends, Landon, Holton-Arms, National Cathedral, and St. Albans. Getting in had already become a feat worthy of cocktail party conversation and jealousy. One of the ways of weeding out the applicants was performance on the Stanford-Binet Intelligence Test, which I was now scheduled to take at the ripe age of four.

A nondescript woman in a rust-colored dress and pearls came to get me from my father's lap in the reception area, where several other parents were protectively clasping their children and glancing at the competition while waiting their turn. I didn't really understand the purpose of the session I was about to undergo. My dad had told me that I would be playing games, which was fine with me. He looked incredibly nervous for a game-playing session, though, I thought as I was led off.

For one hour I put puzzles together, drew pictures, and

answered questions that seemed pointless. Every now and then the benign-looking woman nodded thoughtfully and wrote a few words on the pad in front of her. She seemed fascinated by every move I made, and when I repeatedly asked what games were coming next, she was especially interested, scrawling notes with a knowing smile.

Two months later my parents received a one-page letter from Norwood's headmistress, summarizing my intelligence and personality based on the one hour I had spent there. After reporting on my puzzle-solving ability and overwhelming curiosity, the letter concluded that I had "superior" intellectual skills and that the school would be honored to have me.

My parents were thrilled. Going to Norwood wasn't inexpensive and there would have to be some sacrifices made, but it boded well for the future. The next two rounds—getting into a prep school and then getting into college—would be difficult, but they were a few years off yet, and Norwood was an important step on the path.

I paused for a moment in my writing to stretch and massage my aching hands. I had been hunched over my journal for more than an hour, scribbling sentences and half phrases that flowed through my head. I felt as if I had opened Pandora's Box; some of the scenes I had described were ones I hadn't thought about for twenty years, and each one had awakened companion memories that brought powerful emotions. In remembering the little girl with the blackened tooth, I had been overwhelmed with confusion and grief. Throwing myself against a wall must have hurt a great deal! How could I have been that desperate for approval? Had that self-destructive drive been part of what had led me into the bulimia? My mind felt overloaded with information.

I walked around the apartment, fighting the familiar itch to eat whenever I didn't want to face something unpleasant. It was only ten A.M. I had eaten breakfast at five A.M. and now, five hours later, I was feeling hungry for lunch. But if I ate now I wouldn't have anything to look forward to when the rest of the world's lunchtime rolled around. And the program suggested that three meals a day, with nothing in between, was one of the important ways to control cravings and put food back into proper perspective while learning how to cope with life's daily pressures.

Thinking about eating was making my dilemma worse. I decided to read some of the reams of literature I had collected at the meetings. "Here, take these and keep them by your bed and in your car," one woman had urged me at a recent gathering. "I even carry them around in my purse so that if I ever have a spare moment somewhere I can fill it with program thoughts."

I stretched out on my bed with a bright pink pamphlet on compulsive overeating. In just a few paragraphs I read a perfect summary of my obsession. Whoever had written this description of the overwhelming urge to binge had hit the nail on the head. It said that abstaining from compulsive overeating was more than just a physical act; it was a learned emotional reaction. Whenever I wanted to just have that one little, compulsive bite, I should look at what was going on in my life: Was I depressed? Angry? Scared? Whatever it was, I should just feel the emotions and let them pass rather than dulling them with food. Life was for living, and feelings were a natural part that we didn't have to run away from. It also said that one bite was always too much and that fifteen were never enough. That certainly was accurate.

The pamphlet cautioned that I would experience periodic, powerful urges to have just one little bite of something, but that with time these would completely leave me. Every time I didn't give in to that longing voice I would be building insurance against a future slip.

I picked up the newspaper to divert myself from the very definite cravings that were filling my thoughts. I flipped to the lifestyle section, where there was a big article on England's future queen, Lady Diana Spenser, accompanied by a number of pictures taken of her since the announcement of her engagement to Prince Charles and the birth of her first child.

"What a remarkable transformation!" I marveled to myself as I surveyed the images. In the earliest pictures Diana had a full face and a sweet, wistful smile. She even filled out her clothes. More recent pictures, though, were much different. Her face looked drawn, her clothes hung loosely, and her arms were downright scrawny.

The article waxed rhapsodic about her "new" and "regal" figure, breathlessly reporting that designers were falling all over themselves to drape her in their creations because of her exquisite proportions and majestic bearing. This had all come about after her five-nine body had shrunk from a "puppy-fat" size 12 to a size 6 or 8.

I gulped uncomfortably. I was a size 12. Did that mean I looked as plump as a puppy, too? The last time I remembered being a size 6 was when I was six. How could anyone be that thin at that height? But the article unquestionably left the reader feeling that thinner was more beautiful, and that we American women would be wise to copy Diana's meager intake: some cereal, a bit of tuna fish, and perhaps a cup of yogurt if she wasn't too busy to think of it.

I tossed the paper aside. My jealousy was rising and the little green monster inside was beginning to take over. I didn't like thinking that someone could be as pretty or as thin as Lady Di. I knew I'd never be a size six again even if I devoted my life to it. I loved food too much. I would probably die if I tried to starve myself like that, I thought miserably.

I picked up the phone to call a woman I had met at a meeting. I had learned that the phone was important because compulsive overeating was a disease of isolation, and that staying in close touch with people like myself between meetings was not only supposed to teach me to reach out for help, but it was also a time when I could hear others tell me they had done the same things with food as I had. This latter fact was crucial to me because no one looked or sounded shocked when I related some of my grimmer eating forays. Finally, I was feeling as if I wasn't the strangest and sickest person in the world anymore. If these people could accept and love me as I was, flaws and all, then perhaps I could start accepting myself too, I was beginning to believe.

Sandy would surely understand my urge to eat right now, I decided as I dialed her number. I had heard her speak one night about how she used to drive crazily from one convenience store to another in her nightgown and a raincoat, buying junk food from each one and then eating in a frenzy while she continued on to the next one. At thirty-one she said that she had thought her life was over because she would eat for hours and then fall into a stuporous sleep, waking up the next day bloated and remorseful, and unable to fit into the previous day's outfit. "I don't know why I did it," she told the assembled group that evening, "but I also know that as hard as I tried to stop I was completely powerless over my cravings."

Sandy answered the phone on the first ring.

"Hi Sandy, this is Caroline. Do you remember me from the meeting?"

"Of course I do. How are you doing today?"

"Well, I'm really fighting the urge to eat right now," I said. "I ate breakfast really early and I want lunch now."

"Hmmm. What did you eat for breakfast? Did you have enough?"

Enough? No one had ever asked me if I had had enough. I thought the purpose of a diet was not to have "enough," but to be deprived—to never feel satisfied.

"I think I had enough. I had some cereal and cottage cheese and a piece of fruit."

"That sounds fine. What are you planning to have for lunch?"

I wasn't sure, and I told her so. What I really wanted was a huge salad that would fill me up until dinner.

"You know you're playing with fire by not calling someone every morning and outlining your day's meal plan," Sandy remarked. "I know that I personally cannot afford to simply open the refrigerator door before every meal and then decide what to eat. When I do that I am more likely to have tastes of everything while I'm just standing there, and before I know it I've eaten a lot but I'm not satisfied and I'm not sure just what I've had."

"Do you actually call someone and tell them what you will eat for all three meals?" I asked, somewhat incredulously. I would feel self-conscious calling someone and reciting my meal plan. Besides, everyone had told me for years that I ate crazy foods and weird combinations, so I certainly didn't want to let anyone in on that secret. I didn't need one more person commenting on my food, making me feel stupid and inferior.

"Look," she said simply, "I abused food for years. I spent hundreds of dollars buying sugary and starchy foods and eating until I thought I would die. I bounced checks to get food and went to money machines in dangerous parts of town for binge money when the urge to eat struck. I hated myself and everyone around me. I felt worthless and I couldn't sustain any kind of relationship with a man because my love affair was with food.

"I know that I have lost the privilege to eat spontaneously," she continued. "I have to commit my food to someone else or I'll go back to where I came from. Some days I can only commit general things, like protein and a grain, because I'm going to a restaurant. But I need to have a plan, and I need to tell it to someone else. Somehow, I feel that I'll be letting that person down if I don't stick to my meals. In fact, there are days when that is the only reason I don't change what I've committed.

"You have to be honest with yourself to get well," she concluded.

I hung up feeling chastened. I wasn't willing to tell anyone what I was eating yet. I was feeling better about my meals, though, and I hadn't binged or purged in several weeks. I knew I was on the "pink cloud" that all newcomers who stopped binging floated on. I felt pretty good, but if I stopped feeling good I would try to commit myself to a daily food plan, I decided.

The next night I went to a meeting at a church several minutes from our apartment. "I'm going out for about an hour," I called to Haywood as I put on a loose sweatsuit and brushed my hair. I had just finished dinner and my stomach felt bloated. In my shapeless outfit no one would see my body.

Haywood now knew that I was trying to recover from bulimia through the support group I was frequently attending, and that my tentative confession the previous summer had barely scraped the surface of my long-standing problem. Attending my first meeting had given me the courage to sit him down and tell him how truly sick and out of control I was. While he had been disturbed that I had not told him the complete truth about my condition at first, he had been most surprised that I had been able to continue hiding it from him and everyone else for so long.

I thought back to the night when I had first tried to talk

to him about my struggles with bulimia. He had come home from work one evening and I had curled up next to him on our queen-size bed, screwing up the courage to tell him about my misery. I had spent the entire day eating and vomiting repeatedly, telling myself that every trip to the toilet was going to be my last. Despite my best intentions, though, I had found myself in front of the well-stocked cupboards within minutes after finishing purging, mysteriously starting the eating cycle again.

"Haywood," I began, "I have a secret to tell you." With those words he tore his attention away from the television. "Don't ever keep secrets from me," he had repeatedly told me. "If I can't trust you our marriage will be worthless."

"I think I have a really severe problem with food," I said hoarsely. I had scraped up my throat during the day's purges so talking was painful. I was always making excuses for my sore throats; I had colds year-round, people thought. Besides my raked throat, I had broken blood vessels around my eyes and my stomach was aching from all the abuse.

"What kind of problem?" he asked, obviously relieved that the topic wasn't more serious. Every woman worried about her weight. So what else was new?

"I spent all day throwing up," I said in a rush. "I have bulimia and I think I'd better go to a hospital, or get some therapy or something. Johns Hopkins University has an Eating Disorder Clinic—I saw it advertised in the paper."

I suddenly felt vulnerable and naked. I also was strangely relieved not to have the secret locked inside anymore. I had never told anyone I had bulimia. Whenever I had talked about it, and people had asked me why I was so knowledgeable, I had made an excuse about trying it once before in high school, or having friends who had it. Anything but the truth.

Haywood's eyes widened in shock. He knew enough about bulimia to be scared, because we had discussed friends who had developed goiters, intestinal ulcers, tooth erosion, and ovarian destruction as a result of the disorder. I could see his mind spinning these frightening thoughts. He sat up straight.

"Why didn't you tell me before that you were bulimic?"

He reached out his arms to hold me. I snuggled in, put my head on his shoulder, and started to cry.

"I don't know," I said sadly. "I guess I thought I could control it, or it would go away when we got married. I want to be a good wife and I feel like such a failure!" Sobs wracked my body as he held me tighter.

"What do you do—stick your finger down your throat or something? Is that it?"

"Yes," I sniffled. "And I can't stop even though I want to. It's like something comes over me. I'll just be doing something and I'll think about food, or I'll hear an ad for ice cream, or I'll get nervous about something, and before I know it I'm binging. And once I've eaten, I have to get it back up."

"How much are you doing it?" Haywood held me away from him to look at my tear-streaked face.

"Well, I did it a lot today. But sometimes I can go a whole week without doing it. It's always lurking there in the back of my mind, though, as a way I can relieve a too full feeling."

"Has this been going on for a long time?"

"Since tenth grade. Two of my friends told me how. I thought I could take it or leave it at the time. But I'm addicted now."

"Did you do it at Harvard, while we were dating?" His face was pained. It hurt him to hear that I had been deceptive, and that he hadn't noticed anything amiss. He was probably feeling like a failure, too.

"Yeah—in fact, a lot of people you probably wouldn't guess had it, too." I named a few people he knew. Haywood looked battered as I reeled off the list. This was a lot for him to be hearing.

"Can't you just not eat when you get the urge?" he asked hopefully. "I'll help if you want me to. I'll watch you eat and stop you if I think you're having too much. Will that help?"

I sighed. I knew that if anyone put restrictions on me, I'd find a way out. That was just part of my rebellious nature. I mentioned the Hopkins Eating Disorder Clinic again.

"C," he said, using my nickname, "that would cost a lot of money. You don't have a job yet and I've got two more years of law and business school. Where do you think the money will come from?"

44

I started to cry again. Hopkins was my last resort. I didn't know where else I would go to get well. Seeing my tears, Haywood softened. "Look, we'll find a way to send you there if you really need it. But I just think you need a little more willpower. I don't always eat when I want to—it just takes discipline," he said helpfully.

We talked about it for a few more minutes, and I promised to try harder, but I could tell that Haywood just didn't understand what I was going through. Most men couldn't. They didn't have to pay attention to the ubiquitous billboards and advertisements that stressed that the perfect woman was skinny. Besides, if he wanted to lose weight, he just cut out second helpings. It wasn't fair.

Now, almost a year after that scene, as I was preparing to head out the door to a meeting, Haywood wasn't happy. While he was thrilled that I was taking positive steps toward recovery, he didn't understand why I needed constant meetings and phone calls, especially when they were cutting into our limited time together.

"Didn't you go to a meeting last week?" he said with exasperation as he watched me sling my purse over my shoulder. "How long is this going to go on? I never see you—I don't even feel like you're my wife sometimes. You get up, go to work, go to meetings, and go to bed. Aren't I important anymore?"

"Haywood, this isn't the kind of thing you can take care of with one meeting a week!" I said angrily. "Some people go to one or two meetings a day! I can't recover unless I see and talk to people who are just like me—who feel the way I do and who have done some of the things I've done."

He remained unmoved. "I wish you would stay home. I had a hard day, too. You don't see me running to meetings to tell people. I count on you to be my sounding board. Can't you use me the same way? Besides, you say you haven't thrown up for a few weeks. Aren't you cured yet?"

I sighed. He just didn't understand. People told me I had to be selfish, and that I had to put my recovery at the top of my list of priorities. They told me that unless I could lay aside the food obsession, I wouldn't be much good to anyone—my husband, my family, or my employer. One day, Haywood

45

would grasp the necessity of the measures I had to go to not to eat. But I wasn't going to stand here and try to make him see things my way. That would take time, and I didn't want to be late for the meeting.

"I'm going," I told him firmly as I headed for the door.

"Fine. I'll be waiting for you right here. Hurry home," he said glumly as the door slammed shut.

At the meeting I sank into the corner of a comfortable sofa and looked around. I was a bit early. Around me men and women were chatting happily, greeting each other with smiles and hugs. I still thought there was a little too much touching at these things. It was all I could do to hold hands and say the Lord's Prayer. I hoped no one wanted to hug me. I crossed my arms and waited.

As the grandfather clock chimed eight o'clock, people settled into the chairs and sofas around the room. Some lit up cigarettes while others pulled knitting and needlework from bags and proceeded to busy themselves.

"Hi, I'm Charlene, a recovering compulsive overeater and your leader for this meeting," a middle-aged woman said. "First, will you join me in the Serenity Prayer?"

People's heads dropped forward and eyes closed. "God, grant me the serenity to accept the things I cannot change, courage to change the things I can, and wisdom to know the difference," the group intoned. Whoever had written this comforting prayer had wrapped a lot of understanding of life into a few short lines. I always felt peaceful when I said it.

Several minutes later a tall, beautiful woman named Betsy was introduced as the speaker. Could she possibly have an eating problem? She didn't look as if she'd had a day's misery in her life! I stared at her, fascinated, waiting to hear what she had to say.

Within the space of a few short minutes, I was hooked on her compelling narrative. This woman was singing my song. Not only were our backgrounds the same, but she was talking about endless rounds of binging and purging, punctuated by periods of laxative overdoses, syrup of ipecac, and diuretics.

"It all started with a little diet," Betsy said. "My brother said that he thought I could be a model if I dropped five pounds. I was five-ten and weighed 150 pounds at that time,

46

which was good for my height and bone structure. But after that comment I looked at myself completely differently. I started by cutting out desserts and second helpings, and I began to exercise more. I lost five pounds pretty quickly, but then I decided that that wasn't enough—another five pounds would look even better."

Around the room, people were nodding their heads, affirming similar experiences.

"Soon, I was totally obsessed with food and calorie counts," Betsy continued. "I went through lots of phases with my eating habits; one month I ate only white foods, one month only green foods, one month only vegetables. But the amounts became smaller and smaller, and with each pound I lost I felt more powerful, more superior to the slobs around me who had to eat and who couldn't control their hunger pangs.

"I dropped from 150 pounds to 100 pounds in the space of a year. I kept playing lacrosse and field hockey, but I can see now that I was just doing it to burn off the calories. There was no joy in my activities anymore; I was tired and hungry all the time, but I didn't add any food to my meals because I thought that would have been admitting a weakness."

I studied Betsy carefully, thinking about my own sports history. I had started swimming competitively when I was seven and had continued to compete and practice in long daily sessions until I was nineteen. I had set a number of records in the Maryland area and had been considered a rising star until I was fourteen, when my times had suddenly plateaued. That was when my extreme dieting had taken over my life. Perhaps the two had something to do with my performance. I could think about that later, though. I wanted to concentrate on Betsy's story.

"Before I knew it, I was bulimic," Betsy was saying. One day I got so tired of starving myself all the time that I gave myself permission to have one—just one—tablespoon of peanut butter. Then I went crazy. All my tastebuds went wild and screamed for more. So I ate for several hours, devouring everything in my parents' cupboards and refrigerator. It was like I was standing outside myself because I felt another person inside me just eating, eating, eating."

47

Betsy paused to light a cigarette. She looked reflectively at the floor for a moment, the smoke snaking out of her nose and mouth, framing her delicate face. It was hard to equate the horror story coming out of her with the tremendous beauty sitting across the room. She must have known that people would have killed to have her looks and her family's affluence, but clearly she didn't. Her story was one of self-hatred and low self-esteem, as well as a total lack of perspective on the front she presented to the rest of the world.

For another twenty minutes Betsy spoke, describing endless sessions of binging and purging and wild weight swings. She said that she never knew from one week to the next what size she would be so she had clothes from size 8 to 16 in her closet. I could certainly understand that. During my junior year at college I had worn loose overalls or sweat suits every single day because I was terrified of trying on clothes that had waistlines and that might not fit.

Betsy discussed her stay at a well-known hospital, where she had lived on the eating disorder ward for eight months but had been unable to recover. The doctors had finally discharged her because they said they didn't know how to treat her or keep her from purging. She had then moved back home, where her despairing parents had resorted to looping bicycle chains around the handles of the cupboard and the refrigerator. Betsy said it had only led her to steal their money so that she could drive from one fast-food restaurant to another, vomiting in various bathrooms.

"You know, we all have to hit our own bottoms before we seek help," she continued, "but I'm not sure what mine was. A lot of things added up in my disgust with myself. For example, I remember being mortified when I was caught shoplifting food at a supermarket and the manager took me aside and said that he wouldn't call my parents if I would come back that night and meet him in the parking lot for sex. It didn't stop me from binging or stealing, though. I just got more careful."

Betsy concluded by saying that she had stumbled into the program through word of mouth five and a half years previously. She said her recovery had been a long haul, and that her abstinence from compulsive overeating and purging had not been perfect, but that she had become willing, one day at a time, to be honest with people in the program about her behavior. The result had been more than three years of freedom from bulimia, a stable weight, and a new sense of serenity and happiness that she had never previously experienced.

I was completely blown away. Betsy was one of the first people I had ever seen or heard who said she was totally free of binging and purging, and whose story closely paralleled mine. Most of the people I had known in high school and college who admitted being bulimic said they purged occasionally—"after a heavy meal," one said—and that they weren't worried about that.

But I didn't even want to be an occasional purger. I wanted to get rid of the behavior and never do it again. I still was having shaky days with a lot of food thoughts, but Betsy's story hardened my resolve to do whatever the program suggested as a method of recovery. She had also filled me with renewed hope that food could assume secondary importance in my life.

When the meeting ended, I approached Betsy. A ring of men and women stood around, thanking her for her honesty and praising her for her remarkable recovery. Finally it was my turn to speak with her.

"Thanks a lot for sharing," I began self-consciously. "My name is Caroline and I've got to tell you that I did a lot of the things you said you did, and you are one of the first people I've ever heard whom I completely related to."

Privately I was thinking that I would never have the courage to tell my story to such a large group of people, and I especially admired her for her candor.

"Are you new to the program?" Betsy asked, her eyes taking in everything about me from my lack of makeup to the ratty sweatsuit. I nodded.

"Do you have a sponsor yet? You really can't work the program unless you have some sort of daily contact with someone who is further along than you are, and who can guide you through the highs and lows you are going to experience."

I admitted that I hadn't had the courage to ask anyone yet. Although a book was circulated at every meeting with names and phone numbers of people willing to sponsor people and take calls at any hour of the day, I had felt shy about picking someone. I was afraid I would be a burden to them.

"I'll be your sponsor if you want," Betsy offered. "The program says you have to be willing to go to any lengths to get abstinent from compulsive overeating, and without a sponsor you'll only be working the program half-assed."

I was overjoyed. "Oh, that would be wonderful! I was thinking that you were probably getting calls from lots of people, judging from your story. I'm sure that everyone here —whether they purged or not—related to your need to eat until you popped, and then the compulsion to get rid of it afterward."

"Yeah, we all have the same problem—compulsive over-eating," Betsy agreed. "In fact, my sponsor wasn't bulimic. I had to totally trust in her and the program to get well. But I knew that diets, hospitals, doctors, and therapists hadn't done a damn thing for me, so I was willing to do what she said because I was desperate and she was doing well. And that was the secret."

Betsy's voice took on a harder tone. "Are you willing to go to any lengths to get well?"

I looked at her. Her hair was shining, her skin was flawless, and her slender body was surely the envy of many, including me. I wanted what she had. I wanted the peace and serenity she had spoken of. And I didn't want to purge again as long as I lived.

"Yes, I think I'm willing. What do I have to do?"

"Here, take my phone numbers. Call me at work anytime. If I can't talk, I'll tell you. But I'll call you back. You can also call me at home, and I have an answering machine that takes messages up to five minutes long, so you can talk to that if you can't reach me. Don't be afraid to call. There were lots and lots of people who were there for me when I was getting well, and part of my staying in recovery is to be there for others. You will learn in this program that 'You can't keep what you don't give away.'"

The room was practically empty by now, so we walked outside together.

"Come on, give me a hug," Betsy said as we parted. "Everything will be fine. Just keep coming to meetings and keep listening. The minute your mind closes, you're in trouble. And call me whenever you need me."

We hugged and I walked home slowly. I smiled at the firemen sitting in the spring air outside the station. Usually I ducked my head and scowled as I scurried past, afraid that one of them might make a suggestive comment. But I felt happy tonight and no one was going to spoil it. I felt as if I wanted to hug the world.

"If this is the pink cloud I keep hearing about, then I like it," I thought to myself. "I can't imagine that I will ever be depressed as long as I do what people tell me to do."

How wrong I was. For even as the "pink cloud" enveloped me and kept me buoyed for a while, dark clouds were gathering on the horizon that were to knock me flat and test my commitment to getting well.

FOUR

TWO MONTHS LATER, mid-morning, I sat at work, panicking about lunch. I had a flight to a Midwestern city for a business trip in less than two hours, and I suddenly realized that I didn't know what was going to be served on the plane, and I hadn't called ahead to order a seafood or vegetable plate. That made me nervous.

"What am I going to do?" I wondered as I sat at my desk, pondering the momentous problem. My mind spun to several possible solutions. I could call the airline and tell them that I had a medical problem that necessitated them serving me a salad, despite the late hour of the order. I could just eat whatever they served and trust that I would not gain weight or purge. Or I could go to the mall across the street and get the lunch I ate every single day: a bran muffin and a medium-sized dish of frozen yogurt.

52

The last idea appealed to me the most. I had become quite attached to this particular meal, and I found myself edgy and grumpy if I couldn't have it, if there was a line at the yogurt store that delayed my eating, or if my favorite yogurt flavor wasn't available. The thought of not having my comfortable lunch, especially on a day when I was traveling on business and feeling unsettled, was almost too much to bear.

I looked at the clock—eleven A.M. If I gathered my things now and left, I could get my lunch, wolf it down and still make it to the airport on time. I briefly thought about making a call to Betsy to check out my plan but decided against it. I was doing really well in my recovery and was feeling strong enough to eat certain foods without a lot of anguish, so my calls to her had been less frequent.

"Hey, how're ya doing, beautiful?" Uh-oh. Howard, one of the office's biggest time-wasters, appeared just as I was putting on my blazer. I always cringed when he came by because he never appeared concerned if I was engrossed in something; he simply chatted away as if my activities were unimportant and irrelevant.

The other thing he did that always infuriated me was that he put his hands on my shoulders or my arms when he came close to me. I never put my hands on him, I often thought angrily, so why did he feel free to violate my personal space?

I usually kept silent, however, not sure of the proper way to handle the issue. If I said something, I knew I'd be castigated in the office as frigid and unfriendly. And if I didn't, I could be sure he would continue the obnoxious practice, convinced I enjoyed it. Being a working woman, especially in a predominantly male office, was a double-edged sword.

Howard sat in a chair next to my desk and grinned at me. "Are you going somewhere, hon?"

"I've got a plane to catch. The leasing kickoff is tomorrow." I bent over to pick up my bags.

"You look really pretty today," he continued, unconcerned about my imminent departure. "Is that a new dress?"

Now he had pushed both my buttons. He had not only squeezed my shoulders as he came in, but now he had also commented on my appearance. All the women's success books said that this latter occurrence was a sure sign that my work wasn't taken seriously. The authors emphasized that if a woman's outfit was complimented, it meant her looks—not her opinions—were her most prominent feature. The solution, they all counseled, was to dress like a man in dreadful suits and floppy bowties, something I knew I had to force myself to do more often.

"Thanks. That's a good-looking tie you have on, too." I hoped my voice revealed my annoyance. Perhaps he would understand my point of view if I concentrated on mentioning his suit, his tie, or something else he wore from now on. I left him sitting at my desk as I breezed out the door. I had to get my lunch.

I barely made it to the plane on time. As I collapsed into my seat and the flight attendants began their passenger check, I regretted that I had made the mall detour. The store had only had strawberry yogurt—my least favorite—and I had had to stand in a long line to get it. Although I had briefly entertained the notion of trying something new, like pizza, I hadn't had the courage. So I had quickly eaten the unsatisfying meal while driving to the airport, dripping the sticky yogurt onto the steering wheel and passenger seat, sprinkling crumbs everywhere. On top of that, I had indigestion from running through the terminal with heavy bags slung over my shoulder.

At least this would be a quick flight, I thought with relief as I buckled my seatbelt. Flying frightened me, and my churning stomach wouldn't improve matters any. Flying was only one of my fears. When I had first moved to Baltimore, I had been afraid to drive on the beltway, convinced that I would get lost once out there, or my car would break down and no one would stop to help me. As the bulimia had become more ingrained in my personality over the years, I had also developed other phobias including fear of heights, fear of failure, and fear of new situations.

My beltway phobia had been especially paralyzing when I had started looking for a job in Baltimore. During the long, hot summer after our wedding I had often thought of going for a drive to investigate the local sights, but my fears had kept me chained to the small apartment where I had filled the time with binges, soap operas, and stuporous afternoon naps.

54

Now, because of the self-confidence and encouragement I was getting from people in the program, I could drive almost anywhere, and my other phobias were beginning to dissipate as well. People kept saying "Progress, not perfection" at the meetings, which was helping me not to expect so much from myself all the time. It was nice to start removing the impossibly high standards I had always thought I should meet.

Once we were in the air, the flight attendants began to bustle about, bringing drinks and hot meals. I looked longingly at the lunch trays, trying to summon up the courage to tell the slim stewardess that I didn't want anything. "We have to learn to say no—to put our recovery first," I had heard one man say at a recent meeting about turning down unplanned food.

"Would you like lunch, dear?" the flight attendant drawled, peering at me through mascara-drenched eyelashes. She looked like she had been poured into her size 4 pants, and she had a cute bust to boot. Maybe airline food was good for you.

"Sure," I said, telling myself that I would only let it sit in front of me. The fried chicken, green beans, biscuit, and blueberry cobbler would be a good test of my brand-new abstinence from compulsive overeating.

It had been twelve weeks since I had binged and purged, and I was on top of the world about it. I had never been able to put together more than a week of nonsloppy eating and no purging before, so I was feeling powerful.

I opened up the newspaper to read but within five minutes had dropped the pretense. The food smelled too good to pass up. After all, I hadn't eaten a lot for lunch. Maybe if I just picked at something it would be okay.

"Three meals a day with nothing in between." "Abstain from sugar and refined flour products." "When in doubt, leave it out." Suggestions I had heard drifted through my head as I eyed the tray. I felt as though a gluttonous sinner was perched on my left shoulder and a reasonable, program-spouting moralist was on my right, both tugging at my heart and mind.

The sinner won. The blueberry cobbler had large blueberry chunks in it. That would be my fruit for the day, I decided with lopsided reasoning, convincing myself that there wasn't a lot of sugar clinging to the berries. I could pretty much pick my way around the fattening stuff, I reassured myself.

I started with delicate, slow forkfuls, congratulating myself on my self-control. At least I wasn't eating at record speeds anymore. Before I knew it, though, I had rationalized my way through the whole cobbler and was trying to decide if the biscuit could count as that evening's carbohydrate choice.

I decided it could and I ate it, a little more quickly. But I was still hungry. The beans didn't appeal to me—I had eaten enough of them over the years to keep the Jolly Green Giant in business for life. That left the chicken.

"I must be premenstrual," I told myself as I attacked the chicken. Within a minute it was denuded. I wasn't wild about the meat, but I sure liked the skin.

My family had found out about my skin fetish the hard way. After one Thanksgiving dinner in high school I had volunteered to clear the table and wash the dishes, much to my parents' delight. I had secretly been delighted, too, because cleaning up after family meals is a bulimic's dream. Not only could I appear helpful, but I could also surreptitiously eat any and all leftovers while loading the dishwasher.

While everyone had retired to the den to watch home movies during this particular holiday, I had zoomed around the kitchen, knocking plates together to keep the cacophony up and eating like a wild woman. The turkey had been one of my prime victims, as I had gobbled the entire coating of skin piece by piece, with buttery chunks of stuffing wrapped in the middle.

It wasn't until I had finished the dishes that I realized I had destroyed the week's provisions. In terror of being found out, I had started to slice the turkey off the bones, hoping no one would notice the butchered carcass. Then, running out of time, I had wrapped the entire package in foil instead of plastic wrap because my picking wouldn't be as easy to spot.

Later, after purging and retiring to my bedroom above the kitchen, I heard my mother go in to check on my work and cleanliness. She opened the refrigerator door—a sound that always struck fear in my heart because it meant my binging might be detected—and gasped. She must have un-wrapped the foil and seen the lack of skin and stuffing, be-cause ten minutes later my father was at my door asking what had happened to the turkey.

"Nothing!" I protested angrily. "I didn't eat a thing. At least you could say thank you for all my hard work!" And then I had stonily looked back at my book, determined not to let him think he had rattled me.

The sudden pitching of the plane returned me to the present. We were in for a turbulent few minutes, the pilot warned us over the loudspeaker. I felt myself turning green. My fear of crashing and the extra food I had eaten were mak-ing me extremely nauseous. I stood up and went back to the smoking section where I slipped into a free seat near the bath-room.

I didn't want to purge. I would keep this food down come hell or high water. Although I felt fat and bloated, Betsy had told me that so-called "normal" eaters also felt this way some-times, and that they just loosened their belts and let the feel-ing pass. Not me. Whenever I felt the slightest pressure on my waistband, that was my cue to purge.

"Normal eaters sometimes eat too much, but they don't gain weight," she told me one night. "Don't be so black and white about your food choices. If you feel you've had too much, just let the fullness pass and make different food choices at the next meal. The last thing you need to do is beat yourself up over it. We compulsive overeaters can be awfully hard on ourselves because it is the only emotion we know after eating."

Her reasoning made sense, but I still didn't enjoy feeling bloated after meals, even if it was only on vegetables. "Feel-ings aren't reality," Betsy had stressed time and time again. I decided to trust her. After all, she looked wonderful and had done the same things I had done, so she must know what she was talking about.

So instead of purging now, I decided to have a cigarette, a vice no one knew about. It didn't fit my clean-cut athletic image and Haywood couldn't stand smoke, so I rarely in-dulged. But it was the one thing that calmed my fears and

57

settled my stomach during turbulent, or even slightly bumpy, flights.

I had first tried smoking in seventh grade when I had been babysitting at a house up the street. Both of the parents were smokers and I had been curious about its taste, especially because a number of the girls in my class had either tried cigarettes or were actively smoking on the sly at parties.

My first puff had been dreadful. I had inhaled really deeply and had momentarily felt my head spinning and my knees weakening. My second puff had intensified the dizziness and driven me to the bathroom, where I had been certain I would get sick, but had mercifully been spared.

That experience had effectively ended my smoking career until college, when some of my friends had helpfully told me that periodic nicotine bursts would keep me awake while studying. But even then I had been a moderate dabbler, never inhaling or getting hooked.

A lot of people in the program smoked. They also knitted, crocheted, and chewed gum. "What a compulsive lot of people we are," I had thought to myself one night, surveying the busy hands and mouths around me. I had talked to Betsy about it later, who had said to me about her own cigarette addiction: "Not binging is the most important thing in my life right now. I'll deal with the other compulsions later. First things first."

I was one of the ones guilty of gum and sugarless mint abuse. I wasn't ready to give either habit up because there were days when that was the only thing that helped me get from one meal to the next without snacking. Eventually I knew I'd have to give both up, as well as my coffee and artificial sweetener addiction. But Betsy emphasized that the binging and purging had to be tamed before I tackled anything else.

I looked out the window as the plane bumpily cut through the clouds. My mind wandered back to my babysitting days, when the binging had been especially intense. Not only had this money-making pasttime fueled my addiction, but it had also been one of the ways I had kept the bulimia hidden for so long. If parents only knew how deadly it was to say to the baby-sitter as they sailed out the door, "Help yourself to anything in the house!"

I had usually taken their advice to heart, helping myself to anything and everything, baking when there wasn't enough to binge on. Some nights I just took a complete food inventory of the house, snitching bites of things that I had never tried before, sure that I would never have the opportunity to sample them again. By the end of the evening, though, I would be overcome with guilt and would make a careful list of the foods I had consumed and their calorie counts.

One evening I was horrified to see on my daily food tally that my four-hour grazing while babysitting had resulted in well over 800 extra calories. I had started to panic about my total lack of willpower, as well as the fact that too much time had elapsed since the beginning of the evening's nibbling for me to be able to purge.

So my solution to the dilemma had been to jog around the family's dining room table for an hour, glaring in the mirror at my protruding stomach every time I rounded the corner and thinking hateful thoughts about myself. When the parents arrived home, they commented on my exhausted appearance. "The kids were quite a handful tonight," I responded, smiling my most martyrous smile.

Most babysitting nights, however, I wound up purging again and again, despite repeated vows not to. I would arrive at the people's homes feeling virtuous because I had just had a swimming workout and had eaten lightly, but soon the obscene cravings would outdistance my desire to stay "clean." Then the kids would be hustled off to bed early or pressed into cooking duty. "Won't your parents be delighted to see this chocolate cake when they get home!" I would say joyfully as we began to bake.

More often than not, however, I would binge on the batter and icing, resulting in a misshapen and small cake. And then once the cake was baked I would eat a good portion of it, summoning every ounce of respectability to leave some for the family. If the parents ever tired of having sweet concoctions whipped up the moment they left, they never let on. And if they ever wondered who had done the lion's share of sampling, they never asked me about that, either.

I finally had to put an end to babysitting in eleventh grade after one humiliating episode at a new family's house. I started the evening's binging with several bowls of cereal swimming in cream and bananas, and progressed through the cupboards and the refrigerator, eating randomly from peanut butter jars, marshmallow bags, and Tupperware containers.

After purging every new round of food—promising myself it was the last time—I still felt like binging and turned to the freezer as my last unexplored territory. In there I found frozen tubs of beef stew, which I immediately wanted because I hadn't eaten any beef for several months. "Maybe just a taste," I said to myself.

The stew, however, was frozen solid and a knife couldn't make a dent in it. I stuffed the container in the microwave oven and stared at it impatiently, hoping it would defrost quickly. Then I returned to the freezer to see what I could eat in the meantime.

A foil-wrapped round item caught my eye. Peeling the shiny layers off, I discovered a rich, rum-laced cake blanketed in a thick coat of buttercream frosting. "Mmmmm," I murmured appreciatively as I scraped some icing off the side to taste. "Maybe I can have just a little without them noticing."

Within a few minutes I had eaten a thick layer of cake off the bottom and the top where I thought my nibbling would be less noticeable. But I couldn't stop there. I then took slivers off the sides, turning the cake into a decided octagon.

Finally, I ceased my mechanical activity, staring in horror at what I had done. The cake now had only a thin sheen of frosting where there had once been ample swirls, and it was much smaller in size than when I had first started working on it.

I hastily wrapped it back up, praying that the family would never want to eat the cake. I then shoved it in the back of the freezer, piling packages around it in a vain effort to hide it. If the parents asked me what had happened I would blame the food theft on the dog, I decided. They had a tiny Scottish terrier and I could always say that I had dropped the cake by accident and the dog had attacked it. I didn't stop to think about the clean knife marks I had left. I was too interested in moving on to the now pliable beef stew in the microwave oven.

Although it was still half frozen, I dug away at the stew, eating tasteless icy chunks of carrots, potatoes, and beef as fast as I could cram them in my mouth. Enjoying what I was eating was secondary to totally satiating my belly and keeping my jaws moving.

When I couldn't eat any more, I put the stew remains back in the freezer and retired to the bathroom where I purged for almost half an hour. Bready foods were almost impossible to get back up, and I had eaten so much cake that I wasn't sure if I was being successful. So I was extra vicious to myself, pounding my stomach repeatedly and jabbing my fingers forcefully down my throat. Convinced that I had done the best possible job of regurgitation, I finally gave up and slumped in front of the television set, waiting for the parents to come home.

Later that week at school, a classmate who was friendly with the family approached me chortling, "You're never going to babysit for the Harrises again! Mrs. Harris had a dinner party last weekend and when she pulled the cake out of the freezer she was furious about the way it looked. Did you really eat most of it?"

I turned a bright shade of red and stammered an unconvincing story about the dog. But I was mortified. The episode finally convinced me that I had no control over my eating while babysitting. So I declared to my parents that I was not accepting babysitting jobs any longer. I was simply too busy with swimming, piano, advanced placement courses, and my summer jobs, I said to them with great self-importance. Getting into college would be my absolute top priority from there on out.

I stubbed my cigarette out. I would have to make a belated apology to that poor cakeless family, I thought to myself as I made my way back to my seat and the plane started to descend. The program had a series of steps it encouraged people to follow to recover from compulsive overeating, and one of them was making a list of people who had been harmed by our behavior, and then asking for their forgiveness and understanding. I didn't think I would ever have the courage to ap-

61

proach the people I had harmed and the stores I had stolen from, but people in my group assured me that when the time was right, I would be able to do it, too. The honesty, they stressed, would free me from hidden fears and guilt, and was essential in the process of eliminating food cravings and becoming a new person.

I pushed these thoughts away as the plane landed and we taxied to the gate. I would have to be more honest with myself before making those amends. The airplane lunch was a solid lump in my stomach. I hadn't needed to eat it and I was angry I had made excuses to have it. That wasn't honesty. I should have called Betsy before I left and talked over my day with her. Then this slip wouldn't have happened. But then again, I hadn't purged it either, I reassured myself. That was probably the most important thing.

As I debarked from the plane, I decided to keep my slip to myself. Betsy didn't have to know about it. She would be so disappointed if I told her. If I just focused all my energies on doing the best possible job I could for tomorrow night's event, then I might be able to put food back into its proper perspective. I resolutely marched toward the terminal, determined to make the rest of the trip as "clean" as possible. I'd get to a meeting the night I got home and get right back on track.

The following day passed quickly as I worked with the company's marketing director to set up the presentation and press table for the evening's leasing kickoff. The real estate company for which I was public relations director was building a specialty marketplace in this small, Midwestern town. On this particular night, we would be introducing the retailing concept to area businesses and aspiring entrepreneurs to show them how they could help return life and shopping to abandoned inner cities.

I was still new to the public relations game, having mostly worked as a journalist during my summer jobs. In 1978 I had worked at *Washingtonian* magazine as an assistant to the publisher, learning about production, editing, and feature writing. Following that I had been named editor of my high school paper, had later become an editor on *The Harvard Crimson*, and had then spent a summer apiece at the Washington bureaus of the New York *Times* and *The Wall Street Journal*.

I was especially proud of my work at the *Journal* because I had won the internship over dozens of aspiring applicants, and the position was considered a precursor to joining the staff full-time. I loved my summer there, as I wrote a number of stories that ran on the front of the paper and on the front of the second section. But because my decision to marry would take me to Baltimore—where there was no bureau—I had regretfully ended my journalism career with them. Thus I had fallen into public relations, the only job I had been able to find.

At my age and level of inexperience, I was nervous about every move I made, sure that all the people in the company were laughing at me behind my back. And to complicate matters, I had only the chairman of the company to turn to for performance reviews and other advice because no one else at the small organization knew how public relations worked. The atmosphere was very much sink-or-swim and for a young, shy, and insecure woman, the combination was excruciating.

Despite my fears, the leasing kickoff went very well. More than six hundred potential retailers jammed the ballroom of the downtown Hyatt and oohed and ahhed about the wonderful renaissance they were convinced would soon come to their city. Our chairman, an internationally recognized developer and visionary, gave a stirring speech about city revitalization. The press came in droves and everyone was happy. With relief, I joined the throngs mingling at the reception afterward.

Specialty marketplaces traditionally have numerous dining spots to choose from, ranging from fast-food stands to ethnic eateries to full-service restaurants. To reflect this diversity, the marketing director had arranged for the ballroom to have several stations serving these kinds of foods to the guests. Every kind of cuisine was represented: sizzling tempura, barbecued chicken wings, freshly made omelets, pizza squares, exotic desserts, and more.

I strolled slowly around the room, savoring the delicious smells emanating from each stand. I was not going to sample anything; there was a company dinner at a local restaurant after the reception to which I had been invited. If I ate now, it would constitute a fourth meal, which I was determined not to have. I still felt guilty about yesterday's second lunch, too.

Jill, a company leasing representative, walked by munching on a big plate of fried vegetables. They were golden-brown and steaming. I looked at them enviously.

"Aren't you going to eat anything, Caroline?" she asked in surprise. "Don't miss these, whatever you do. They are divine." Her slender body disappeared into the crowd.

"Oh, to be normal and able to eat like that!" I thought wistfully. At the same time I remembered to try to avoid any self-pity about my disorder. "When you get on the pity pot you can be sure that you are that much closer to a binge," Betsy had warned me. "Get out of yourself and your ego when that happens."

I was trying to do this when Bob, a development director, appeared at my side, holding a plate of chicken, some imported cheese chunks and my favorite—the fattening tempura.

"You did a great job tonight," he said. "We'll get a lot of coverage. Your follow-up calls really made a difference in getting the press out. Here," he smiled, "take this plate. You deserve it after working so hard."

With a parting smile, Bob left me with the plate. The tempura's grease was staining the thin cardboard. The food looked wonderful. My internal battle about what to do began.

Two weeks previously I had been in a similar situation. I had been at an afternoon wake where the pushy host had asked me repeatedly if I had sampled his wife's cooking, especially her famed chocolate cake. Each time he passed me, he had inquired about my intake, insisting that I try the cake so that her feelings wouldn't be hurt. Every time I politely refused, saying that I had just had lunch two hours earlier.

Just when I thought I was safe, he had appeared at my side with a huge slab of the chocolate concoction. "Come on, honey," he cajoled. "You need some meat on your bones. My wife will be upset if you don't have one bite."

My fury had risen at his incessant and thoughtless prodding. "Thank you," I had snapped as I took the cake and strode toward the bathroom. There, I dumped it into the toilet, flushing hard. "Why does everyone equate having a good

64

time with eating?" I had angrily thought to myself as I watched the crumbs swirl away.

Now, as I stood in the Hyatt ballroom, I tried to resurrect the same anger. But I couldn't. It was after seven P.M. and I was hungry. Dinner wouldn't be for another hour. Maybe just a bite would tide me over until then.

My first crunch into the tempura was wonderful. I hadn't eaten a morsel of fried food in weeks because of my tendency to binge on fatty things. I savored this unexpected treat. The hot grease filled my mouth as I finished off the crispy pieces and tried to talk myself out of getting more. But it was no use. I was off to the races.

I spotted the tempura booth and headed there quickly, noting with annoyance that a line of people was waiting to be served. The pizza stand next door was comparatively empty, so I sidetracked to fill my plate with little pepperoni and sausage squares. Next stop: the chicken wings.

For the next twenty minutes I made a grand tour of the room, stopping where access to the food was easiest, not even tasting what I was shoveling into my mouth. Several retailers stopped to ask me where they could get more information about the marketplace, but instead of helping them myself, I directed them to another company person standing nearby. "Stand back while I'm eating," was my battlecry at times like this.

Finally I was sated—and horrified. I paused to mentally total the calories of my frenzied eating. The pizza squares were at least 50 apiece, the chicken wings were 75, and the tempura was probably 100. And I had eaten a stupendous quantity of each. I felt like crying. I had blown the whole evening. I saw no solution to my agony other than to somehow get rid of the food.

There was no way I was going to go to the company dinner now. I would look stupid sitting there sipping a Diet Coke, not eating a real meal like everyone else. Besides, I was going to have to work fast if I was going to be able to fit into my clothes tomorrow morning.

I gathered my brochures and papers, placing them protectively over my bulging stomach, and slipped out of the ballroom, hoping that no one would notice me leaving.

Vomiting wouldn't work tonight; the pizza and tempura would never come up without sustained effort and I wasn't willing to lean over the toilet for an hour. Not only was I too tired for that, but I didn't want to have the tell-tale puffy face and scratchy throat tomorrow. Tonight would have to be a laxative night.

Thank goodness the hotel drugstore was still open. I hurried in there, hoping no one I knew was there to see me buy the laxatives.

Good, the store was empty. I put two packages of Ex-Lax in front of the clerk and told her to charge it to my room. She looked at me with amusement. "Traveling is tough on the stomach, isn't it?" she chuckled. "Harder than you think," I thought grimly to myself, outwardly laughing affirmation.

My weapon in hand, I rode the elevator to my room wishing I hadn't ruined the evening. I felt pangs of self-pity that I wouldn't be able to join everyone, but I pushed the thoughts away, telling myself that no one liked me anyway. I knew this because no one in the company ever joked around with me or included me in their discussions. More often than not I felt like an outsider looking in on a party I wasn't part of. That was pretty much the way I had felt all my life: a lonely misfit.

I stopped at the soda machine in the hallway to buy a diet drink to wash down the pills. I wasn't looking forward to this purge. But I had to get rid of the food. That was all that mattered.

Back in the room I lay down on the bed and took a deep breath. "You were doing so well, Caroline," I thought disconsolately. "Why did you take that first bite?" They were right at the meetings when they said that the first compulsive bite was all it took to get back on the binging roller coaster. While I was angry that I had been forcibly handed the plate of food, I was angrier at myself for my weakness in not refusing it.

I opened the laxatives and cradled eight of them in my palm. "Here goes," I thought disgustedly as I sat up. I gulped the bitter white pills, chased with a few swigs of Diet Coke to kill the horrible taste. I repeated this ritual three times and then lay back down, exhausted and unhappy.

Now I had not only binged, but I had also been unable to call anyone before beginning the purge, something the program advised doing. Part of me knew that calling before binging or taking the laxatives would not have been helpful, though. When I wanted to eat or get rid of the food, there was nothing anyone could possibly say that could alter my actions.

I looked at the clock. Maybe I could at least make a call now to someone. But I didn't want to call Betsy. I didn't want to let her know that all of her advice, support, and love had been for naught. And besides, I felt guilty for not calling her every day recently, as she had suggested. I would just call someone else now and chat for a while—maybe not even tell them about the binge.

I picked up the phone and tried a few phone numbers, but no one was home. "Probably all at a meeting," I grumped. Finally, having exhausted all the numbers except for Betsy's, I decided to try her, hoping she wouldn't be there.

No such luck. On the second ring she picked up. "Hello," I heard her deep voice say.

That was all it took to make me crumble. I completely fell apart, gasping between sobs that I was out of town and that I had just swallowed a box of laxatives. "I'm a total failure," I wailed in desperation. "I've wasted your time and there's no hope for me. I'll never get well now!"

"Calm down," Betsy said comfortingly. "You don't have food in your hand now and that's all that matters. The binge is over and you are going to be okay."

I let her words wash over me like a soothing balm. I had expected her to reject me or yell at me, but she was doing neither. She was telling me that she had done the same thing before, but that the important thing was that she had gotten back on the wagon and had continued reaching out for help. Her binges had gotten fewer and farther between, she said, until the cravings had subsided completely.

"Look," she said, "you are completely missing the good thing about this whole episode. First, you have gone twelve weeks without binging or purging. You had been totally unable to do that for seven years. Three months is nothing to sneeze at.

"Second, you have learned that traveling is tough for you. The next time you go away, you'll know that there is added pressure and you'll be more careful. If you have to make a call before getting on a plane or going to a reception, then so be it.

"I could tell you were heading for a fall, but I didn't want to say anything," she added. "When your calls weren't as frequent, I sensed that you felt in control again. But that's something you had to find out the hard way. You may have thought that eating extra on the plane yesterday was okay, but in situations like that the dishonesty catches up to you sooner or later, and you have a full-blown binge, like tonight. You've got to get on the phone or get to a meeting immediately when you have a slip.

"This is a learning experience for you," she continued. "It doesn't matter so much that you binged. What matters is what you do with it as far as teaching yourself how to react next time a similar situation occurs, or you are handed a plate of food you don't want.

"You are the quintessential people pleaser," she laughed. "What if you had told Bob you weren't hungry? He most likely wouldn't have given a damn. But you probably thought he wouldn't like you for some reason if you said 'no.' And I know that because I am a people pleaser, too, and I've been guilty of the same thing."

I sheepishly admitted that I had taken the food out of fear of not being accommodating, as well as of being the only one not eating at the reception. I hadn't wanted to be different, or to stick out like a sore thumb.

"When are you going to learn to put yourself and your needs first?" Betsy asked. "You have to make recovery the most important thing in your life without exception. This disease is cunning, baffling, and powerful, and it will kill you unless you treat it with the proper respect. You are not a normal eater and you never will be. You have to be vigilant all the time. That is the nature of this thing, so you might as well forget trying to eat the way other people do and accept your condition."

I wanted to argue with her, but I was feeling more and more fatigued by the minute. The laxatives were not only making mincemeat of my intestines, but they were also making me very drowsy.

"There's a meeting tomorrow night," I heard Betsy say.

68

"Why don't you plan to meet me there, and afterward we'll go out for coffee. We need to do some more talking about your commitment to getting well. For now, just relax and don't beat yourself up over this. It's over. Tomorrow is a new day. And we can only take our recovery one day at a time. You can abstain from binging for at least twenty-four hours. Don't think about forever and ever."

"One day at a time," she repeated with emphasis as she wished me a restful sleep and hung up.

I replaced the phone in the receiver and turned on my side to ease the severe cramping that was beginning to rack my stomach. I thought about the comforting words Betsy had just spoken. While she hadn't condoned my actions, she hadn't judged me or made me feel inferior either. She had simply stressed that life was a journey, not a destination, and that sometimes recovery was rockier than we might want or expect.

I had been so enveloped in the "pink cloud" of the past three months that I hadn't seen the gathering storm of arrogance about my belief that I could handle any situation with ease. Cocky is what I had become. I had not truly admitted my powerlessness over food, which is what the program urged as a prerequisite to getting well.

But I didn't want to admit I was powerless; I wanted to feel in control of things. That was the only way I had been able to function all these years: I had always seized control of situations and rammed my way down others' throats. To admit I was powerless over anything was frightening.

But if I was in control, why was I hunched over on the bed again, despondent over food? This stuff wasn't harmless—it was dynamite in my hands. It was capable of destroying my self-esteem, my job, and my life, if I allowed it.

"To gain power, you have to admit powerlessness," I remembered hearing someone say at a meeting. It had seemed incomprehensible at the time, but now it made sense. I felt a dawning realization. If I was powerless over food, it didn't mean that I was weak. It simply meant that I was respectful of its potential power over me.

"At least I've learned something," I thought as I drifted off to sleep. "Betsy's right. I've abstained from binging and purging for twelve weeks, which is amazing. If I keep going to meetings and working this program, she promises I can abstain for life. That alone is worth giving the program a few hours a week when I might otherwise be eating."

Several minutes later I was asleep, fully clothed, but hopeful again that I wasn't destined to a life of endless eating, unresolved guilt, and baggy clothes. These people I barely knew had given me the hope that I might someday be well. That slender thread of hope was my lifeline.

FIVE

THE FOLLOWING NIGHT, Betsy and I walked across the street after our meeting to a popular neighborhood restaurant that had recently caught the California nouvelle cuisine bug. All of the entrées included steamed baby vegetables and dabs of goat cheese in the salads, and the coffee was not only freshly brewed, but it came in flavors like chocolate amaretto and Viennese cinnamon. As long as I couldn't have real sweets, I let myself indulge in these extravagant coffees, which I always laced with several packs of artificial sweeteners.

"I'll have decaffeinated cinnamon coffee with milk, not cream," I said to the waitress after we settled into the booth, emphasizing the latter part of my order. I always requested milk instead of cream out of fear of additional calories, but more often than not the waitress brought cream anyway, defeating my purpose.

"I'll have herbal tea, please," Betsy said, pulling the ashtray closer as she lit a long, slender cigarette.

"Okay," she said as soon as the waitress moved away, "let's talk about powerlessness. Do you agree that you are powerless over food, and that you are willing to go to any lengths now to get well?"

I paused. "I think so. But explain powerlessness. I think I understand the concept behind relinquishing control over the food, but what happens then? Who's there to take care of you if you can't control something through sheer willpower and determination?"

Betsy asked a direct question. "Do you pray?"

"No. I don't believe in God. I'm an atheist." My last statement was uttered with pride. It made me feel superior to all the people I knew who went to church. Church was for weak people, I had decided. And God was just a crutch for those who were incapable of dealing with life's pressures and misfortunes by themselves.

"Back up a minute," Betsy said, laughing at my answer. I was a little hurt that she found me amusing. I liked to be taken seriously. "When did you become such an earnest do-it-yourselfer?"

I started to explain. "I went to church a few times when I was younger. My grandmother is a Christian Scientist and she believes in God and all that stuff. She is always preaching at me about love and being grateful for all my blessings. But I stopped going to services with her when swimming workouts and competitions interfered. Besides, my parents never go to church, and they don't ever talk about religion or God, so I just don't believe. Plus, what proof do I have that God exists?"

As I spoke to Betsy I thought of my early efforts to embrace Christian Science. It preaches that evil is a false state of mind because God is everywhere, and that a loving God would never condone illness or disease. Ergo, they simply do not exist—"error," they are called. My grandmother firmly believed in these things, and when I hurt myself or was depressed, she would squeeze her gentle, cornflower blue eyes shut and say, "God is all. God is all. You are His perfect child and He wouldn't let anything that is not good happen to you."

I didn't doubt that this mysterious religion that scorned doctors and other health professionals was good for Donny because she managed to look radiant and youthful even as she reached into her sixties, seventies, and eighties. But I had always found it difficult to believe that some nebulous force was looking out for me, and that it would heal me if I only asked for help.

My final straw with Christian Science had come one Sunday morning at the children's meeting of the church my grandmother attended. After singing a hymn this particular day, we broke down into a number of smaller groups consisting of boys and girls of the same age. The woman leading our small table in discussion about the day's topic, "Mind over Matter," had long, scarlet fingernails that she clicked emphatically on the table with every point she made.

Although I was bored, I suddenly interrupted her dialogue with a question that I thought was pertinent to our subject. "What language did Jesus speak?"

The woman was momentarily taken aback. Not only had I disturbed her spiritual train of thought, but she clearly was not prepared for my question.

"Why, er, when he spoke with his disciples he used the language of the time," she faltered. "Aramaic, I believe. Yes," her face brightened, "it was Aramaic, a derivative of Hebrew. Does that help you, dear?" She beamed at me, pleased that she had regained control of the table.

"Is Aramaic anything like English?" I looked at her stubbornly. "I mean, would I have understood Jesus if I had heard him talking?"

"Well, of course not. People didn't speak English in that part of the world two thousand years ago." She looked displeased with my questions.

Jesus had dropped from my life at that point. If he had materialized in my bedroom, I would not have understood a word he said, and God was nowhere to be seen. I decided that Christian Science was for the birds, and my grandmother stopped taking me with her on Sunday mornings.

When I entered National Cathedral School in 1970, my parents breathed a bit easier, assuming that my religious training would be taken care of through the frequent chapel services and weekly services at the Cathedral. While I did learn some pretty songs, and certain prayers became like second nature to me, I never managed to embrace a faith or a belief in a power greater than myself during my nine years there.

The only reason I ever looked forward to attending the Cathedral on Friday mornings was to use the forty-five allotted minutes to catch up on sleep or homework, which I surreptitiously did in a back row while the school's chaplain droned on. If for some reason, a teacher spotted me reading a book or cramming for an exam and took my papers from me, I looked around the church with boredom, fascinated only by the shifting patterns cast on the marble floors by the magnificent stained-glass windows lining the clerestory level.

One school clique that puzzled me was a group of very religious girls whose main extracurricular activities outside prayer meetings were madrigal singing and bell ringing. They did things I didn't understand, like holding hands and praying, wearing crosses around their necks instead of the latest fad of jewelry, and gathering frequently to discuss the Scriptures. They also seemed to be happy and above the petty jealousies and intrigues among the different school factions.

Although there were times when I envied them their apparent serenity and rock-solid faith, I derisively called them "the God Squad." Where I loved to gossip, they preached humility and understanding. Where I used expletives, they counseled not taking the Lord's name in vain. I found them pious and holier-than-thou, and I had a wonderful time making fun of them and their beliefs.

To my great disgust, my sister joined a subset of the God Squad in ninth grade when she took it upon herself to get baptized and confirmed. As Liz became more religious, I was spurred to go farther in the opposite direction with my outrageous and rebellious behavior. Teachers were always surprised when they discovered that we were from the same family. "You're an Adams, too?" they said in disbelief when they realized they had taught an entirely different kind of girl the previous year.

Perhaps the best thing about National Cathedral in terms of religion was that I was exposed to every faith known to

74

man. My class contained a mixture of Catholics, Methodists, Baptists, Jews, and Muslims. And because so many foreign ambassadors' children attended the school, we had frequent assemblies about different religious traditions and ceremonies.

One morning the Jordanian ambassador's daughter explained the Muslim religion, which intrigued me because of the unquestioning belief that whatever happened was supposed to happen: they called this the will of Allah. This complete acceptance of fate and its consequences certainly took a great deal of responsibility off people's shoulders, which appealed to me. I also liked the idea of chanting and praying five times a day on pretty prayer rugs. But I quickly lost interest in the faith when I heard that the month of Ramadan—which fell around September—was the month of fasting. You could eat before sunup and after sundown, but not in between. That was unthinkable to me, so I continued my half-hearted search for a tradition or meaning to life that I could live with.

One religion that captivated me for years was Mormonism. When I was thirteen, the glittering and palatial Mormon Tabernacle opened on the outskirts of Washington, its gilded spires poking into the heavens. It was strategically placed off the beltway surrounding the city so that as you came over a certain rise, its gleaming white towers and blinding gold tips were suddenly visible. Cynics called it "Our Lady of the Highway."

Shortly after the building was completed, tours were held for the curious nonbelievers. During this brief period, people came from all over the country to view the interior of the awe-inspiring church, which would soon be declared forever off-limits to those who did not espouse the Mormon faith. Just the mere idea that it would be so difficult to gain admission later on had appealed to my elitist nature.

The day my family chose to tour the Tabernacle was a wet one, but that did not dissuade the Mormons from standing out in the pouring rain, grinning happily as they handed out literature about their religion. I was impressed with their faith; there weren't a whole lot of things I was willing to stand in the rain for.

Several things inside the church also made an impression on me. The first was the gargantuan mural covering the wall opposite the front-door entrance. It dramatically depicted the second coming of Christ in vivid colors, using everyday people to show who would be saved and who would be destined to everlasting hell.

"Is this what happens when you die?" I asked my father, gazing curiously at the figures being forcibly yanked toward the lighter, or "good," side of the picture by those already there. "No, dear, it's just a symbol," he answered. Nevertheless, the scene remained with me, the harsh judgmentalism giving me cause to fear for my own fate.

The opulence of the temple also surprised me. All the floors were covered with what seemed like a foot-thick carpet, and no expense had been spared in the intricate details of the rooms. Doorknobs shone, stained-glass windows sparkled, and anything that wasn't made of gleaming mahogany was gilded. I felt like I was in a four-star hotel.

The money for the extravagant trappings came from the church members, my parents explained later, who were required to give ten percent of their income—called "tithing"—to the church no matter how poor they were. This dictate somehow didn't seem right to me; nor did the expensive decorations. Did God like pretty buildings? Did that make Him happy or more willing to help the church's members? If so, Christian Scientists were doomed. Their buildings were hovels in comparison, my grandmother's unpretentious brick church particularly standing out in my mind.

I didn't completely write off Mormonism until my freshman year at Harvard, after I cornered a Mormon classmate of mine at several meals and quizzed him about the religion. I had had more than spirituality on my mind; he was tall, blond, handsome, and an internationally acclaimed swimmer, and I would not have minded dating him a few times. The only thing against him was that his personal habits were impeccable: he didn't smoke, drink, or swear, and at parties he often stood shyly in the corner with a glass of milk. People that pure made me nervous.

Nevertheless I sat down with him in the Freshman Union one evening after our respective workouts. "So Mike," I began as I dug into a mound of stir-fried vegetables, "tell me about what it's like to be a Mormon." My tendency to not mince words and go straight to the heart of the matter was disconcerting and off-putting to many, but Mike seemed pleased with my interest. Perhaps he saw this as an opportunity to convert me.

"It's really wonderful. I think it is the finest and most God-fearing way to raise a family," he said reverently. For a moment my mind skipped ahead a few years. I liked family men, and Mike and I would probably produce tall, blond athletes if we got married, which wasn't an unpleasant thought.

"Tell me more," I said smiling, encouraging him with my appreciative voice and eyes.

Mike talked for a while about the lengthy Sunday services and some of the ceremonies of the church, including one where the congregation had held a service in which they had married his dead grandparents in the Mormon faith—in absentia, of course.

"How in the world can you marry dead people? Why would you even want to?" I was confused.

"To save them. If they didn't marry in the Mormon faith, they won't go to heaven with us, so we can do it for them after they die."

I wasn't sure what I thought of this practice, but I didn't say anything. I also didn't want to raise his hackles by bringing up what I saw as the sexism of the church, which was ruled with an iron fist by a bunch of old, white men.

"One of the things we do for the church is spend two years as missionaries, converting others," Mike continued. I knew about these people. They had come to our front door once when I was young and my mother had invited them in to talk. They had been dressed in simple dark suits, and had been clean-shaven and well mannered. They had also gotten to our house on bicycles, which had intrigued me.

"Are you going to take two years to be a missionary?"

"Yes. I'll probably take the next two years off and travel in South America."

"What about college? Your friends? The Olympics?" I said with obvious surprise, putting my fork down. "Will you come back to Harvard as a sophomore when we're all seniors? You wouldn't enjoy that, would you? Also, what about training? Will you be able to swim during those two years?"

Mike explained that the church expected him to put its tenets before his life, and that swimming would have to be shelved along with Harvard while he answered the call. He wasn't even allowed to swim for recreation during the two years he'd be away because there was a statistic about people dying while swimming that the church didn't like.

"They don't expect you to put your life on hold, do they? I mean, won't you be upset to just start here and then leave?" I was astonished.

"It really doesn't matter. What I want is not important because there is a lot of God's work to be done in the world."

With that comment, I returned silently to my vegetables, convinced that all religions were stupid. They had silly rituals, suffocating rules, and lots of hypocrisy. I didn't even like a lot of the people who regularly attended church; some of them were the meanest people I knew. No, I would have to find a religion that didn't require a lot of me. Mormonism involved too many sacrifices for others.

Mike left school after our freshman year, never to return to Harvard. The last I heard, he was enrolled at Brigham Young University in Utah following his two-year mission, and his name was rising again on the list of world-ranked swimmers. I thought of him often, wondering if his mission had benefited him, or if he missed us and the Harvard experience. Although I admired him for his strong commitment, I was turned off by our conversation and the imposition of the religion on his life.

In many ways, it reminded me of the stranglehold the Pope had over most Catholics and the way they lived their lives. At one point, however, that religion held a strong allure for me, too. All of my Catholic friends went to church every single Sunday, which was impressive in itself, and some of my fellow swimmers even sought out churches on Sunday mornings when we were competing in other cities. They also did something strange when they were on the racing blocks before the starter's gun: they made the sign of the cross. I thought that was pretty neat. I figured they had a direct line to God because most of them swam well after the quick blessing.

But a couple of things started to bother me as I got older

about the Catholic faith. For one, most of my churchgoing Catholic friends didn't attend services because they wanted to. They did it out of rote or fear. Many also didn't follow the Pope's dictates about birth control. In fact, I didn't have a single Catholic friend who didn't use contraception or who didn't approve of abortion in certain situations. Despite these obvious breaks with the church, however, they still remained Catholics, attending church in body if not in spirit.

Annulment was another bizarre Catholic concept to me. How could the Pope declare that a marriage had never taken place when it obviously had, and when there were often children to show for it? And why couldn't the Catholics in question remarry in the church without going through the lengthy annulment process? It seemed awfully harsh to me. What about forgiveness, and the fact that sometimes people made mistakes?

My final straw as far as religions went, however, had been when a born-again Christian had shattered our friendship one day by telling me that she was praying for me because my soul was "hanging in the balance." Because I had not accepted Jesus Christ as my personal savior, she said, I was not going to go to heaven.

Well, who was going to make it into eternity? I asked, bewildered. And what about all of the people in other religions—like the Jews—who lived very spiritual lives, yet who didn't see Jesus in the same light as she did?

My friend had just shaken her head sadly. The Scriptures clearly said only people like herself would sit on God's right hand, and if I read the book of John I would see things her way, she promised. I just distanced myself from her and her beliefs after that conversation. Any religion that promoted exclusivity and an attitude of superiority wasn't for me. I had decided at that point that atheism was the most viable path.

"So you see," I said to Betsy as I sipped my coffee and related these episodes, "religions stink. They are controlling, hypocritical, and they inspire fear in their members. I mean, wars are being fought in the Middle East over religion and God! If we all go to the same place when we die, why is there so much competition and hatred among different faiths to prove that theirs is the only way to reach God?"

"You've really gotten bogged down in details," Betsy said, mashing her cigarette in the ashtray and pouring a fresh cup of ginger tea. "No one said that you have to have a religion to believe in God. Why do you think you have to go through all kinds of difficult channels and services to reach Him? Don't you think that there's something greater than yourself watching out for you now?"

"No, I don't."

"Well, then, you can forget about getting and maintaining any kind of abstinence from compulsive overeating if that is your attitude."

"Why?"

"Caroline," she sighed, "don't you see how badly you've messed up your own life by trying to do things yourself? All this emphasis on dieting *your* way, eating *your* way, and running things *your* way has gotten you into trouble. Look what you did to yourself last night, for example. You thought that you—and you alone—had been responsible for not binging for twelve weeks, so you decided that you had a firm grip on things. You were in control.

"So you got cocky," she continued. "You weren't abstinent in a serene way; you were stark-raving abstinent!"

"What do you mean by that?" I asked, laughing at the image of me being stark-raving anything.

"Not eating by the skin of your teeth. Hanging on by your fingernails. Thinking more about what you would and wouldn't eat than changing some of the reasons why you ate in the first place. You were bound to have a slip," she said evenly. "You haven't developed a Higher Power that will help you get well."

I bristled. Her words sounded preachy and suspiciously religion-laced. "Are you telling me that I have to have a belief in God to get well?" If that was a prerequisite, I didn't want any part of this group any longer. I wasn't going to be one of those weak people blindly bowing to the will of God; nor was I going to go to church.

"You weren't listening," Betsy replied. "I said a Higher Power; I didn't say God."

"Oh, I thought they were the same thing."

"Well, for most people they are. But not everyone. A

Higher Power is simply a force greater than yourself upon which you can rely to help you recover."

"Why do I need to do that? Can't I just do it myself, with help from you and other people? That seems to be working."

"How well did it work last night?"

She had a point. But how could I guarantee that something outside myself could make those binges get better, or disappear? I asked Betsy that question.

"You just have to trust. You have to look around you and decide who you want to be like. Then you have to do what those people have done to get well. You can't do everything Caroline's way. Look where that route has taken you."

"So you believe in God, huh?"

"I didn't at first," Betsy said carefully. "I had trouble just trusting that another person would care enough about me to talk to me at any time of the day, and who promised that if I did what she did then I could stop binging. And, as I told you, my first sponsor wasn't bulimic. She was just a garden-variety compulsive overeater who went on starvation diets after binges instead. But she looked great and said that she had stopped binging one day at a time, so I decided to do what she was doing: three meals a day with nothing in between, none of my personal binge foods, and lots of telephone calls and meetings."

"What about God, or this Higher Power stuff, though?"

"I'm coming to that. Like I said, I had trouble with that concept, but my sponsor told me that if I trusted her enough, then I could make her and the group my Higher Power. She said to just rely on the group for strength and to believe that the forces that had worked through her and others would certainly work for me. That's how I first was able to turn my will over to something greater than myself, and that's when the real recovery started, and the habits and beliefs that had led me to binge and purge began to disappear."

"So do you believe in God now?"

"Now I do, but it took some time. Once I decided to stop struggling and to follow the instructions of the program to the letter, then miracles started to happen. The desire to stop eating compulsively and purging began to be lifted, one day at a time. I stopped shoplifting and was able to plan my daily meals and stick to them. And while it was hard at times, and I desperately wanted to eat sometimes, I just kept trusting in the power of the group and things kept getting better.

"Soon it was hard *not* to believe that there was a God who was looking out for me, doing for me what I couldn't do for myself. And when I looked around me and saw people who had also tried everything in the world to stop eating, but who had never been successful until they had turned their will and their lives over to a Higher Power, which many called God, then I really knew that there was a powerful, omnipotent force around me."

"Betsy, maybe I can make you and the group my Higher Power, but I don't know if I'll ever be able to trust in a loving God that wants me to get well. There were times when I prayed in desperation to stop binging, but I never was able to get well. Besides, He'd never forgive me for some of the things I've said and done over the years. I mean, I've stolen, lied, said cruel things to people who love me, and I've been ungrateful for a lot of gifts and talents I've been given. I'm sure God is fed up with me, if there is a God."

"First," Betsy said, "all those times you prayed to stop binging I'm sure you didn't believe that something was out there to help you. You have to at least act as if there is a Higher Power waiting to pick you up and carry you through the rough times.

"Second, you have to state what the condition is to get results. Did you just pray to be normal, as opposed to saying that your life was completely unmanageable and that the food had driven you to your knees? You have to state accurately and honestly what the condition is before you can pray for the solution.

"Third, do you know the story of the prodigal son?"

I did, indeed. My grandmother had taken me to the National Gallery of Art when I was small, and I had sat transfixed in front of the famous painting for many minutes while she had told me the biblical story of the son who had gone out and squandered his inheritance but had been welcomed back as a pauper by his father anyway. The story had touched me tremendously, as had the painting, which dramatically showed the aged father embracing his raggedy son.

"That story is just an analogy for the love that God has for us," Betsy insisted, leaning forward to emphasize her point. "He is always waiting to welcome us back into his arms and forgive us for our past transgressions. But He gave us free will, so we have to ask Him into our lives; He can't come in where He's not welcome."

What had I gotten myself into? All I wanted to do was stop binging, and here I was discussing theology in a trendy restaurant! It was absurd! But Betsy was making sense to me. My way had indeed gotten me nowhere with the food. Trusting that something outside myself could help was certainly appealing but very scary.

Betsy interrupted my silence. "Look at that vacuum cleaner," she said, pointing at the machine now whirring around the deserted restaurant. "You can vacuum and vacuum all day, dragging the thing around, but it won't pick up anything until it is plugged into a Higher Power—an outlet!"

I had to laugh at her comparison. She was right.

Pleased with my laughter, she continued. "When you go into a room and it is dark, you don't question that the light switch is going to work either. You just assume that the electricity will illuminate the room when you flick the switch. You never stop to question why it happens. That's called trusting, too."

I was tired, and my mind was swirling with unresolved thoughts. I didn't quite know what to make of this whole conversation, but I felt on the verge of something big. This was an opportunity for me to challenge a lot of my past assumptions, and to admit that I didn't know everything. But relying on a Higher Power was frightening. I had never allowed myself to become dependent upon anyone. Even in my most intimate relationships, I had always kept a lot of my thoughts and feelings to myself because I was terrified of becoming too reliant on anyone. Usually when I had made the mistake of opening up too much about my thoughts, or caring too much about someone, I had gotten hurt. Totally trusting in something else, especially about an issue that was destroying my life, was going to be difficult.

But I was also tired of fighting. I was sick and tired of the food obsession. Of being unable to eat out at restaurants unless there was a salad bar, or a bathroom where I could purge undetected. Of feeling inferior to almost everyone else. Of hating to look in the mirror, or have my picture taken. There had to be a better way.

"Do you think I could stop binging again for good if I had a Higher Power?" I asked Betsy doubtfully. I wanted to recreate the clean feeling I had enjoyed for the last twelve weeks, but I also wanted to let go of the food obsession more completely. Betsy was right: I had been stark-raving abstinent.

"I did," she said simply.

Again I studied her face carefully. She wasn't lying. I had heard her story at meetings, and she had shared even more sordid details about her decade of binging and purging with me on the phone. If she could recover, so could I. My competitive fires flamed again. I could do it, too.

"Okay," I said, "where do I start? Do I have to pray yet?"

"No," Betsy laughed, putting down a few dollars for our beverages and standing up. "Why don't you start by just writing down what you would like your God to be like? Your Higher Power should be a God of your own understanding— warm, funny, omniscient, male, female, concrete, nebulous, whatever! Just define a source outside yourself and try to become comfortable with that. When you are ready, then you can pray.

"By the way," she added impishly as we stepped outside, "when was the last time you got on your knees?"

"I scrubbed the kitchen floor last week."

"Good. Then it won't be too difficult for you to get on your knees and pray to your Higher Power, will it? And you can even talk out loud!"

With that Betsy started a slow jog down the avenue to her apartment as I turned down a side street and headed for my place. There was one more person I wanted to discuss this Higher Power stuff with before I made any decisions. I opened and shut our apartment door quietly, hoping Haywood was asleep and I wouldn't wake him up. I crept to the phone in the dining room.

"Diana—did I wake you up?"

"No, I'm just making the kids' lunches for tomorrow. In

fact, I'm glad you called. Standing here late at night is so tempting for eating. It would be so easy to just lick the tunafish spoon, but I know I can't allow myself that anymore. So what's up?" she added cheerfully.

"Well, after tonight's meeting I went out with someone in the program and we talked about Higher Powers and God, and how I have to develop something outside myself to recover. I know that you're studying Hebrew and the Bible, and I was wondering what kind of conclusion you have come to about God."

"Boy, that was a real toughie for me," she laughed. "I really resisted the whole concept in the beginning because both my parents survived Auschwitz, but they lost all their brothers, sisters, and other relatives there. I mean, I don't have any aunts, uncles, or cousins. So I grew up furious with God for letting that kind of barbarism happen. I saw Him as distant, uncaring, and judgmental, and I couldn't conceive of how I could possibly turn my will and my life over to Him."

"Wow," I said softly. "Are your parents the same way?"

"No, that's the wild part! They have so much faith in God it's unbelievable. It was because of them that I started to try to understand more about the Bible and God."

"So when did you come to believe?" I knew Diana had a strong faith now because I had heard her talk briefly about her former spiritual struggles at a meeting.

"Several months ago I was bitching to someone else about how I had been coming to meetings for four and a half years and I had not been able to lose and keep off any significant amount of weight," Diana answered. "She asked me if I prayed for strength, and I told her that I just couldn't do it yet. Then I realized that for four and a half years I had tried everything but surrendering my will and life to a Higher Power and that absolutely nothing had worked. In desperation about the weight, I prayed one night for the willingness to believe in something greater than myself that would take the obsession away, and my life has been a series of miracles since then. I've lost weight, my compulsion to binge is lifting, and I'm finally free to start enjoying life. I'm just so mad that I waited so long to trust in a Higher Power."

As I listened to Diana, I was reminded of a slogan I had

heard at a meeting. One man jokingly said that he had lived through three distinct phases in the program. He called them, "I came. I came to. I came to believe."

"Do you pray on your knees? And talk out loud?" I asked Diana dubiously.

"Oh, sure," she replied. "I feel so much closer to God when I talk like I'm talking to a friend. And that's what He is to me now—a friend."

I thanked Diana for her insights and hung up, staring out into the inky blackness of the night. I looked up at the sky, trying to make out the Big Dipper and the Little Dipper. When I was young, my parents had often taken me, my sister, and my brother outside after dinner, where we had all huddled together under the rough tarp on our trampoline and tried to spot the different constellations. I had never seen anything but a jumble of stars, although occasionally I thought I had seen a dipper. Tonight the sky was twinkling brightly, but if there was a dipper, a hunter, or a bear, I sure didn't see them.

Who or what had created this beautiful firmament? I wondered, as I scanned the heavens. Intellectually I wanted to believe the Big Bang theory that we all evolved from a whirling mass of crazed electrons and protons. But there was so much that was still unknown about the world, and just when textbooks were being printed with these complex theories another discovery was made throwing everything into disarray. It would be so simple to just trust that there was an infinite power that created me, the world, and the heavens, but not being able to understand it scientifically went against all my years of schooling.

"Quit struggling, Caroline," my inner voice commanded me. "Just trust. Don't make everything so damn complicated." The same prompting that had informed me I was going to get well after my first meeting now instructed me to relax and have faith. Maybe I was going crazy, but my conscience, or whatever the source of the words now filling my head was, now told me to get on my knees.

"I can't believe I'm actually doing this," I thought as I sunk onto the hard wood floor, wondering what I could possibly say to God. Other people said that they asked their Higher

Here I am at age four, a happy child and obviously not concerned about my weight or appearance. But it's clear from my dead tooth that my willful nature is already in evidence.

Here are my older sister, Elizabeth, my brother, Billy, and I, the picture of the perfect family. I had no reason to suspect that I wouldn't always be this happy and carefree.

At age twelve I was a swimming champion and held local and state records in breaststroke and individual medley events. This is one of the last times I can remember not being overly concerned about my body and my weight.

With Olympic gold and silver medalists as ancestors, it is no wonder that the Adamses spent a lot of time in athletic pursuits. During the intense summer swim season, we averaged three to five hours daily in the pool. So much time spent in a bathing suit fueled my obsession with my body.

In my senior year at Washington, D.C.'s National Cathedral School, I was editor-in-chief of the school newspaper and one of the lucky few granted early admission to Harvard and Yale. No one looking at my credentials would guess that I was already two years into bulimia and miserable inside.

Powers to guide them throughout the day and to help keep them abstinent. "I think of the acronym "K.I.S.S." when I talk to God," one man said at a meeting. "Keep it simple, stupid."

Okay, I'll keep it simple, I decided. I shut my eyes and laced my fingers together. "God, I'm desperate. I've lost seven years of my life to my food addiction and it has made everything insane. Please take away my obsession and make me better." I said my short prayer softly, afraid Haywood might hear me. I tried to think of something more profound to say, but my mind was blank. "Thank you," I added, wondering if my words would do any good.

Suddenly the room was flooded with light. For a moment I thought God had decided to visit me in all His glory, and my heart beat so fast I felt faint. Hadn't He said, "Let there be light!" in the book of Genesis?

"C, what in the world are you doing?" Haywood stood in the doorway, looking at me as if I had gone slightly mad.

"You don't have to look at me like that," I said haughtily as I got to my feet, embarrassed at having been seen in such a humbling position. "I was just . . ." I wasn't sure if I could get the last word out, but it followed reluctantly. "Praying!" I uttered with finality, sweeping past him into the bedroom. "And I don't want to talk about it, either!"

Haywood got back into bed, grumbling about my late meetings and phone calls, but he didn't mention the praying. I undressed and snuggled onto my side, turning my back to him to discourage any further conversation. As his breathing became deeper and more regular, my embarrassment lifted and a warm sensation entered my body. I thought I felt a powerful pair of arms encircling me, but I knew it was only my imagination. I fell asleep at peace.

SIX

I STARED IN HORROR at the ugly numbers: $518.62. How in the world had I managed to spend that much money in such a short period of time? I tried to conceal my rising panic as I quickly scribbled my name on the charge slips. I looked at the various items being carefully folded and placed into the store's trendy shopping bag: three identical silk shirts in pink, green, and white; black flannel pants that buttoned smartly up the side; a vibrant purple and green imported sweater; several silk handkerchiefs; a "power" black linen suit; a colorful pleated wool skirt; and a huge belt that drooped toward my knees.

I hadn't even intended to come into this chic women's clothing store. My destination in the mall had been the gourmet delicatessen to buy coffee beans, but the sale sign in the

88

store's window had lured me in where a fast-talking sales-woman had flattered me endlessly and convinced me that everything I was buying was necessary for my well-being and future success.

"Oh, darling!" she said ecstatically every time I re-emerged from the tiny dressing room wearing something she had culled from the racks. "I've never seen anyone carry off that outfit the way you do! You must take it!"

I had let her talk me into trying on things I normally wouldn't consider buying, like the black suit. "Don't you know that every woman must possess one of these?" she asked me incredulously, amazed at my lack of business savvy. "How can you get any man to take you seriously if you don't wear black every now and then?" she scolded.

I had bowed to her fashion judgment, especially when she pointed out the "darling" kick pleat in the skirt and the vents in the back of the jacket. "So chic," she murmured as she made me spin in front of the mirror and the other customers. Giddy with the praise, I happily submitted to her ministrations, enjoying the ego pampering, however false. The only item I drew the line at were the eelskin pumps; although I was fully capable of living in a leather world, twenty dead eels on my feet didn't turn me on.

"Uh, I'm sure I won't need to do this, but are these things returnable?" I asked with a weak smile as I put my charge plate away and picked up the bags.

The saleswoman frowned at me. Suddenly, I felt like a rancid piece of meat. "You do not like your clothes?" she asked with surprised disdain. "Or you are, perhaps, worried about the bill?" Her dark eyes, rimmed with jet-black eyeliner, stared disapprovingly at me.

"Oh, of course I can pay the bill," I said airily. I didn't want her to dislike me for my apparent lack of wealth. I wanted this saleswoman to admire and accept me, to let me fit into the affluent group of women who shopped here. I smiled placatingly. "It's just that I let my husband veto some of my purchases. You know, it's no use wearing something your husband can't stand!"

"Actually, everything you bought is on sale, and it can only be returned for store credit. I'm sure he'll like what you bought. How could he not? You look so divine in everything," she cooed, drawing the word *divine* out. "And think of how much money you saved! If you had bought everything at full price, the total would have been much higher, so you really got some bargains!"

I smiled meekly as I left, assuring her I would return soon to check out the fall shipment. If these saleswomen were on commission, she had certainly made some good money off me. I didn't really like everything I had bought, but I hadn't figured out a nice way to say no every time she thrust a new outfit into the dressing room. Just as I had been a pushover with Bob and the plate of food he had given me a few months earlier at the leasing kickoff, I had been unable to resist the saleswoman's blandishments. I was just a people pleaser, pure and simple. I wanted everyone to like me, and that meant never saying no to anyone.

I angrily berated myself as I left the mall, vowing not to spend any more money that month. My shopping was getting out of hand. It seemed that every time I walked into a store, I bought something whether I needed it or not. Records, jewelry, shoes, towels, pens, kitchen supplies—the list was endless. I found something Haywood or I "needed" every day, justifying the purchases by declaring that I had seen an article saying that it was an item no couple could live without. "This juicer is supposed to be the best in the country," I told Haywood one night while I pulverized a mound of carrots and celery for him to sample with dinner. "We'll be healthy forever!" He had gotten angry even before he had tasted the orange liquid, spitting it out in disgust and getting a beer while muttering about cutting my charge cards in half.

I knew that I had simply switched compulsions from eating to shopping, which I had heard was a fairly common occurrence for people like me. The instant gratification of the new item and the fleeting pleasure of signing a charge slip was similar to the beginning of a binge, as was the subsequent "out of control" feeling and the guilt about overdoing it. Some of the people in my program attended meetings for compulsive spenders but I didn't feel ready for that yet. Not only had I not hit a shopping "bottom" yet, but I also felt that

90

buying clothes was therapeutic atonement for my years of store avoidance.

When I had first become obsessed with my weight and my body ten years earlier, I had stopped buying new clothes because I hated to look in the store mirrors at what I thought was a fat body. The pendulum had swung the other way now, though. I was so delighted that I could wear a decent size and not look bloated all the time that I was indiscriminately buying everything that fit. As I locked my new purchases in the car trunk and started the drive home, I thought uncomfortably of all the people in the program who had said that true recovery meant moderation in everything: sex, shopping, smoking, coffee, and more. Damn. I knew they were right, but I didn't like hearing it.

My mind meandered back ten years to when I had become so dissatisfied with my body. Although many people had hated the National Cathedral School uniforms of drab, shapeless sacks and unflattering seersucker dresses, I had eagerly worn them, grateful that they camouflaged my body and gave me an excuse not to shop. Dreaded times were "free dress" days when we were allowed to wear regular clothes: opportunities that others took to show off new, stylish wardrobes. Thankfully, these days were kept to a minimum, though, because school administrators wanted to avoid clothes competition among the students. With so much genuine cutthroat competition over grades and extracurricular achievements, clothes were just one more arena where we could have waged war.

To my great dissatisfaction, the school's uniform regulations were relaxed during the Carter White House years when low thermostats were the rage. A political group of students banded together and lobbied the headmaster for warm corduroy pants during the winter months. In a patriotic fervor, the measure passed. Thus dark-colored corduroy pants became the uniform for most of the year, causing me tremendous consternation. Not only was a bloated, postbinge stomach tough to cram into most pants, but I despairingly observed that the size tags on the backs of the pants—which I surreptitiously took note of—revealed that my waist was larger than just about everyone else's.

I'm sure I wasn't the only one who took note of these silly measurements because it was a rarity for a girl not to be on a diet of some sort. Starting in fourth or fifth grade, we made comments about one another's bodies, sparing no feelings. If a girl tended toward pudginess, we wasted no time in telling her. If she was very thin, she was put on a pedestal. And if at lunch one of us made the mistake of taking a helping of mashed potatoes, another would quickly chime in that it was fattening, and that a lake of butter in the center—with 100 calories per tablespoon—would make her even more corpulent. With this kind of peer pressure operating, I don't see how anyone could escape from Cathedral—or any other girl's prep school—without an eating disorder or obsession of some sort. Just as competition in classes was taken for granted, competition for the trimmest figure naturally followed.

Somehow I managed to avoid the extreme dieting phase until I got into Cathedral's middle school: seventh and eighth grades. At that time, just about everyone was talking about boys and bodies, and I learned quickly that a good body attracted a guy, and fat was a turnoff. Figurines, scale numbers, and various bizarre diets became universal concerns. Whenever I heard that someone weighed less than 100 pounds, I flew into a tizzy. Although I could never be described as chubby, I was taller than almost everyone in my class and outweighed most of my peers by ten to fifty pounds. It never clicked that taller might equal heavier; I just wanted to be the same as everyone else.

Having a good body—good enough to attract one of the prized St. Albans boys—involved being more than thin, however. It meant having breasts, too. But the Adams women were not known for their curves and I was no exception. I often soothed myself with the knowledge that as a competitive swimmer I had less weight to drag around in the water. It didn't erase my strong yearning for a Raquel Welch bustline, though.

I was probably the last girl in the class to buy a bra, which my mother finally insisted was necessary. One Saturday morning when I was thirteen, we went to the Saks Fifth Avenue lingerie department to acquire this important item.

"My daughter needs a bra," my mother greeted the saleswoman loudly. "Do you have anything in her size—probably a 32A?"

I wanted to die. Not only was 32A the closest size to a training bra, but I was sure that everyone in the store had heard her pronouncement of my deficiency. I looked around for a rack of negligees to hide in.

"Of course, madam," the woman said, motioning us over to the counter where she began pulling various lacy undergarments out. "We have a lovely Olga bra that is fiber-fill. This will give the young lady a nice shape."

My mother held the bra up, then draped several that appealed to her over her arm. "These are nice. Let's go try them on, Caroline."

I snatched them off her arm, casting a dirty look her way. "I'll do it myself," I said with finality. "After all, I get to make the decision—not you!"

I did wind up with the 32A fiber-fill, which did give me a nice shape but did not win me any boyfriends. In fact, boy-girl parties became the bane of my existence. While everyone else seemed able to snare and keep a boyfriend, I remained dateless, gradually convinced that I had a fatal personality flaw, a defective body, or both.

I could tell my parents were equally stymied by the lack of male attention. One night, after returning home from yet another party where I had sought refuge in the cake and pretzels after watching everyone else pair off in the corners and bedrooms, I went into my parents' room to let them know I was home.

"How was it?" my mother asked tentatively, half expecting me to burst into my familiar storm of tears.

"Awful, as usual," I said mournfully, trying my best to not cry.

As I closed their door and headed down the hall to my room, I heard my mother say worriedly to my half-asleep father, "Bill, have we done something wrong?"

Not having to worry about dates, however, brought several bonuses, not the least of which was having the phone silent most of the time. The other benefit was the time it afforded me to pack my résumé with good grades and college application-enhancing jobs and hobbies. Getting good grades at Cathedral was no easy feat, though. The sixty-plus girls in my class had achieved mightily to even gain admittance, and those same sixty now sought to rise to the top of the class and outdo one another in every possible way.

In seventh grade I started to drink coffee, not because I liked it, but because it gave me an added boost in studying for the frequent tests and exams we faced. One of the most dreaded courses that year was medieval history, which we had been warned about by older students as one of the toughest classes we would ever encounter. This fact was driven home to me in one of the first sessions.

"How do you spell 'medieval'?" one unsuspecting girl asked.

"It has 'die' in it," the teacher answered, only half jokingly.

The class moved at a fast pace, covering everything from the fall of the Roman Empire to the Byzantine period. Homework assignments ranged from lengthy readings in difficult religious books to creating a mosaic masterpiece from construction paper scraps. But what had really given me the most trouble was memorizing the various routes the Visigoths, Huns, and Crusaders had taken over the centuries. The night before the biggest exam of the year I burst into tears, terrified that the multicolored routes on my maps would never register in my brain.

I walked into my parents' bedroom, tearfully holding the stained maps. "Will you love me if I don't get a good grade on this exam?" I asked my father. "I'll never learn all of this by tomorrow."

My dad took a look at the map and simply said, "You can learn it. You can do anything you set your mind to." He had also made a point over the years of telling us that he had been number two in his high school class but that he should have been number one. The message was clear; I went back to study for a few more hours until, exhausted, I fell asleep.

The rest of high school was filled with courses like medieval history, our grades becoming increasingly more important. We knew that the cut-off year for getting "bad" grades—anything below a B, many of us thought—was eighth grade; in ninth grade everything went on a transcript that would be

94

sent on with our college applications. And admission to the Ivy League institutions, or places of comparable reputation, was the Holy Grail of which most of us were in hot pursuit.

Sometimes this college scramble led people, including me, to do and say things about others that resembled guerrilla warfare. Once a girl in my English short-story class received a rave review from our attractive male teacher about a composition of hers. She was a talented writer, but her good grades became suspect, and before long a rumor about her and the teacher was making the rounds, always ending with a smirky comment about the way she earned her A's.

In eleventh grade, my obsessive focus on getting into the "right" college reached a new height. The first major hurdle my classmates and I faced were the Preliminary Standard Achievement Tests (PSATs), affectionately known as the "peesats." Taken near the beginning of the school year, these innocuous multiple-choice exams had the potential to make or break students' college applications and self-esteem. Doing well on them could vault a student into the National Merit semifinalist ranks, while poor performance could drive her into a self-doubting abyss of despair followed by enrollment in the expensive SAT-preparation courses.

The day the scores were available at school, a long line formed outside the college counselor's office. I joined the throng, my heart beating impatiently. Perhaps the numbers would bear me out as an intellectual fraud, which I felt I was a great deal of the time. I could BS on the essays and exams we were given as well as the next person—usually getting the required high grades and laudatory comments from teachers —but there was no fooling the multiple-choice sheets and number-two lead pencils.

Finally it was my turn to enter the counselor's office. "You did very, very well, Caroline," she said, smiling brightly. "You are in the ninety-eighth percentile of the country in intelligence!"

I glanced at the two numbers, quickly doubling the verbal score and adding the math to it. The total indicated who would be without honors, commended, or a semifinalist. "Will I be a National Merit semifinalist?" I asked hopefully.

"No, you'll be commended. The District of Columbia's

cut-off this year is higher than ever. You fall short by four points."

My heart sank. "But I live in Maryland!" I protested.

"That's true, but because you go to school in the city you are judged on those standards. If you went to school a few miles down the road, you would be a semifinalist, but then you wouldn't have the privilege of getting the education you are getting here."

One of the privileges of going to Cathedral was hammered home as I left the office and immediately had the test results yanked from my hands by one of my classmates. "We have the same score!" Sheila chortled, holding her results next to mine. Everyone in the line looked at us as she told them what we had gotten. I was furious, partly because she had invaded my privacy and partly because everyone would now know I was "only" a commended student. Angrily I grabbed the precious scores and headed for the phone to call my parents with the news.

Later that day, I chanced upon the nosy Sheila in study hall, going from one member of my class to another, asking them their scores and revealing all the ones she knew about. Such is the stuff of private schools.

National Cathedral was not unique in this sense, however. Other schools had stories that rivaled the ones circulating in our halls, but we liked to think that our classes, our students, and our college acceptance results were better than those at other local private schools. And we liked to talk about the plethora of ambassadors, senators, and Cabinet members whose daughters graced the school, as if the line of gleaming black limousines and chauffeured cars outside the school every afternoon justified the grim competitiveness that permeated every minute of the long days.

By the time I reached eleventh grade, bulimia was an ingrained part of my coping mechanism. Whenever I felt overwhelmed with schoolwork, my swimming career, twice-a-week piano lessons, and the never-ending quest to get into an Ivy League college, I turned to food to let off steam. As long as I didn't feel I could rebel in any other way, the binging and purging was a violent release of my fears, frustrations, and anger.

96

I never discussed my bulimia with Cheryl or Gina after they taught me how to purge. It just never came up, and I didn't want them to know that I, too, had succumbed. I also never confided in anyone else about it. As I became more adept at getting my food and covering up the binges, though, I noticed a number of other girls in the school who had the marks of a bulimic: sore throats, watery eyes after visiting the bathroom, massive consumption at lunches, hours of exercising, and that haunted, hunted look that I had come to know so well. Whenever I saw someone I suspected of bulimia, however, I consoled myself with the thought that I was less obvious than they were, and that I could stop whenever I wanted. I just didn't really want to yet, I told myself.

National Cathedral couldn't be faulted for not doing something about the growing problem because little was known in the mid-1970s about bulimia, and even less on how to treat it. Plus, bulimics were almost impossible to spot, unless they had anorexic tendencies as well. Anorexics—of which Cathedral also had its share—simply stopped eating and started compulsively exercising, and their skeletal frames made them impossible to ignore. One girl in my class wasted away to seventy pounds before the school intervened and she was hospitalized. Until then, though, I stared at her in fascination at meals, where she played with a lettuce leaf coated in mustard for hours, and in the library, where she did her homework standing up so that she could burn off as many calories as possible.

I often wished I had more anorexic tendencies, because once I discovered binging and purging, the idea of depriving myself of anything was anathema. I did have an anorexic phase in eighth grade, though, when I subsisted on several hard-boiled eggs and cottage cheese every day. The more weight I lost, the more compliments I received. I was almost too sick to appreciate them, however, because whenever I stood up quickly, the room spun around me and black spots danced before my eyes. My swimming performances also deteriorated. I had no energy to complete the grueling workouts, but I never equated my diet with my lack of stamina. All I knew was that getting into a bathing suit was much more pleasant as I got lighter.

My high school reverie was suddenly broken. I angrily jammed the brakes on my car, leaning on the horn at the offending driver who was now impeding my fast progress home from the mall. She had tried to merge into traffic in front of me and I was having none of it. I angrily cursed the woman, shouting obscenities as I passed.

Almost immediately I felt guilty as I settled back into the fast lane. I had heard people say at meetings that they made a point of letting people into traffic and of not being angry about it. Betsy had explained later that doing nice things for people was one of the key ways of alleviating compulsions because it got us out of ourselves. The program suggested doing at least one nice thing a day for someone else without getting found out. Not getting found out also developed humility. Some of the ways I had heard suggested besides letting people into traffic were feeding expired parking meters, paying for the car behind you at a toll booth, sending an anonymous floral bouquet, and starting a subscription to a magazine for someone else. This was an area I would have to work on. Every fiber in my body craved recognition for my good acts. When I complained to Betsy that I would never be humble enough, she just said, "Progress, not perfection. We aren't saints—we're just willing to grow along spiritual lines."

I checked my watch. Haywood and I were due at a barbecue in less than an hour. I was going to be late as usual. My inability to be anywhere on time was another of my glaring character defects that Betsy had told me would have to be eliminated. Selfishness and self-centeredness went hand in hand with compulsive overeating, and making people always wait for me was definitely selfish. I pressed harder on the gas pedal as my mind wandered back to National Cathedral and my senior year.

Shortly after that school year began, I became convinced that I was headed for a nervous breakdown. Although my résumé said all the right things, I was still terrified that if I didn't get into the "right" college, my life would end in humiliation and ignominious failure at the tender age of seventeen.

The college counselor tried to allay my fears by assuring me that my credentials were impeccable. I was still an excellent swimmer despite the toll dieting had exacted, and I had held leadership positions at school, including president of my class twice and editor-in-chief of the school newspaper. In addition, I was in my tenth year of piano lessons and competitions, and my résumé listed a phalanx of jobs and activities that surprised even me when I perused them, wondering where I had fit everything in.

One of my activities had been a three-and-a-half-week stint on an Outward Bound course in the rugged Sierra Nevada Mountains after tenth grade. I had been accepted under the age cutoff of sixteen for this challenging test of survival skills and leadership abilities. While it had been an extremely difficult and valuable experience, my primary interest in going had been to lose weight while hiking in the hot, California sun. In fact, I had been so sure that I would return from the trip svelte that I had eaten heartily at every meal. The three-day "solo"—a solitary period without food or water—had not been enough to negate my gluttony during the other twenty-five days, though. In fact, the first thing my father said as I stepped off the plane when I got home was "Gosh, you look heavy, dear." I had been so angry and hurt that I had barely said a word in the drive home from the airport, much to his chagrin.

Because of my high marks and numerous activities, the college counselor recommended that I apply for an Early Decision at Princeton, Harvard, and Yale. Early Decision was a mixed blessing; if you were admitted in December, you could relax for the rest of the year while other students impatiently waited for regular April notification, earning their envy. But if your application was tabled for further discussion, feelings of inadequacy and fear haunted you for months. A number of the students vied for admission to the same places, too, which unleashed jealousy and gossip about who had lied on her application about being president of nonexistent clubs, or who had gotten her parents to write her essays. In my class of sixty-three students, about twenty applied to both Harvard and Yale.

One gray day in December, the Early Decision results arrived at home. Some people didn't even bother to come to school during the week the letters were expected; others simply glued themselves to the pay phones, calling home many times every day to see whether or not the mail had arrived. Parents were renowned for doing all kinds of things to find out ahead of time whether or not their daughters had been admitted to their schools of choice. One mother in our class simply moved down to Washington, D.C.'s central post office to await mail shipments in the hopes of intercepting the letters early. Others relentlessly called every contact they had who had attended the school in question, pressing for inside information.

I was at school on the fateful December afternoon in question. As I did every day, I staked out my pay phone and called home, only to get my giggling grandmother, who had been keeping up the college vigil with my mother for several weeks.

"Donny, what's going on?" I demanded, as I tried to find out what was so funny. "Did the mail come?"

"Wait, wait, your mother is coming to the phone. She has letters from Harvard and Yale. I don't know what they say, but . . ."

My heart started to pound so loudly I thought the hallway must be reverberating with the sound. My throat was so tight that I could barely utter the words.

"Mom, what do they say?"

"I don't know dear, but I held the Yale one up to the window and I think it says 'congratulations' in the first sentence."

Every ounce of my body screamed with exhilaration. The long wait was over. I could finally, finally relax. I wanted to sob with relief.

"Open them both," I ordered. "Read them to me."

My mother started to cry happily as she scanned the contents. She read both letters aloud, which offered me spots in their classes of 1983. As I listened to her sniffling, it dawned on me that she had been under the gun, too, in this mad college dance. All the years of driving me to workouts, activities, and jobs, while demanding nothing out of me in the way of household chores so that I could study more, had paid off. I had done the work, but she and my father had made the opportunities possible. I hung up with a big smile on my face and a perspiration-soaked shirt.

News like mine at Cathedral was impossible to keep quiet. Within an hour the whole class seemed to know everyone else's fate in the Early Decision roulette. Yale had accepted three of six applicants and Harvard had taken about the same number. No one had heard from Princeton yet, a fatal flaw in their acceptance process because people tended to feel warmer toward the schools that informed them the soonest.

My joy at the glad tidings was soon dashed on the rocks of pettiness, however. I just happened to be in the bathroom when I overheard a conversation between one of the girls who had been rejected by Harvard, and several others who were planning to try their hand at second-tier schools in the regular admission rounds.

"Did you hear that Caroline got into Harvard and Yale?" one said.

"Yeah," another unidentified voice responded. "She only got in because she's a swimmer. The Ivys are looking for blond athletes this year."

"Her parents really push her," another commented. "I'll bet they wrote her applications."

I listened quietly as I heard the other lucky girls get savaged, one by one. Finally the group left and I burst into tears. Why was everyone so mean? I couldn't wait to get out of this place. Only six more months, I consoled myself, then I'd be free of this competition forever. I was sick of going head to head against the same girls in class after class for nine years, and I desperately wanted to get away from these people whom I knew as well as myself.

Soon after hearing from Harvard and Yale, I scotched plans to apply anywhere else. Princeton wound up deferring decision on my application until the regular admission round, but I settled on Harvard and informed both other schools to withdraw my name from consideration. Some of the other girls who fared well in the early decision process didn't do the same—they played the college scalps game. Although a good number of them knew where they wanted to attend, several kept their names in for the regular round of April notification, mostly to see how many admissions they could rack up. By the same token, lots of people applied to more than ten schools—many of which they didn't want to attend—to achieve the same ego-gratifying result. Some pleaded needing a back-up college as the reason, never stopping to think that they might be denying a fellow classmate a spot at the school. For a few girls it was genuinely true; for others, it wasn't.

Was Cathedral responsible for developing my eating disorder? I pondered this question as I turned down the street where we lived and pulled into a spot in front of our apartment complex. After listening carefully at meetings and examining my own personality over the last six months, I had decided not. While the pressures of an achievement-oriented school undoubtedly contribute to the difficulties a young girl faces, I had internalized a lot of the stress and peer pressure to be thin, and had not sought healthier outlets for my fears.

The school had probably only hastened the onset of the disease, I now believed, as my perfectionist personality would have undoubtedly led me to bulimia or another addiction later. I tried not to engage in analysis of why I had become bulimic anymore, though. "Look back, but don't stare," was a phrase I heard often at meetings. Again and again it was said that we didn't really have to understand why we were compulsive overeaters; we just had to concentrate on today and change ourselves so that the destructive behavior could be eliminated.

I looked at my watch again as I hurried inside: four P.M. Haywood was probably furious that we would be cutting it close again. The barbecue was at the home of the senior partner at the law firm where he was working this summer. Every move he or I made was being scrutinized at the frequent gatherings the firm hosted. Being a good lawyer was only part of the reasons someone would or wouldn't be asked to join this established, old-line firm. Other criteria included contacts, sports, hobbies, and the ability to relate well to others. And spouses—mostly wives—were watched, too. I hoped I was an asset to Haywood's career, despite my tendency to speak my mind.

"Where have you been, C?" Haywood looked up from the television, annoyed, as I breathlessly entered the apartment.

"We're going to be late, as usual. Can't you ever be on time? Hurry up and change. We're going to leave in ten minutes. I'm timing you." He tapped his watch for emphasis.

"I was buying coffee beans." That wasn't a complete lie. I *had* been buying coffee beans; I just conveniently didn't tell him about the new clothes in my car trunk. "We have to be rigorously honest in all our affairs," Betsy had often cautioned me. "Lying—to yourself or others—will lead you back into the food." I thought uncomfortably of her warnings. But no one was that honest! A little white lie never hurt anyone, I silently defended myself.

I went to change. What to wear? This was always a grave predicament, capable of ruining even the best of days. For if the chosen outfit didn't fit properly, or if I thought I looked too fat, I either didn't go to the occasion, or I thought miserably about my horrible body for the rest of the day, vowing to be more Spartan in my food choices from then on.

My first combination was a jersey dress with a belt. Within seconds it was off again; it clung too much and made me look hippy. Next outfit: a sleeveless summer dress. No way—now my arms looked heavy. All that sagging skin under my biceps! Maybe I should start lifting weights. But that would make my weight go up because muscle weighs more than fat. I'd worry about my arms later.

Four outfits later—each one discarded after looking in the mirror and turning this way and that, never finding an acceptable view—I was nearing a panic state. Where had the serenity from today's clothes shopping gone? I hadn't been upset about my body while buying all those new outfits! Why did my acceptance of my body careen crazily from one extreme to the next within a few short hours? Was I insane?

"Ten minutes are up!" Haywood bellowed from the living room. "Let's go!"

"Go without me!" I screamed back. "I'm not going! I'm fat!"

"What in the world is wrong with you?" Haywood stood in the bedroom doorway, looking from the heap of clothes on the bed, to disheveled me, and back. "You're not fat; you're beautiful." He was used to these scenes, although they had declined in frequency lately. Sometimes he could talk me out of my fit of pique and disgust with a few soothing phrases, but I was having none of it today. I knew that if I put on a burlap sack and caked my face with ashes, he would tell me I looked gorgeous. He was lying to me.

"I'm fat!" I screamed again. "Nothing fits! I'm not going!"

Now he was exasperated. "I'm tired of this. Your clothes fit fine and you weren't fat yesterday. What changed overnight?"

"I don't know," I whimpered. "All I know is I look terrible in all that stuff." I waved my hand at the bed.

"Wear this," Haywood commanded, taking a shapeless tent dress from the closet. "It's a swimming party anyway, and everyone will be casual. Take your suit, too."

Bathing suit? He had to be joking. I would be mortified if anyone saw my body that exposed. I was still very private about letting anyone see me unclothed. Despite my steady recovery from bulimia, I saw fat everywhere when I had a figure-revealing suit on. I couldn't believe that I had once spent nearly half my waking hours in a bathing suit.

The dress was loose and comfortable. It would pass. But I still felt fat. I'd have to talk to Betsy about my menu planning. Maybe she would have some insights on how I could feel slimmer or lose some weight. Her focus thus far had been on having me just learn to keep food down comfortably and to forget about the weight. Although a number of people said I didn't have to lose weight, I still felt that being a few pounds lighter wouldn't hurt.

Halfway to the party, I realized I didn't know what was going to be served. But Haywood had promised to call and find out so that I could carry something acceptable with me in case none of the food choices were comfortable.

"What did they say was the menu when you called?" I turned to look at him.

Haywood turned a bit red but kept his eyes on the road. "Uh, there will be vegetables and grilled chicken. You won't have any problem with the food. It sounded like everything was stuff you're used to."

Relieved, I sat back. Going out into the unknown was frightening for a food addict like myself. Many times I had heard people talk at meetings about calling restaurants and hostesses to learn what the menu would be. One woman had laughingly related that she had sat down at a restaurant, opened the menu, and then walked out when she saw that there was nothing she could eat serenely. "I know my recovery has to come first," she said. "I have to stay away from people, places, and things that threaten my abstinence."

We mingled at the party for an hour or so before dinner was announced. I went to the dining room with an empty plate, salivating at the thought of vegetables and chicken. The vegetables would calm my ravenous stomach. I knew I could eat as much as I wanted in that food group—within moderation—and not gain weight.

I froze at the table. There was nary a vegetable in sight; nor was there the promised grilled chicken. Instead I saw a pile of hotdogs, a tub of coleslaw, and baked beans. I couldn't eat any of those things. All of them were fattening and I wasn't ready to try to incorporate them into my meal plan.

I stomped outside and cornered Haywood by the pool. "You lied to me! You said there would be salad and chicken, and there isn't a thing I can eat here!" I hissed between clenched teeth, trying not to let anyone overhear my predicament.

"I forgot to call. I'm sorry," he pleaded. "How was I to know they wouldn't have any vegetables? This is the first cookout I've ever been to that didn't have a salad or something. Do you want me to ask Mrs. Landis if she has any carrots? I'm sure she wouldn't mind."

"Great idea," I growled. "That would really draw attention to me. Why didn't you just tell me the truth? My whole evening is ruined. I'll just have to wait until I get home to eat! And if I binge because I'm so hungry, it'll be your fault!" I flounced off, thinking evil thoughts of divorce.

The ride home was made in stony silence except for a heated exchange. "You don't take my eating disorder seriously," I charged. "You don't care whether I get well or not!"

"C, that's not true," he said wearily. "I didn't know it was that important to know what was being served. It's hard for me to understand your compulsion. I just can't imagine having that strong a draw to eat and throw up. Why can't you just eat a little bit of some of that stuff? What's so wrong with hot dogs and cole slaw?"

"Never mind. It would take too long to explain," I huffed before lapsing into silence.

At home I made a beeline for the phone. "Betsy, do you have a minute? I'm just so angry that I have to talk to someone."

"Sure. What's up?"

"I just got home from a party where there was nothing I could eat, and it was worse because Haywood told me that there would be salad and stuff, and when I got there I found out he hadn't called after all. All they had were potato chips, pickles, hot dogs, cole slaw, and other fattening stuff. It was awful. Why don't people serve things everyone can eat?" I grumped.

Betsy sliced right to the heart of the matter. "When are you going to start taking responsibility for your problem? Why does Haywood have to call ahead? Don't you know how to operate a phone?"

"What do you mean?" I was flustered. I had expected sympathy and that wasn't what I was getting.

"Caroline, grow up. Stop blaming everything and everyone for your problem. One sign of maturity and getting well is to take responsibility for your disease. No one made you put the food in your mouth and no one ever made you purge. You'd better start accepting the fact that if you do the footwork and ask for help from your Higher Power, you will make it. Expecting other people to look out for you all the time is just admitting powerlessness over getting better.

"Furthermore, you can't afford anger—which is dripping from every word coming out of your mouth. People like us who have mental obsessions coupled with physiological addictions can't handle anger, justified or not. Resentments are better left to people who can handle them. That and fear are the two things that will lead us right back to the food. Avoid them at all costs."

As usual she was right. How well she understood me! I felt penitent as I thought of Haywood in the other room, baffled at my vehement outbursts and accusations. I couldn't go on hurting the people around me. This *was* my problem—not anyone else's.

"Caroline, are you there?" Betsy's voice had softened. "I'm sorry I was harsh, but sometimes that's what egotistical bitches like us need to get through the facades." She giggled. "You're okay, kid. I see so much of myself in you, and I just don't want you to fall into the same traps I did."

"It's okay," I said. "I was just thinking that you're right. I'll have to go apologize to Haywood." I didn't like admitting I was wrong about anything, but I had heard again and again from Betsy and others that we needed to take daily inventories of our behavior, admitting our wrongs promptly and making proper restitution.

"Good for you," she responded. "You'll feel better afterward and you'll be less likely to eat out of anger or whatever else is going through your head right now. One other thing, though, before I let you go. You'll have to get used to foods like the ones you saw at the party tonight. I was terrified of adding those kinds of things to my meals, but I had to do it, one food at a time, because the fear was holding me back from all kinds of situations—parties, restaurants, and so on.

"My sponsor told me that she ate those kinds of things and didn't gain weight, so I trusted her and tried new things once a week or so. The next time you see coleslaw, have a spoonful. That won't make you fat—it's ten spoonfuls that will make you fat. You just don't know what a normal portion is. Watch other people who are normal and try their portion sizes. But don't ever go back for seconds. If you do, make it a rare, rare occasion. It's that 'just a little bit more' mentality that triggers most of our binges, right?"

"Yeah, you're right. I'll try it, but I'm scared. Should I have something other than salad and cottage cheese for dinner?"

"Are you still having rabbit food every night?"

"Yes," I said, somewhat guiltily. I was still caught up in the diet mentality, but at least I was keeping the food down.

"Look—try a salad with a crab cake tomorrow night. Go to the delicatessen and buy a backfin crab cake, and eat it slowly and enjoy it. Next week we'll add in some quiche."

Crab cakes? Quiche? Those two foods were so scary to me

that I wasn't sure I could promise Betsy anything of the sort. Fried foods and cheesy things like quiche would make me corpulent. But then again, Betsy ate them and she wasn't fat. I sighed.

"Okay, I'll give the crab cake a shot tomorrow night. We'll discuss quiche another time."

"That's right—one day at a time," Betsy said as she hung up.

Before I could make my dinner I knew I had to apologize to Haywood. I felt remorseful about my angry outburst, but saying the simple words "I'm sorry" was going to be tough.

I walked into the bedroom. "What are you watching?" I asked with feigned interest. I despised television except for a few news programs, but Haywood found anything that was in color and moved entrancing. Even the old Roy Rogers movies on Saturday mornings could cast a spell over him that was impossible to break.

" 'The A-Team.' " His voice was flat and sullen, and his eyes didn't stray from the screen.

I scooted into bed next to him, laying my head on his shoulder and entwining my fingers through his. "I'm sorry about what I said tonight. I don't know what got into me at the party. Will you forgive me? It's just that living without the food is difficult, and I haven't learned how to be abstinent in those kinds of situations yet."

Haywood's anger melted immediately. He wasn't used to me asking forgiveness, so he hastened to meet me halfway. "I shouldn't have lied," he said. "I just didn't think it was important what was being served."

"I should have called. It's my disorder, not yours. I've got to take some responsibility for this thing or I'll never grow up," I countered, now eager to come completely clean. It felt good to admit my shortcomings. I was surprised.

"No, no—I shouldn't have lied to you," he emphasized. "That is absolutely the worst thing anyone can do. You don't lie to me anymore, do you?"

My mind guiltily returned to the trunk of my car where my new wardrobe was hidden. "Hardly ever," I responded, aware that I would have to come clean on that score soon. But first things first. Tonight was the food problem; tomorrow we'd have to discuss my spending. "I'm getting better and better and better," I said truthfully.

And I was. Life was unfolding before me with miracles and serenity that I had never before thought possible. I was beginning to believe that there was no food good enough to replace the happiness and contentment filling my life with increasing regularity. A year ago, I couldn't have bought new clothes, gone to a party without binging, or said I was sorry to anyone. I wasn't perfect yet, but I *was* making progress.

I happily padded into the kitchen to fix my abstinent dinner, thinking about how exciting it would be to have crab cakes again.

SEVEN

"I THINK YOU'RE READY to chair your first meeting. Why don't you plan to lead next Monday night's meeting?"

I looked at Betsy incredulously as we walked to our cars after a Saturday night meeting at a local hospital. Since the barbecue debacle last month, I had been working on the program harder than ever, and Betsy had commented several times that I was making a lot of progress. She always urged me to raise my hand and talk at meetings because of the benefits of sharing thoughts and feelings with others. But I didn't feel ready to actually lead a meeting.

"Me? Chair?" I couldn't fathom the idea of me sitting in front of dozens of people and telling them chapter and verse about my eating disorder and the terrible things I had done to support my habit. It was one thing to tell people individually and on the phone about my past and the struggle not to binge, but it would be too frightening to address a group with the rigorous honesty I was continually told I had to practice in every area of my life.

"I don't think I can," I apologized. "Maybe another time."

"Well, I've already volunteered your services," Betsy smiled at me. "You'll be surprised at how relieved you'll feel when it's over. Furthermore, you owe it to some of the new-comers to tell about your struggles with different parts of the program and how you resolved them. It never fails that the speaker at a meeting hits on topics that are of immediate concern to the audience."

I gulped hard. I had nine days to prepare my talk. Most speakers talked for about twenty minutes and then left the balance of time for sharing from the group. I didn't know if I could talk that long.

"What will I say? I haven't ever spoken publicly!"

"Now don't be such a perfectionist," Betsy laughed as she unlocked her car door. "Just be simple. Talk about where you've come from, what you did to change, and where you are now. Don't even prepare anything," she said, reading my mind. "The best speakers just pray that the right words will come to them when they begin. It's just one more way of surrendering to your Higher Power and asking for guidance."

I thought about my new, daunting task on the way home. There were so many things I could talk about: my unhappy high school years, the pressure at Harvard and all the eating disorders there, my shoplifting, my former fears of eating at restaurants without salad bars, and on and on. I would have to prepare an outline of sorts or I'd just ramble, I knew.

When I got home, there were no lights on. Haywood was obviously out with friends. Since I had made it clear that I would be going to a lot of meetings no matter what he said or thought, he had begun to spend more time with his law and business school friends, which I felt was healthy. The last thing I wanted to have was a marriage where both partners were incapable of doing anything without the other one. In fact, one of my friends was in the middle of a divorce from her husband of nine years for that exact reason: their inability to do anything separately had led to general dissatisfaction and boredom, and divorce was the only remedy they could come up with. All the togetherness had taken its toll on my friend; there were very few people she could call friends or confidantes, and because of that I encouraged Haywood to do as much as possible without me, and vice versa. When we were together, we enjoyed each other that much more. And when we went out to dinner, our conversations were animated, unlike some couples I observed who spent their meals in silence, staring idly at the walls and other people.

I went into the kitchen to prepare my dinner. I had decided on a simple meal—a crab cake, a large salad with diet dressing, and half of a cantaloupe. Betsy had been right about the crab cake and quiche; since I had tried them and found that I wasn't gaining weight, I had been able to diversify my meals both at home and at restaurants. It was a miracle to me that I could walk into a restaurant now and not panic about whether or not I could get a salad, whether or not I would be full enough after the meal, what the bathroom was like if I had to purge, and on and on. It exhausted me to even think about the mental gymnastics I had had to perform for years to do a simple task like eating.

I opened the refrigerator and took out my salad makings. I enjoyed this part. Touching food, shopping for it, and baking it was a very sensual act for me. I still loved food, but I was learning to love it without abusing it. I briefly thought about my former obsession with baking in high school. It had really flowered during my anorexic phase when I was thirteen: I had pored over cookbooks and the "Food" section of the newspaper, trying recipes out on my family while eating nothing myself. Later, when the bulimia had taken hold, I had continued to cook and bake, but I had liberally sampled the fruits of my labor.

I glanced over at my ignored recipe box, which was jammed with the yellowing recipe clips—mostly for rich desserts. I doubted I'd ever use them now because the less time I spent in the kitchen, the better. Besides, I was finding all kinds of fun things to do that didn't involve cooking or eating, which was amazing to me.

I surveyed my salad. It was gigantic—enough for a family

of four. I thought guiltily of Annette's honesty at tonight's meeting. She had talked about her massive salads and vegetable concoctions, and how she was striving to eliminate the bulk of noncaloric foods from her diet. "It's heartbreaking to realize that you don't need that much food to live," she had laughed as she described the "trough" she used to make her salads in. "And giving up that huge amount of food is like giving up a friend," she had continued. "But at least now I can go out after meals without feeling as if I have a balloon in my stomach, and I can enjoy making love to my husband. It's tough to feel sexy when you have two heads of lettuce in your stomach!"

I had laughed at Annette's reference to intimacy. Food had come between me and Haywood, too. Like many bulimics, I had entered the program terrified of closeness and the vulnerability of sex; food had been my lover. Some people avoided making love by stuffing themselves with food then pleading heartburn or indigestion. Others, afraid of smelling like vomit after a purge, carried around breath mints, spray, mouthwash, or toothpaste to mask the unpleasant odor if they had to kiss someone. My feelings about my body and my sexuality were changing slowly but surely as I recognized these destructive patterns in my life and discussed them honestly with Haywood and my program friends.

But I was still eating far too many vegetables at times, I thought uncomfortably as I replaced the salad makings in the refrigerator. In the back of my mind I was still scared that if I didn't eat until I no longer felt hungry, then I would die before the next meal rolled around, or I'd have to snack to keep my energy up.

I knew exactly when my vegetable obsession had begun. In eleventh grade I had become convinced that if only I knew correct portion sizes and lost weight, then my bulimia would magically disappear. I had decided that Weight Watchers was the answer, but I didn't have the money to join and pay for the weekly meetings, so I had convinced my grandmother to join and get the diet guide for me.

"Donny, will you join Weight Watchers for me?" I asked her one afternoon after she brought me home from a swimming workout. Donny did everything for her three grandchildren that she possibly could, but this was the strangest request I had ever made of her.

"Why? Do I look like I need to lose weight?" She touched her stomach protectively. My mother was always poking my grandmother's stomach, telling her she looked heavy, but I thought she looked just like a grandmother ought to—slightly plump with soft skin. I couldn't wait to be a grandmother because then I wouldn't have to diet anymore. Grandmothers were allowed to be heavy; people my age weren't.

"No, no, not at all," I said soothingly. "I'm just having a little problem with my stomach. It's kind of bloating out and I think I ought to lose some weight to make it look better." My stomach was actually a source of great concern to me. All the binging and purging had left it distended, and getting into a bathing suit every afternoon was becoming more and more difficult. I couldn't tell Donny that, though. She'd tell my parents and all hell would break loose.

"All right," she said reluctantly. "I'll call tomorrow."

The next time I saw my grandmother she gave me the multicolored Weight Watchers booklet containing all the food groups and accepted portion sizes for weight loss. I was thrilled. Perhaps this would be the key to alleviating my misery.

"Wait, I have something else to give you," she said as I got ready to get out of the car. "I got worried when you said that your stomach was bloating, so I looked up every reference to 'puff' or 'air' in the Bible." She pulled out a sheet of paper covered with references. "I want you to get the Bible and look up all of these quotations and meditate on them. Ask God to relieve you of your bloat through understanding the words."

Her blue eyes were fastened intently on me. I had no idea where my Bible was, nor did I plan to look for it. But she had joined Weight Watchers for me, so I owed her one. "Okay, I will," I promised as I edged out of the car with the sheet of paper.

"Oh wonderful, darling," she exclaimed. "Just ask God for His help. He'll always help you no matter what your difficulty is. But you have to invite Him in; He won't come unbidden."

Needless to say, Weight Watchers hadn't done a darn

thing for me except teach me that certain vegetables were "free"—i.e., they could be eaten any time of the day or night in gargantuan quantities, and weight loss was still promised. I loved that idea, so I set about eating vast quantities of every "free" food on the list, except for the ones I couldn't find, like kale. The net result was that my bloat had intensified, I hadn't lost an ounce, and I had thrown the booklet away in despair. The deadly dance with bulimia had simply continued.

I smiled in my kitchen as I remembered that scene in Donny's car. I shook my head silently, marveling at what I had made others do for my food obsession. So selfish. And the lies! I had to lie to cover up for the food I stole or ate, and I had to lie to cover up for the lies. They had become like second nature to me, and even now I still had to watch for the glib half-truths that dropped from my mouth so easily. Honesty was tough.

I was about to shut the refrigerator door when my eye fell on a jar of peanut butter. It was Skippy Super Chunk—my favorite kind. I hadn't allowed myself any for a long time because it still reminded me of all my binges that had usually incorporated peanut butter in some way. Once during high school I had awakened in the middle of the night and crept down to my family's kitchen where I had eaten half a jar of peanut butter, the huge spoonfuls alternately embellished with chocolate syrup, butter, and grape jelly. I had been unable to sleep after my nocturnal binge, my thoughts whirling around with such questions as: Should I purge? Will someone hear me if I do? If I keep it down, will I get fat? How many hours of swimming will I have to do to exercise it off? And on and on.

The other reason I was laying off the peanut butter was because it was loaded with sugar, which probably explained part of my obsession with it. Many people in the program advised cutting sugar out entirely because of the belief that it created or enhanced food cravings. Betsy had warned me about hidden sugar to look for. "Anything that is above the fourth listing of ingredients in a product that says either sugar, maltose, dextrose, corn syrup, or honey should be avoided," she had said. I had been shocked when I had started to examine my "abstinent" foods—including my daily lunch.

I had had to eliminate lots of them: yogurt, bran cereal, peanut butter, catsup, and muffins among them. I had undergone definite sugar withdrawal, but it had worked. My cravings to binge had lessened tremendously.

Until now. Just a spoonful wouldn't hurt, I told myself as I picked up the peanut butter. Maybe I could just eat the nuts out of it and make that my protein for dinner. I was starting to unscrew the top when I heard Betsy's strident voice infiltrate the Skippy fog.

"All it takes is one bite—one compulsive bite—and you might not be able to stop. This is life or death, Caroline. Don't forget it!" Her warnings were dire. This program had ruined my binges. I found myself unable to binge, or think about binging, without someone's words coming back to me.

The hell with everyone. I'd just have a spoonful and stop there. No one would know, and I still resented the implication that I couldn't control my eating through sheer willpower if I wanted to.

I went to get a spoon—the biggest one in the kitchen. As I held it poised over the glossy, alluring substance I heard Betsy again. "You are powerless over food. Think about that when you want to eat. Ask for your Higher Power's help. And don't forget about the aftermath of a binge. It starts as fun and ends in misery—bloating, guilt, swollen face, bloody throat, shoplifting et cetera. Is it really worth it?"

No, it really wasn't. I didn't want to spend the rest of the night eating and purging, or having to go out to buy laxatives and more food. I dug the spoon in the peanut butter and shoved a hunk down the disposal. Out of sight, out of mind. Many people in the program didn't have anything dangerous in the house. I was playing with fire by having it around. I turned the disposal on and went to work.

Within minutes the peanut butter was gone, along with half the refrigerator and cupboard contents. Haywood's ice cream and chocolate cake disappeared into the whirring jaws of the disposal. So did the strawberry jelly, cream cheese, potato chips, oatmeal pies, and other taboo foods. Most of them were for Haywood, but I was sure he'd understand. I just couldn't have them around.

Soon I breathed a sigh of relief, not unlike the overwhelming peace I had once felt after purging successfully. The kitchen was clean. Nothing remained except salad makings, crackers, cottage cheese, and other healthy foods. I felt good that I had been able to redirect my binge thoughts to constructive actions. I picked up my dinner and headed into the bedroom to eat.

Within minutes, Haywood was home. "Hey, C, I'm home!" he yelled.

"Hi, honey! How was your day?"

He came into the bedroom, shrugging off his clothes as he related the day's activities. "Oh, by the way," he added, "Dave might be calling you soon. I told him about your bulimia and he wants to talk about his sister. She's a little younger than you are, but she's already been hospitalized for bulimia. Now she's living alone and insists everything is fine, but he says that she's still binging and disappearing into the bathroom after every meal. I told him about your group and he just wants some more information."

"You told Dave?" I asked incredulously. Now everyone in Baltimore would know I was bulimic. I wouldn't be able to look Dave in the eye at the next party. The thought that I had once forced myself to vomit after meals probably made him think less of me.

"What's wrong with that?" Haywood asked with obvious surprise. "You're on the phone, day and night, telling everyone about your problems. Dave isn't going to tell anyone else."

"Haywood, you don't understand. Those people I talk to are in my program. They're recovering compulsive overeaters, too, and they are all bound by the tradition of anonymity. If it weren't for the fact that you are supposed to hold what you hear at meetings and in phone calls in confidence, then there is no way I'd be able to talk there about things like the shoplifting! Dave isn't restricted like that! What if it spreads around your law firm that I stole things? Who knows what people will think or say about me or about you? People are petty, Haywood. I've seen it again and again."

Recently I had lunched with an image specialist who had filled me in on the gory details of being a businessman's wife. I had been shocked—or naive—to think that we were judged

117

separately, or that what I did had nothing to do with Haywood's career. "Whatever you do," she had cautioned, "dress down, wear little makeup, and keep your mouth shut at firm gatherings. Look demure. The last thing you need is to have the boss's wife find you threatening and give her an excuse to urge her husband not to promote Haywood."

I had sputtered, "But that's not me! I like bright colors! I like to laugh! Am I supposed to just conform to 1950s expectations of a perfect wife? Haven't you heard of the women's revolution?"

She had regarded me calmly with a knowing smile. "Listen, Caroline, I'm not telling you what you have to do. I'm just telling you what I've seen and experienced in my time. You forget, too, that Baltimore is terribly provincial and very chauvinistic at times. Just play the game and keep your eye on your goals."

After that conversation, the last thing I wanted was to be perceived as defective goods at the law firm, and I repeated my convictions to Haywood.

"C, you worry too much about what other people think. Relax. Dave is just concerned about his sister. And isn't one of the goals of your program to 'carry the message' to the person who still suffers?"

He was right. He had already picked up the program lingo, which amused me. "Okay," I said reluctantly, "I'll tell Dave as much as I can when he calls."

Haywood abruptly changed the subject. "What's for dinner? I'm starving."

"Uh, there's all kinds of stuff in the refrigerator," I said, remembering all of a sudden my frenzied "house cleaning."

Haywood and I had an agreement about food. We each made our own meals, which surprised a lot of our friends. Most people simply assumed that the wife was responsible for the cooking, so when they found out I ate salads a lot, their first reaction was usually "Does Haywood like that kind of food?" That always annoyed me because not only did it presume that I was on kitchen duty, but also that despite my busy job I somehow found time to cater to someone who had two hands and more free time than I did. Besides, he loved to create his meals. With a microwave oven, cheese, and spa-

118

ghetti sauce, he could perform gustatory feats that even impressed me.

"C, what the hell is this all about?" Haywood had reappeared in the doorway, holding a Baskin-Robbins container in one hand and the empty peanut butter jar in the other, his face twisted in disgust. "Did you purge tonight?"

I started to laugh. "No, no—I was thinking about it, but instead I decided to just get rid of the food that tempted me. You don't mind, do you?" I asked sweetly.

After a few seconds of indecision, mixed with relief that I hadn't binged or purged, he said, "No, I guess not. If that's what you need to do, I'll eat things that don't bother you. The other stuff isn't good for me anyway. Besides, you've gotten a lot easier to live with since you got into this program, and I don't want to go back to the other way."

He retreated to the kitchen. "Thanks, love," I called after him. "I knew you'd understand."

I went back to my dinner. Just as I was about to take my next bite, the phone rang. I sighed. These calls were coming fast and furious at every hour of the day and night. We'd have to get an answering machine or we'd go crazy.

"Hello?"

"Caroline! I'm so glad I reached you!"

An old friend was calling—one of the ones I might not see for several years, but who I could pick right up with as if there had been no interruption.

"Celia!" I said happily. "What's up?"

The last time she had been in town, I had sat her down and confided in her about my bulimia and all the secret binging and purging I had done over the years. Like my family and friends, however, she had never suspected or noticed my aberrant behavior. She had listened to my confession sympathetically, clucking at the right times and saying that if there was ever anything she could do for me, all I had to do was ask.

"Well, I'm in Washington for a week or so and I know your birthday is coming up, so my present to you is to take you to the restaurant of your choice for an elaborate dinner. Don't even think about prices; we'll go wherever you want."

I groaned inwardly. She, of all people, should know better than to ask me out to dinner as a present. The last thing I wanted was to celebrate with a meal. I'd feel obligated to have everything from soup to nuts, and she was the kind of person who would wave the dessert cart over after dinner and pick two of the most extravagant pastries on it for us without batting an eye or asking my opinion.

"Um," I paused, "that's great." I hoped I sounded enthusiastic. I quickly tried to think of an acceptable place in town where I could order light, abstinent food.

"Look, just think some about where you want to go," she said. "Is Friday okay? I'll come pick you up at seven P.M. Will Haywood mind?" she added as an afterthought.

"No, he'll find something to do, I'm sure," I answered. We said our good-byes, but by the time I hung up I was seething.

"How dare she do this to me after I've explained my bulimia to her?" I thought angrily to myself. "Is she just one more person who doesn't take eating disorders seriously? Would she take an alcoholic friend to a bar without asking if it was comfortable? Maybe she's even jealous or has an eating disorder herself and she doesn't want me to succeed." My thoughts occupied me until I went to sleep.

Wednesday was my birthday, but I was sure no one at work would do anything for me. The people who were remembered were the ones with secretaries who made a point of having a party for their bosses, or the ones whom other people in the company had a crush on. One young attractive man had received not one, but three cakes on his birthday, complete with cards, hugs, and kisses. I had no secretary and no one had a crush on me.

Therefore it was a shock when I walked into a dark room in the afternoon for a "meeting," only to have thirty people scream "Happy birthday!" As the lights came on, I saw a huge chocolate cake in the center of the table, with my name scrawled across the top in blue icing. I knew I couldn't have sugar, but I wasn't sure how I was going to get around this one.

I began to slice the cake in huge hunks, hoping it would run out before I got to myself. No such luck. The first piece was handed to me as one of the bookkeepers took over the slicing. "You have to try this cake," she said. "I made it myself because I know how much you love chocolate."

I smiled weakly as I thanked her for her thoughtfulness. Maybe I could lie and say I had recently developed diabetes. Some people in the program did just that when they had no alternative. I didn't have the nerve, so I just started to circulate, hoping the conversation would distract people enough so that I could drop the piece in the trash can without being noticed.

"Delicious cake!" Howard boomed. "Why aren't you eating any?"

I turned away from him and looked in the other direction. Standing against the wall was Deirdre, her eyes devouring the cake although she was refusing any herself. I was sure she had an eating disorder—probably anorexia. Everyone whispered about her fainting spells, her miscarriages, her extreme weight loss, and her refusal to eat, but no one did anything to help her that I was aware of. I knew that many companies had Employee Assistance Plans that arranged interventions for people with drug and alcohol problems, sending them off to treatment centers while holding their jobs until they returned, usually after a month. That was very rare with people like me or Deirdre, though. After all, how do you confront someone with bulimia, whom you usually can't spot, or an anorexic, who isn't showing up drunk or high at work, but who is probably angry, dizzy, and weak nonetheless? If I ever kicked this thing for good, I vowed to myself, I would help people like me and Deirdre get restored to wellness in a professional capacity.

Before long the party was over. I had mashed my cake into little pieces, pushing it around the plate and hoping no one was noticing my avoidance of eating any. Aside from Howard's loud comment, I thought I had gone undetected. This abstinence stuff was not easy. There was always a situation waiting to catch you off guard and test your willingness to stick to your food plan.

As I returned to my office, I mulled over people's habit of celebrating with food or liquor. I was continually catching myself falling into the food-as-a-gift trap, so I knew I was as guilty as the next person. For example, I had recently visited a friend in the hospital, and my first reaction had been to take a big box of candy. Just as I had been about to buy it, however, I had thought about what my reaction would have been if I had been the one in the hospital bed. I would have wanted books, flowers or magazines, so I had changed my purchase. But it was a continual process of re-education, and for people who didn't have eating problems, it was probably even more difficult to understand the desire not to receive food—especially sugary things—as a gift.

It was getting easier and easier, though, to withstand the pressure to eat at social gatherings. At a wedding I had just attended, I had had to refuse the wedding cake seven times from the endlessly circulating waiters. Standing next to me had been a high school friend who was recovering from drug addiction. She had had to fob them off with equal dexterity, although she had been busy avoiding the champagne because part of her recovery included ingesting no mood-altering substances. We had laughed about the suspicious stares we had gotten from the smooth waiters—they probably thought we were incredibly boorish—as we had exchanged stories about sticking to our respective programs in the face of such pushiness.

The day after my birthday, I flew up to New York for a dinner honoring a member of our company. I felt proud that I had had something to do with the publicity the award had generated, and I was thrilled to be one of the few participating in the festivities. Several of the top people at the company had also been invited to join the black-tie affair. My only concern about the evening had been the menu for the dinner, which I had had to talk through with Betsy before leaving.

"Betsy, this thing is going to be seven courses, and part of me wants to give myself license to eat it all because it's a special dinner and the food will be wonderful."

"How do you know it will be seven courses? Are you sure you're not projecting?"

"Absolutely. I called up there on another pretext and found out what would be served. The P.R. person told me there would be lobster bisque, filet mignon and vegetables, salad, palate-clearing sherbet, cheese and crackers, chocolate mousse, and then coffee and some little cookies."

"Good Lord!" she exclaimed. "Okay, let's take it one course at a time. What do you want to eat? And what will you be able to eat and keep down comfortably without guilt?"

"I don't want the soup," I said. "That'll spoil the main course. But I want some filet because I haven't allowed myself that kind of food for years. I also want the vegetables and the salad. The rest I don't want."

"Okay. When the soup is served, drink a diet drink and keep talking to someone. People probably won't even notice if you're not having the soup. If they do and they ask you why, tell them that you don't like lobster, or just that you're not hungry for it. And leave it at that. Then eat as much of the main course as possible, have the salad, and skip the rest. Beg off with diabetic complications if you have to. But stick with your plan and you'll feel wonderful at the end of the night. Disappear to the ladies' room and pray during the fifth course. But don't take that first bite. Once you start, as you well know, it's tougher than nails to stop."

As I sat at the dinner I found it easy to do what Betsy and I had discussed. I knew it was essential to have a plan now for my meals, and I was beginning to write down in the mornings what I was going to eat every day. Removing the spontaneity from my preparations made it much easier to keep food in its proper perspective. I found myself relaxing and enjoying the bantering around me, grateful for the freedom I was feeling from the bondage of food.

When the dinner was over, the speeches began. The man from our company accepted his plaque and began to speak about the company's philanthropic mission. Everyone at our table beamed, pleased to be associated with such a laudable organization. Just as the speech was winding down, he looked at the table and said he wanted to introduce the key people in our company—"the men and women who make things happen."

I preened a bit. What an ego boost to be introduced to a ballroom full of real estate and engineering executives! "You've come a long way, Caroline," I thought admiringly to myself as I remembered that just one year previously I had been unable to find a job. I felt like a debutante at a cotillion as I awaited my introduction.

One by one, the people at the table were asked to stand as they were glowingly praised. The spotlight in the back of the room focused on each one with intensity as they rose and blushingly listened to the enconiums. I started to perspire as my turn neared.

But it wasn't to be. Everyone at the table except me was standing, basking in the glare of the lights and the admiring stares of the audience, when the man at the microphone concluded, "And there they are. The best people in the country in their jobs!"

I was crushed, and I had to bite my lip to keep from crying. Had the oversight been deliberate? Was I no good at my job? Was he trying to put me in my place for some reason? I tried to hold my hurt feelings in check. People probably thought I was just someone's wife. The "wife of so-and-so" was something I dreaded becoming, so I always planned to work outside the home. I couldn't imagine being identified in other people's minds as simply a man's appendage with no discernible talents of my own, but that was probably exactly what the people in this room thought. I started to get angry.

I flounced back to my hotel room after the dinner, poutingly refusing invitations to continue the revelries with the other company members. I had to talk to someone about this horrendous and unforgivable slight. I wouldn't be able to sleep until I did.

"Betsy, did I wake you up?"

"No, no—how was the dinner?" she asked sleepily.

"Awful."

"Why? Did you purge?" She was suddenly awake, her voice laced with concern.

With surprise I realized that the dinner had been manageable. I had felt comfortable with what I had eaten, and I had even left some food on my plate. That was a new occurrence. Usually, leaving food felt like cutting my arm off, but tonight I had stopped when my hunger had subsided.

"No, the food was fine," I reassured her. "I ate what I told you I'd eat, and I even left some food and didn't feel deprived."

"That's wonderful! Can't you see what a miracle that is? You weren't able to do that several months ago!"

I hadn't thought about that. I had just focused on my hurt feelings. "Yeah, I guess you're right. But it was something else that was awful." I went on to describe the humiliating scene to her, embellishing a few details and magnifying my woundedness.

"Welcome to the King-Baby club!" Betsy laughed. I was annoyed. Betsy never gave me the strokes I wanted and expected. She always managed instead to confound me with some observation about myself that turned the situation upside-down and put the blame squarely in my lap.

"What do you mean by that?" I asked, irritated by her reaction and my confusion.

"The King-Baby syndrome is common to people with addictions. It means you have a huge ego and low self-esteem, and that when you allow your expectations to become grandiose and they aren't fulfilled, you start feeling insecure, as if something is wrong with you."

Once again she was right. I had blown my importance to the company out of all proportion, and when my ego hadn't been stroked, my self-esteem had plunged and my feelings had gotten hurt.

"Let me tell you something my sponsor told me," Betsy continued. "Whenever your feelings are hurt, look inside yourself to see what's wrong, because there's something wrong with you if you allow someone else to affect you like that. A lot of times when I'm angry or my feelings get hurt, it's because of my own faults—I feel guilty, I've pretended to be something I'm not, I've lied, or whatever. But remember this: when troubled, look within. You'll be surprised at what you'll discover about yourself if you are rigorously honest about your motives and actions."

This damned rigorous honesty was hounding me again. But thus prodded, I answered Betsy truthfully. "Perhaps I'm not as important to the company as I'd like to think I am," I said. "Do you think I built myself and my accomplishments up too much?"

"Caroline, how long have you been with that company?"

"About a year."

"How old are you?"

"Twenty-three."

"And you want recognition, glory, and fame to deposit itself on your doorstep now? If you get everything now, what will be left when you're thirty?"

I had to laugh. I was one of the newest company employees, and I was the youngest by many years. In fact, the next oldest person at the dinner was twelve years older than me. Who in the world was I to expect the same thing as people who were older and had accomplished much more?

"Oh, God, you're right," I said resignedly. "Now I'm embarrassed about what I did after the dinner. Everyone was going out for drinks and I just turned on my heel and left. What a baby I am!"

"Caroline, you lost seven years of your life to bulimia. While everyone else was growing up, you stayed stuck at the emotional level of a fifteen-year-old. It's going to take you a while to catch up to other people your age. You're going to have to learn a lot of things about emotions, appropriate reactions, love, friendship, men, and so on. But don't be so hard on yourself. Once you put the food down and start dealing with life on life's terms, everything gets better and better and better."

Again she was right. Although everyone had always described me as mature for my age and poised, the truth of the matter was that I had to constantly wear a mask to cover up for my massive insecurities about my looks, my body, my abilities—everything. The false maturity was my way of taking myself too seriously and not letting anyone close enough to figure me out.

"Thanks, Betsy. I can't tell you how much it means to talk to you. I don't always like what you have to say, but you're usually right." I looked at the clock: it read eleven-fifteen P.M. "Oh my God! Go back to sleep! I didn't realize it was so late."

"Don't worry about it. Every time I take a call and help someone else, I'm taking out insurance against going back into the food myself. Your calls help me as much as they help you. And when you're sponsoring people, you'll find that the same thing will happen to you. I'm so grateful I'm well that I'll do anything to help someone who really wants to get better. It is our responsibility to ensure that we continue to carry the message of recovery."

"Do you really think I'll be able to sponsor someone one day? I don't feel like I've learned enough to do that."

"Caroline, you can't see it, but I can see the tremendous growth in you since you came into the program. In just the last few months you've made a lot of progress: you've been able to stop binging, change your food choices, confront things about yourself, and move on with a minimum of angst. You have a long way to go, but I'd be surprised if someone doesn't approach you Monday night after you chair the meeting and ask you to sponsor them. People need to hook up with others who are a little further along in recovery than they are, and you're definitely further than some of the newcomers."

Oh no. I had temporarily forgotten about Monday night's talk. "Are you sure I have to go through with that?" I asked.

"You'll never get better if you don't share on that level. Don't worry about it. Besides, it's several days off and you've got a bunch of twenty-four-hour periods to get through until then. One day at a time, dear!"

With that, she hung up. Monday was a few days off, but I was too keyed up and compulsive to rest. I pulled a chair up to the desk and started to outline my embarrassing history with what I hoped was rigorous honesty for Monday night's talk.

EIGHT

"HI, MY NAME IS CAROLINE and I'm a bulimic and compulsive overeater."

There. I had gotten through the hardest part of my talk. I still had an occasional urge to deny that I was a bulimic or compulsive overeater, and sometimes I even tried to tell myself that maybe I wasn't as sick as I thought, and that one day I would return to "normal" eating. These were fantasies I knew I could not afford to indulge. I had to continually state that I was a bulimic to remind me of my disease, and to give me a much-needed dose of humility. An expectant hush fell over the room as fifty pairs of eyes looked at me, waiting for me to continue.

"I'm a little nervous," I said haltingly. "This is the first meeting I've chaired, so forgive me if I have to look at my notes while I talk."

"A little nervous" was an understatement. My hands were so sweaty that the ink on the crumpled outline in my hands was staining my palms. Betsy had patted my back comfortingly before the meeting and told me to "let go and let God" when she noticed my fear. I tried to do that now.

I wasn't sure where to start, but as I had repeatedly mulled over my talk, memories of things I thought would be appropriate to share had flooded my mind. Situations I had buried forever—or so I thought—had returned, reminding me how much my food obsession had dominated my life. I wanted to include them all: stealing food from my family and college roommates, being a compulsive cooker and dieter, lying to cover up for binges, driving around late at night in search of food to binge on when the urge struck, purging in bathrooms I would shudder to go into now, and on and on. As I sat in front of the group I realized that I just had to "turn it over"—meaning to let my Higher Power guide me in my choice of words. There was too much to tell, so I'd just have to fit in what I could.

"I think I've always been a compulsive overeater," I plunged in. "I've always loved food—especially sweets—and I was always the child who wanted second helpings of dinner. Part of this was because I was a big girl, but part of it was definitely because I just loved to eat. My dad once commented that he might have been responsible for my love of eating, because when I was just a baby, he stuffed me with oatmeal so that I would sleep through the night. Perhaps the seeds of my compulsive overeating were sown in the crib.

"Nevertheless, the kitchen was always my favorite part of the house and I often gravitated there to sit and read, do my homework, or watch television. In my mind, food equalled love, companionship, and security. Whenever I stayed home sick, I got to eat whatever I wanted because everyone knew it would make me feel better. I never stopped to think about my eating being a problem, though, until I was about eight, when food all of a sudden became a very important issue and I started to think about being fat."

Here I paused to relate the Howard Johnson's story of my father telling the waitress that the vanilla milkshake I had unwittingly ordered at lunch went to the "heavy" one. Several people chuckled, nodding knowingly. I relaxed a bit with the laughter, gathering steam as I pressed forward.

"I went to a private girls' school in Washington and quickly learned that to be accepted by the "in" group, you had to be thin and pretty. In fifth grade, one friend of mine told me I was developing a pot belly and I was devastated. I had already begun to educate myself about calories, but at that point I tried even harder to avoid cookies and other sweets.

"When my family drove out to the West Coast the following summer on vacation, I kept a journal in which I not only described some of the magnificent scenes we encountered, but I also talked about my food intake and the fit of my clothes. I remember that the day we spent in Disneyland, I jubilantly wrote in my journal that I had eaten nothing all day and that my skirt felt looser. I had then lain down on the floor of the hotel room and done sit-ups to end the day on a good note. This was at eleven years old!

"What is so amazing to me as I look back is that I can see now that I was not a fat child. I was taller and larger than all of my peers, but I was not heavy. People always called me an "Amazon" or "the Jolly Green Giant," though, so in my mind I assumed gargantuan proportions. I was also uncomfortable and envious when my classmates discussed borrowing each other's clothes; I knew I could never do that. In fact, I couldn't even get into my sister's clothes because although she was older, she was shorter and smaller-boned. Every time she wore something of mine that was baggy on her, my jealousy grew and my self-esteem plummeted.

"There was a definite diet mentality in our house. My six-foot-tall father was at one time about 220 pounds, and the summer we drove west he decided that he wanted to be thin again —especially if he was going to encounter his Stanford University classmates out in California. He ate very little—mostly cottage cheese and pineapple sprinkled with bran cereal—and talked a lot about his weight loss as the pounds kept falling off. On the cross-country commute we kept a huge cooler in the back filled with ice and his diet foods. One of the only things I remember about his rigid regimen was opening the cooler one morning and seeing swarms of ants on the sticky pineapple cans.

"Starting when I was about eight, I began swimming competitively, but practices became more intense when I was ten or eleven. Once or twice a day I had to get into a bathing suit and train long hours. This went on during the school years and throughout the summers. I loved swimming because I was big and strong and I won a lot of races. In fact, when I was twelve and thirteen I was considered one of the area's top breaststrokers, and I held a number of local records.

"I began to be more and more obsessed with my size, though, which made going to workouts hellish. When I put the bathing suit on, my thoughts were always: Is the suit tighter than it was yesterday? Is my stomach sticking out? Are my thighs fat? Am I the biggest one on the team? And on and on. Weigh-ins were awful because no matter what the numbers were, I felt they were too high and that I needed to lose weight. I couldn't pass a mirror without turning sideways and sucking in my stomach. I was obsessed with my body and I saw flaws in it everywhere.

"When I was twelve, a new bathing suit hit the world scene. Called the 'skin suit,' it molded to swimmers' bodies like a second skin, leaving absolutely nothing to the imagination. I hated these revealing things, but competing in them was a must because they sliced seconds and minutes off race times from reduced drag in the water. I used to sit at meets and envy the tall, sinuous girls who looked so wonderful in skin suits, convinced that I looked fat and dumpy by comparison. Back in the privacy of my bedroom I would peel the suit off and pinch my body hard until the skin was red and angry, declaring my figure 'ugly' as I vowed to start a new diet. Then I would go out and buy a diary and put a goal weight a month or so ahead and then back up day by day with what I would have to weigh to achieve that."

More people were nodding as I spoke, laughing in parts. There were times when I wanted to think that my story was unique, but clearly it was just like many of theirs. I still occasionally wanted to stand out and be different from everyone, but I knew that I would have to let go of that kind of grandiose thinking. "You're just another Bozo on the bus," someone had once said to me. Trying to be just a Bozo rather than the bus driver was tough, but I was starting to see that I was no better, no worse, and no different from anyone in any of these meetings. I continued.

"When I was thirteen, I began dieting in earnest. I was planning a trip to the beach after the swim season, and I wanted to wear a bikini, which I had never before had the guts to buy or wear, so I ate little and counted calories. I lost about ten pounds—which made me really thin—and I wore the bikini with an incredible sense of pride. I bored the people around me by talking about food and thinness constantly, telling them that they could all afford to drop a few pounds, too. I wore my newly baggy jeans like a badge of honor, silently scorning those with tight clothes. They did not have my willpower, so I was superior to them, I told myself.

"That low weight didn't last long. Soon I was eating a lot again, but because swimming burned up so many calories, I didn't pack on the weight as quickly as I would have if I didn't exercise. But I did steadily gain weight, to the point where I was the heaviest I had ever been. My parents began to make comments, especially comparing me with my older sister, whom I began to hate with a passion. Even at my thinnest points, nothing in her closet ever fit me, which enraged and embarrassed me. To get back at her, I competed in other arenas: swimming, piano recitals, grades, test scores, and so on, flaunting the results if I came out on top. Needless to say, our relationship deteriorated quickly, but I'm just now recognizing that my jealousy about her body started the whole thing going."

I took a deep breath and looked at my watch. I had been talking for about ten minutes, but I didn't feel uncomfortable or at a loss for words. This was a subject I knew cold. My outline was long forgotten—in fact, almost nothing I had said thus far was on it. I was even enjoying this self-revelation; I felt a load beginning to lift off my shoulders as I told this group things I had never before verbalized about myself. I went on.

"My dad tried to be helpful when he noticed my expanding size. He suggested that I go on the Dr. Stillman diet —you know, all the protein you can eat and eight glasses of water a day. I underlined that book, read it and reread it, and followed it to the letter. Soon I began to lose weight, but not without side effects. My personality changed dramatically, and I stopped smiling and laughing about anything. When I woke up in the morning, the first thing I did was feel my stomach. If it was flat, I was happy; if it wasn't, I resolved to eat even less. I would then jump out of bed, run into the bathroom, and weigh myself stark naked. If I didn't lose a pound a day, I was unhappy. The numbers on the scale totally dictated my self-worth. If I was lighter, it was a good day. If I was the same or higher, the day was shot and I was nasty to everyone who crossed my path.

"I even began to have blackouts and dizzy spells. If I stood up suddenly, the room would spin around me and I'd feel light-headed. I later learned that this is common when your diet is predominantly protein-based. I became quite extreme about eating no carbohydrates and gradually reducing what I ate of the unlimited protein. After all, I reasoned that if I was eating as much cottage cheese and hamburgers as I wanted and losing weight, then I could eat less and lose more.

"Thus I entered my anorexic phase. During the worst of it, I was swimming one to three hours a day—I have no idea where the energy came from—and eating nothing but a hard-boiled egg and some cheese. Some of my schoolmates asked me about my wonderful secret because they said I looked so fabulous, so I passed out my diet book and told them sternly to follow it to the letter. One girl who tried to follow it avoided me in the dining hall because she always cheated and had sweets, and she told everyone else not to tell me. She was just weak, I thought to myself. The old superiority feeling reared its ugly head a lot in this period.

"Something I'm just beginning to understand now is that all of the dieting and concern with weight affected my memory during those years," I continued. "There are huge gaps in what I am able to remember, but I do know that it always puzzled me that I didn't know what a book had been about a week after I finished it. Nothing stuck in my head, which I think was a result of all of the dieting and the deep depression I was in most of the time.

"Another side effect was that I never got my period. While part of me was grateful that I didn't have to deal with that monthly mess, another part of me was embarrassed that I wasn't a 'real woman.' I never told anyone about my condition because I felt like such a freak. It wasn't until I got into this program that my body started to be a little more normal, and I hope I haven't done any kind of lasting damage to my body. I've read that some women's bodies are so traumatized by the years of dieting, purging, and exercising that they can destroy their ovaries and become infertile.

"As I reached my thinnest point near the end of ninth grade, I decided that I needed to have my tonsils out. Now this wasn't because of a medical necessity: I just remembered reading that when you had your tonsils out you didn't eat for three days afterward. I thought that this process would be a super way to lose even more weight, so I cajoled my doctor into arranging for them to be taken out. Every sore throat I had was because of my tonsils, I insisted. Although reluctant, he finally agreed to do the operation.

"Well, I didn't eat for a few days after the operation, and I hit what was probably my lowest weight in years. In fact, the first thing I did when I got home was rush to the scale to see how much I had lost. Then, sick of all the deprivation, I started to eat again with a vengeance the next day. After nothing but protein and water for so long, I craved fattening, rich, and sweet foods, so I ate them openly and secretively. People with sore throats are supposed to have ice cream, so I had my license to eat ice cream given back to me for a while. My weight came back on, with interest.

"I was not alone at school with this diet obsession. Almost every girl read the fashion magazines voraciously and cut out pictures of skinny models and pasted them on the inside of their lockers. Goal weights were taped up, and I often took my cue from what a fashion model my height said she weighed. Most of the time, however, they weighed about thirty pounds less than me, so I despaired of ever being pretty and thin.

"Girls around me began to develop health problems from their dieting. A year didn't go by that people weren't pulled from school and hospitalized for anorexia. In fact, one girl in my class just didn't come back after Christmas vacation. I had noticed that she had gotten thinner and thinner, and that she did all her homework standing up rather than sitting down because she said it burned more calories, but I hadn't put two and two together and realized she had anorexia nervosa. When she came back to school after the hospitalization, she was slightly heavier, but still ate very little—if anything—at lunch, and tapped her foot on the floor incessantly in class so that she could continue burning calories even while sitting.

"Many girls simply got fashionably slender. In hindsight, I am certain that some of them were binging and purging, because they ate loads of food and spent a lot of time exercising or in the bathrooms. One girl started to run long distances every day despite her lack of athletic background. The more weight she lost, the more people told her how marvelous she looked. The school even presented her with the 'Runner's Award' at the Athletic Banquet for her dedication to the sport.

"I became bulimic in tenth grade after two girls binged in front of me and then purged in a bathroom while I listened. They weren't embarrassed at all about it. In fact, one of the girls said that her mother—a former model and wife of a senator—had shown her how to stick her fingers down her throat to get rid of fattening foods and stay slim. I thought that I had discovered *nirvana*, but soon the destructive behavior took over my life. I occasionally got frightened about what I was doing, but I couldn't stop no matter how hard I tried.

"One of the excuses I gave myself for the bulimia was that I was under a lot of pressure at school, and that once I got into college, my eating would certainly become more normal. This is the same thing I told myself when I got to college and didn't get any better. Marriage would release me from the bulimia, I then thought. I was always blaming people, places, and things for my eating, never stopping to think that it was I who needed to change.

"During my senior year in high school I was binging and purging several times a week—sometimes several times a day —and I had also discovered laxative overdoses to help keep the weight off. I was shoplifting huge amounts of food, too. In fact, I often went to the grocery store and took a cake off the shelf on one aisle, ate the top off it while pushing the cart around, and then stuck it back on a shelf in the next aisle. I also ate out of bulk food bins all the time. When I went to health food stores, I'd eat to my heart's content. 'Just sampling,' I'd tell the annoyed clerks as I stuffed dried peaches, granola, natural peanut butter, and raw bran into my mouth.

"Around this time I got worried that I had seriously screwed up my body because my stomach bloated out all the time, even when I hadn't eaten anything. I was terrified that I had permanently damaged my stomach, or my intestines, or something, with all of the food and the purging. I cried a lot in my bedroom, standing in front of the mirror and pounding my stomach, screaming that I looked pregnant. I wore big, baggy clothes to hide my body and tried to avoid going to workouts.

"Finally, my parents got so tired of my moaning that they took me to our family doctor. My mother sat right next to me as I talked with this genial, white-haired man, who barely asked me any questions and who didn't examine me. He did tap my stomach once or twice with his knuckles, though, pronouncing me 'gassy.' 'Caroline,' he said solemnly, patting my hand, 'you are swallowing air. You are under too much pressure. Take one or two Mylanta tablets a day and try to breathe evenly when you feel under stress. You'll get better fast, I promise.'

"I wanted to scream and cry when he said that because I knew I wasn't swallowing air. But I figured he didn't know anything about bulimia, and I was too embarrassed to ask him if that might be the culprit, especially with my mother sitting right there. So I nodded dumbly and promised to try to breathe better and take the Mylanta. But the tablets didn't help at all. Two never made any difference in the bloating, so I would go to the store and take a bottle off the shelf and eat the entire thing—usually one hundred tablets—and never feel any better.

"My complaining got worse about my stomach, so we went back to the doctor, who simply prescribed a total barium series, which included the less-than-pleasant barium enema. The tests were awful and humiliating, but my only worry before taking them was that I couldn't eat or drink for twelve hours before the tests. I didn't like that. Just the thought that I couldn't eat made me want to eat.

"They didn't find anything on the tests and I didn't get

any better. Right around this time, though, I got into Harvard and, as I mentioned, decided that once I got there the problem would go away. One thing I thought would help me be more normal would be having guys around me—even in the dorms —twenty-four hours a day. I had never once been on a date, and I thought that getting some male attention might put the food back into its proper perspective.

"But I got to Harvard and my bulimia got worse. I was surrounded by girls with eating disorders. Most of my room-mates, the women on the sports teams, and my other friends were preoccupied with their bodies and practiced some kind of strange eating behavior to get thin or stay thin. Food in the dining halls was unlimited, and Cambridge was infested with candy and food stores where people could stock up on good-ies. With all the easy access to food, the overwhelming bril-liance of the men and women around me, and my deepening feelings of self-hatred and low self-esteem, the binging and purging accelerated.

"I never sought help, though, or confided in anyone. Much as a fat person goes to a party and looks around for someone who is fatter to feel superior to, I looked for people who were sicker than I was, and whose binging and purging was so apparent that it was easy to spot. There was one girl in particular whom I singled out for derision. Painfully thin, she swam on the team despite her emaciated condition and medio-cre performances, never once missing a workout. Her lips often turned blue and her body was wracked with shivering even when the pool was warm. Once I noticed in the locker room that she had sprouted a mat of fine hair on her stomach, which was nature's way of trying to insulate her. After work-outs she helped herself to plate after plate of food, often disap-pearing from the dining hall with a mountainous bowl of ice cream slathered with toppings.

"When the team competed against Dartmouth, we ea-gerly raced to their dining hall after the meet because word had it that Dartmouth had the best food in the Ivy League. Indeed, all the food was freshly baked, there were self-serve yogurt and ice cream machines on every floor of the building, and the students even ate off china, which we managed to steal pieces of as mementos. I ate heartily like everyone else, thinking that I would slip away to purge before we left.

"My plans were thwarted, though, when we were herded back onto the buses early because of an impending snowstorm. Angry and frantic, I tried to think of a way to get rid of the food without anyone noticing, but there was no way to do it. What made me angriest, however, was that this other girl *did* manage to leave the dining room to find a bathroom. While the team languished on the buses and the coaches went to find her, my annoyance mounted that she had gotten away with her purge and I hadn't. When she finally got onto the bus looking thin and serene, I made several nasty comments to others about her obvious problem.

"There were all kinds of disorders at Harvard, and it wasn't limited to the women. I heard stories about male wrestlers, boxers, and members of the crew teams who regularly vomited to make weight, and who were hooked on laxatives and diuretics. I even heard that the top runners on the cross-country team ate and purged together as a social pasttime. And then there were the girls who took huge trays of food, chewed their food, then spit it into their napkins, making countless trips to the trashcans with fistfuls of napkins containing regurgitated food. Perhaps this last category thought that no one noticed them raising their napkins to their mouths after every bite. At least, I consoled myself, I practiced my disease in the privacy of my bathroom!

"I started to think seriously about suicide during this period. I yearned for a time when I wouldn't have to wake up and worry about my weight, if I'd eat, what I'd eat, where I'd purge, how I'd shoplift, whether anyone would notice, and so on. I never had any fun or went anywhere spontaneously because I was afraid my clothes wouldn't fit from one day to the next. Once I was so lonely and depressed that I sat in a closet, hoping that people would miss me.

"To help relieve some of the pain I sought solace in drugs, which were plentiful on campus. Cocaine, marijuana, LSD, uppers, downers—the choice was unlimited. I didn't drink regularly, but that was only because of the calories. If I was really going to escape from my misery, I wanted to do it noncalorically so I ended up smoking a lot of marijuana. I

138

loved getting stoned. One or two hits of a joint was enough to make me giggly and disoriented, and most people got stoned together, so it was a very social thing to do. Trivial things became fascinating when I was high, and I vaguely remember carrying on eloquent discussions about all kinds of things that in the next day's hard light made no sense.

"Smoking a lot of pot, however, worsened my bulimia, because when you are stoned, you get the 'munchies'—an irresistible urge to eat. When the munchies attacked, I convinced myself that eating was okay because I wasn't in my right mind. So I would go out on eating forays with other stoned friends, consuming gallons of ice cream, cookies by the box, and potato chips by the barrel. If I happened to wake up in the middle of the night after such an evening and remember what I had eaten, I would run into the bathroom and try to purge, although too much time would have elapsed to be successful. Then I would sit on the cold bathroom floor at three A.M. and cry about the craziness of my life.

"I tried cocaine, too, because I heard it kept people from eating. The first time I leaned over a mirror and snorted a line of the white powder, I felt like I was on top of the world. As I wiped my nose, enjoying the extreme euphoria, a coked-out classmate happily informed me that his father—a successful North Carolina doctor—had told him that cocaine was the least addictive drug known to man, and that that was why he did so much of it. I remember nodding and thinking that if it was nonaddictive and kept me thin, then I wanted to keep doing it, too. As it happened, though, coke was too expensive for me and I just kept food as my drug of choice.

"I compulsively exercised throughout this whole period, too. In addition to purging and occasionally dieting, I made myself run long distances every day, incurring knee and ankle problems in the process. Every day as I jogged up and down the Charles River, rain, sunshine, or snow, I passed other women doing the same thing, all wearing the same unhappy, tormented look we eating-disordered people seem to have. In fact, I would venture a guess that most people who run are simply people who want to eat a lot without paying the caloric price. I know I was.

"I truly believe that there is nothing I wouldn't have

done to get the food out of me. I remember reading about singer Karen Carpenter's death in 1983 from syrup of ipecac poisoning and complications from her years of anorexia and bulimia. The only thing I got from the article was that she used syrup of ipecac to purge her food. I didn't pay attention to the fact that the emetine poison in it had built up in her heart lining and contributed to her fatal cardiac arrest. I just figured that I had a new way to purge my food.

"So the next time I was home on vacation from college and felt I had eaten too much at dinner, I went to my parents' bathroom, where a bottle of ipecac had been sitting on the medicine cabinet shelf for twelve years. The expiration date was 1966, but I paid no attention to that, or to the instructions to take one or two teaspoons. Within seconds I swallowed the entire bottle and sat on the floor, waiting for the vomiting to start. Five minutes later, my body began to writhe in agony, and I felt so sick that I thought I was going to die. I crawled to the toilet and hung my head over it, letting the food come out of me in wrenching waves. Finally the convulsions stopped, but instead of being frightened of what had happened, I simply absorbed the fact that I now had a new way to get rid of my food."

I looked down at my watch. Lord, I had spoken for half an hour! That wasn't the only thing that surprised me, though. I had just revealed some of the most disgusting and damaging things about myself that I could think of. But no one had gotten up and stormed out of the room in revulsion, and the police weren't hovering outside waiting to slip handcuffs on my wrists for my stealing. In fact, everyone looked rather complacent.

And I was feeling great—better than any drug high I had ever experienced and much better than any double chocolate cake had made me feel. Someone had once said to me about the program's cathartic process of sharing, "We're only as sick as our secrets. Get things you think are awful out in the light and you'll feel better, you'll be one step closer to not returning to that behavior, and you'll give hope to someone who has done the same thing as you and needs to hear that he or she isn't alone." I now wondered why I had resisted chairing a meeting for so long.

What was nice, too, about the program was that I knew what I said would stay in the room and not be repeated. There was a tradition of anonymity—indeed, I didn't know most people's last names, even the ones I called on the phone—so I was confident that I could say anything that was on my mind and not worry that it would be all over the streets of Baltimore the next morning. And for some of the community's most prominent people, anonymity was the only fact that enabled them to seek help here and in similar places for alcoholism, drug addiction, and gambling.

I decided to wrap up quickly. "Anyway, I got married right after college, moved to Baltimore, and plunged into a deeper depression than ever before. I couldn't find a job, I was afraid of going out anywhere, and I ate and purged compulsively all day, every day. I couldn't go to restaurants, I was filled with resentment toward everyone for real or imagined slights, I cried at the drop of a hat, and I bought lots of diet books, convinced that a slender body would solve my problems. When I finally told my husband in desperation that I was bulimic, he tried to be understanding and supportive, but couldn't give me what I needed emotionally to get well. So I floundered around for six more months, stopping the bulimia sometimes, but always returning to it as a way of dealing with every emotion I experienced.

"For some reason, my Higher Power was working in my life one day and I saw an announcement about this group in the newspaper. I decided that I was at the end of my rope and that it couldn't hurt to attend, especially if it was free. My first meeting was on a Friday night at a local church, where I heard people discussing their compulsions to eat, fear, anger, bulimia, dieting, and all kinds of things that I didn't think anyone talked about, at least not that openly. I had no reason to trust anyone there, or to believe that a simple program based on eliminating binge foods, eating moderately, making amends for past wrongs, and helping other people get better, would work. But there was joy, serenity, and hope in that room, and those were three things I knew I needed or I was going to die.

"So I came back to another meeting, and I kept coming back. I got myself a sponsor, I read literature all the time, I went to meetings, I started calling other people, and I began trying to eliminate all sugar and other binge foods from my diet. Although the binges didn't stop right away, they started to get smaller and less frequent, which gave me a lot of hope. And one day at a time, I have felt the compulsion to eat and purge leave me.

"I'm not perfect, though. I still react like a spoiled child when my feelings are hurt, but I'm learning. My sponsor keeps telling me 'Progress, not perfection,' and 'One day at a time,' and I listen because she hasn't binged or purged for years, and that's the kind of life I want. My meals aren't perfect—I still eat too many vegetables and not enough of other kinds of foods—but first things first. I've got to keep things down comfortably, and that is my top priority. One day at a time I'll add in different foods.

"I'm changing in ways that are unbelievable to me. I came into this program an atheist, and I now believe that there is a Higher Power—which I choose to call God—doing for me what I could not do for myself before. It's not important to me anymore to understand the complexities of what God is like, where He is, or any of that. I just pray in the morning and try to turn the workings of my life over to Him on a daily basis, and the miracles keep happening. The only trouble I get into now is when I snatch my will back and try to run things Caroline's way.

"Not only do I have a Higher Power, but I'm eating three meals a day instead of fifteen, I'm able to go out spontaneously and not worry about where my next meal will be, I try to help other people to the best of my ability when I can, and I am developing honesty.

"I am a good friend to people now, or at least I'm starting to be. I don't lie or take their things. If I tell them I'll be somewhere at a certain time, I'm there now. Before I was always canceling, making excuses for not going somewhere because I was ashamed of my body or I had just binged, or something. I'm not an angry driver anymore. If I'm stuck in a traffic jam, I whip out my literature and read. I let people into lines ahead of me. And I just keep feeling better.

"I have a long way to go. I have lots of apologies to make to people I harmed over the years, and there are still a lot of things I don't like about myself that I need to work on. But I'm not flagellating myself anymore or beating myself up about what a terrible person I am. My self-esteem is rising and my huge ego is starting to diminish. But one day at a time, with people like you helping me along, I'm getting better and I'm grateful to be alive. Thank you for letting me share with you tonight."

I stopped. There was no applause, just a rustle as people shifted in their seats. One attractive slender woman raised her hand to talk. "Hi, my name is Annie and I'm a compulsive eater and recovering bulimic."

"Hi, Annie!" the room responded.

"It was really good to hear you talk, Caroline," she said. "I remember the first night you came into the program and you sat in the back of the room with your arms crossed and looked angry. I noticed you because I remember how angry I was when I first came in. I was angry because I didn't want to have bulimia, and I wanted to get well overnight. I didn't understand how this prayer stuff, sponsors, and cute little slogans worked, but like you, there was something in the room that told me I'd never find the answer anywhere else, so I kept coming back."

Annie then went on to talk about her relationship with her fiancé, and some of the difficulties they were having in living together and planning their wedding. "The bottom line, however, is that I'm not running to the store or the refrigerator when I'm upset anymore. I'm just letting the problems surface and get worked out. Normal people have problems, too, and that's what life is all about. I'm not interested in running away from my emotions anymore, because even my worst days of abstinence from compulsive overeating and purging are better than my best days before this."

Next a heavy-set black man spoke. "Hi, I'm Michael, a struggling compulsive overeater."

"Hi, Michael!"

"I'm feelin' pretty good today because, you know, I'm not a fat man anymore. I may look fat to some people, but I've lost sixty pounds in the last eight months and I feel pretty good, you know? It's like I'm not Michael, a dumb, black cab driver, anymore. I have some self-esteem back, you know, and my

sponsor is helping me see what I have avoided doing throughout the years because I thought my size made me unaccept-
able. I never learned how to read, you know, and now I'm
going back to school to get my diploma. I'm forty-seven years
old, man! But abstinence feels so good. When I'm not eating
compulsively, getting fatter and fatter, I can live life, you
know? And right now I don't think there's anything Michael
can't do. Thanks for listening."

Next a thin, dark-haired young woman spoke. "Caroline,
thanks for telling your story. I felt like you did when I first
came into these rooms. Some people looked at me like I didn't
need to be here because I had been bulimic for years, and
although my body didn't reflect my sickness, I know that if I
had kept down half the food I used to eat I would have
weighed over two hundred pounds.

"What you said about drugs really hit home with me.
When I was about sixteen, I started snorting coke, partly because I liked it and partly because it took away my appetite.
Then I moved in with a dealer and started doing it all the
time, even free-basing. Once I stayed awake for three days and
three nights without eating—just doing line after line of coke.
I dropped to eighty-nine pounds but thought I looked great.

"My family got worried and found out what I was doing,
so they put me in a treatment center. I had to change everything about my life: my friends, my attitudes, everything. But
one of the hardest things about getting off the coke was gaining the weight back. I've gained thirty pounds, and although
people tell me I look thin, I still feel really fat, and sometimes
I want to get back into the coke, not because I miss it so much
anymore, but because it made me thin.

"I started to be bulimic when I got off the drugs, and it
scares me. It's harder for me to stop doing that than it is to put
the coke down, because I have to eat every day, three times a
day. I never have to drink or do drugs again, but damn it, I
have to eat, and I feel out of control sometimes and have to
vomit. It's getting better, but I'm still scared, and I know part
of the problem is that I haven't gotten myself a sponsor yet. I
need help.

"I'm also scared because I just found out I'm pregnant.
The idea that I have to gain weight for the baby is upsetting. I

don't want to gain anything! I wish I weren't pregnant, and I'm having a lot of resentment toward my husband because he wants to have a child, and now he's policing me and following me into the bathroom to make sure I don't purge. I just do it when he's not around instead, and it upsets me that I'm getting sneaky again and that I might be hurting the baby. I just needed to get all that off my chest," she concluded. "Thanks for listening."

"Keep coming back," the group said in unison.

Several more people spoke, sharing their thoughts and frustrations about various things: their marriages, their jobs, parking tickets, and so on. It was always so interesting to me that many of the things that were said at meetings weren't about food, weight, and calories. People instead talked about what it was that made them eat, that drove them to abuse themselves with food and unrealistic ideas of what they ought to weigh.

Now I understood why someone had once said to me, "The only thing you change in this program is everything. People come in here hoping for another diet and calories club, and they stay because they change themselves emotionally, physically, and spiritually, and the weight comes off as a fringe benefit." I certainly had not expected any of this Higher Power stuff, or working on amends to people I had harmed, when I had started coming to meetings. I had only wanted to stop thinking about food twenty-four hours a day, and about where and when my next binge or purge would be. I was hooked on this program now, though. I liked the person I was becoming.

The meeting closed, as usual, with the Lord's Prayer. As people turned to talk to each other, Betsy made a beeline for me. "Hey, kiddo, you were great. But we have some work to do. It's time to start your inventory of character defects."

Damn. Why did she always have to take the wind out of my sails? I changed the subject. "I really like speaking. When can I do it again?"

"Oh, my. Caroline's big ego is surfacing again," she said with a smile. "You have some more listening to do. As they say, go to a lot of meetings and take the cotton out of your ears and put it in your mouth. You have a lot of resentments, envy, and fears to get rid of. But we'll work on it one day at a time. Progress, not perfection!" She gave me a quick hug and went to talk to the pregnant woman.

Several other people came up to thank me for my honesty. "I needed to hear about the shoplifting," one middle-aged woman said guiltily. "I did that, too. What I did was take my kids to the store, put them in the carts, and then eat food off the shelves as I pushed them around. They usually held the food because that way it looked like they were eating it. And I never paid for any of it. I just put the empty bags on the shelves. Just hearing that someone else did that makes me feel good."

A cute, tiny girl with big eyes was next. "God, you really rattled my cage," she said excitedly. "I was a gymnast, and my coach used to make me put a nineteen-inch band around my waist to remind me that I couldn't eat or gain weight. I learned how to vomit after eating from some other girls on the team who said it helped them keep their weight down. We made it a big party, too. After workouts we'd go to fast-food places and pig out, and then take turns throwing up in the bathroom. We called it 'scarfing and barfing.' We're all still hooked, even though we're not competing anymore. But I could really identify with your fears of getting into a bathing suit. Getting into my leotard every day was torture, and I tried so hard to think of excuses why I didn't have to go to workouts."

We talked for a few more minutes and exchanged phone numbers. She was in a competitive bank training program, and the pressure of the long hours and high expectations were bringing on occasional binges. "I'm purging less and less," she said hopefully. "One day, through this program, I know that I'm not going to have to do it ever again. And I know how lucky I am to be here. There are a few girls I work with who definitely have eating problems, but they don't want to talk about it. When the time is right, I'll tell them about this group."

The lights were flicking on and off to get us on our way. I felt high as a kite and I wanted to stay and savor the feeling. I reluctantly headed for the door. A pretty blonde with flawless makeup and stunning clothes was waiting there for me.

146

"Can you talk to me for a minute?" she said, her voice edged with desperation.

"Sure, let's sit on the steps outside." She was clearly bulimic; all the tell-tale signs were there: broken capillaries around the eyes, fine lines etched around her mouth, a puffy face, and swollen salivary glands. She kept clearing her throat. Her last binge must have been recent, judging from the congestion.

"You're the first person I've felt I wanted to have sponsor me," she began as we settled on the hard concrete steps, keeping her blue eyes fastened on the ground. "I'm tired of the vomiting. I lie awake at night in bed and my heart beats crazily. A couple of weeks ago I stayed up all night, terrified that I would die if I went to sleep and my heart went out of control. I can't bring myself to tell anyone about it. I ask my mom not to have foods that set me off in the house, and she keeps getting them. She swears they're not for me, that they're for my dad. But he doesn't need ice cream, pretzels, and all that stuff! He just had a heart bypass operation!"

"I know what you're talking about," I responded, relating the story about my friend who insisted on taking me out for my birthday when I had just explained my fear of food and restaurants. "Sometimes there are going to be people who are going to stand in the way of your recovery for one reason or another. You just have to be firm about saying no."

"But she keeps buying the stuff! I've even offered to do the shopping for her!"

"No one is making you eat," I said sternly. "You have to take responsibility for your eating disorder. Blaming someone else for it is just going to keep you stuck in it." I surprised myself with these words. Betsy was a good teacher. I couldn't have said these words, let alone thought them, a year ago.

"Yeah, you're right," she sighed. "Intellectually I know what I have to do. It's just that I'm holding on to the food; I don't really want to give it up."

"You haven't taken the first step yet," I said gently. "You've got to admit that you are powerless over food, and that your life is unmanageable. Don't you think your life is unmanageable with all this binging still going on?"

"Unmanageable isn't the word. Deadly is the word. I

went to the emergency room of a hospital today because I thought my stomach was going to burst. It all started because I went to a vending machine and couldn't stop buying the stuff—candy bars, crackers, peanuts, everything. It's like I was in a frenzy. I *was* in a frenzy. The nurse calmed me down, but they had to pump my stomach. I cried and cried and told her that I had bulimia, and she asked me if I had tried this program. I told her that I had come to meetings sporadically throughout college, but that I had never really worked it. So here I am again. I want to stop. I'm sick of this." She started to cry, burying her face in her hands.

I reached over and put my arm around her thin shoulders. "Don't cry," I said. "You'll be okay. I was hopeless a year ago and I wanted to die. I would drive over bridges and think about how easy it would be to just flick the wheel to the right and careen off the side. That way I would be out of my food misery. But I'm slowly learning to put the food down and live instead. It's not easy, but like Annie said in the meeting, my worst days now are better than my best days when I was still into the food."

She stopped crying and blew her nose. "I believe you. I'm just scared. I don't feel as if there's any hope for me. I can look around and see other people losing weight and getting over their food fixations, but it's hard for me to think I might be well one day, too."

"Do you have a Higher Power or a God?"

"You mean besides food?"

I laughed. At least she had a sense of humor. That would help in the recovery. "No, a force you pray to?"

"No, that's a problem. I'm scared of God. I'm Catholic, and I know all about God and the Trinity and all that, but I feel as if I let God down again and again. Every time I binged, I prayed to God to relieve me of my compulsion. But He never did, and I felt I was a failure. I also struck deals with Him. For example, I told Him if he could help me stop purging I'd make my bed every morning, or something like that. But nothing has gotten better. It's getting worse. And I feel like God has turned His back on me out of disgust and frustration."

Her despair and loneliness were palpable. I told her how

I had come to believe in a Higher Power despite great reluctance. "I didn't believe He'd take care of me, either. But one night I got on my knees and just asked for the compulsion to be lifted. No lightning bolts or visions happened, but I've started to get better. And it makes sense to me that I screwed up everything so badly by myself that it can't hurt to toss the load onto someone else's back. My sponsor just tells me to turn everything over to my Higher Power and to stop worrying so much about the state of the world. It sounds stupid, but it works."

"How do I know He'll help me this time?"

"Just trust. Just trust that you've been led into this program for a reason. He wouldn't bring you this far and then drop you cold. When you recover you'll be able to help people out of their own despair, and every experience you've had will be useful for people who are in the same bind."

"Will you help me?" Her eyes looked pleadingly at me.

"You can't keep what you don't give away" rang in my ears. Someone had recently said this at a meeting, explaining why she spent so much time on the phone with other compulsive overeaters. "If I'm not constantly telling people what others told me, I'm that much closer to getting back into the food," she had warned. My decision was made.

"Sure, I'd love to. But you'd better tell me what your name is," I said, laughing.

"Lisa." She broke into a big smile. "Thanks a lot. I feel like if I can talk to you on a regular basis I might get better. If you can get well, maybe I can, too."

"Wait a sec," I said as I stood up. "I'm not perfect and I have a long, long way to go. There are lots of character defects in me that I'm not proud of, and I have all kinds of amends to make to people for things I've done. But I can help you up to where I am now."

"That's all I needed to hear," Lisa said. "Can I have a hug?"

As I hugged her, I thought about just that one change in my life. Before I came into the program, touching—God forbid, hugging—had been taboo. Why was our society so insulated? Leo Buscaglia was making a fortune teaching people how to hug each other again. It was incredible to me that something as simple as touching was so difficult to do.

I started to walk home. "Call me tomorrow," I called to Lisa as she headed to her car. "We have work to do!"

I started to hum as I walked past the fire station. I smiled at the men lounging outside. Why had I once been so afraid of them? All of a sudden a song from a musical came to me. "Wonder of Wonder, Miracle of Miracles," from *Fiddler on the Roof,* burst into my head. The song talked about a man who had been transformed by God from a lump of clay into a real man.

Change those lyrics around a bit and that was the way I felt. I was a miracle—a living, breathing miracle. Maybe Betsy was right about me having a lot more work to do, but right now I was feeling wonderful. To paraphrase a famous poet, God was in heaven and there wasn't a darn thing wrong with the world.

NINE

THE PEACEFUL STILLNESS of my early morning breakfast was suddenly shattered by a loud crash. I dropped my spoon in surprise, closed my *Just for Today* meditation book, and stood up. The new glass shelf in the bathroom must have fallen to the floor and broken. Maybe I could clean it up before Haywood woke up—if the sound hadn't already awakened him, too.

The screws must not have been tightened enough, I thought with annoyance as I carried my cereal bowl into the kitchen and put it in the sink. So much for breakfast. This was my favorite part of the day and now it was over. I loved waking up while it was still dark outside and eating my simple meal with no interruptions. I also felt as if I was getting a jump on the day if I started while the vast majority of the world lay snug in their beds. I didn't understand people who claimed they could sleep until eleven or twelve in the morning; the day was half over by the time they deigned to greet it.

I tiptoed through the living room, trying to make as little noise as possible. But as I neared the bathroom I heard a strange sound, one that I had never heard before. Something was wrong. Terribly, terribly wrong.

My mouth dropped open in horror when I got to the bathroom door. Lying on the floor, wedged between the sink and the white porcelain bathtub was Haywood, violently thrashing about. Broken glass, cotton balls, shaving cream, and various makeup vials were strewn all over the small space. With every motion he brought another container crashing to the ground, scattering its contents all over. Low, guttural noises were coming from him and spittle was drooling from the side of his mouth. The cords in his neck stood out prominently as he arched his head back, crashing it repeatedly against the tiled floor.

I stood speechless, watching the horrible scene, trying to fathom what was happening. The only thought that came into my head was that he was having a stroke. His grandfather had had a stroke ten years previously and now moved and spoke with great difficulty, his left side totally useless. Haywood was going to be paralyzed. I started to scream.

"Don't! Haywood! Don't!" My hysterical voice came from somewhere deep inside me. I felt divorced from my body. This wasn't happening. What was happening? Nothing I had ever heard or read about could have prepared me for this moment.

I lunged forward and tried to hook my hands under Haywood's arms to drag him out into the hallway, but he seemed to possess superhuman strength. His thick, powerful legs jerkily kicked at everything in sight, which made me afraid to pursue moving him. "Don't!" I screamed again, but the writhing continued unabated, his hands curled protectively at his chest, fingers clenched in birdlike claws. As I watched, his lips turned blue and his face became grayer and grayer. He sounded as if he was choking to death.

I lost control. "Stop it! Stop it! Stop it!" I started to cry. But Haywood didn't hear a word I was saying. His eyes were rolled back deep in his head and his face displayed no sign of recognition. The thrashing went on.

I was terrified. Was this my strong, brave husband? My star athlete and All-American lacrosse player? Often when I looked at him, I thought he resembled a Greek god, his handsome profile chiseled as if in stone. He would always be there for me, or so I had thought. Now he was going to die a horrible, agonized death before my very eyes, or at the very least be a vegetable for life.

I let out a bloodcurdling scream. "God, help me!" Nothing happened, but it released some of the anguish I was feeling. Suddenly I thought of the firemen next door. They could be here in a moment with a medical kit. They would surely be the crew sent if I called the emergency number. I ran into the bedroom, snatched up the phone, and dialed 911.

"Hello—emergency."

"Hurry, my husband is dying! Come fast!" I gave the operator directions to where we lived, screaming, "Please hurry!" at the end.

She went over the address with me again and told me someone would be there in minutes. I hung up, quickly put a sweat suit on over my nightshirt, and ran back to the bathroom. The convulsions were subsiding and Haywood's labored breathing was evening out. His face and body were wrong somehow, though. It looked as if everything had been pulled out of place and then frozen. His face particularly disturbed me. It wasn't Haywood's face. It possessed none of the traces of his personality: no impishness, joy, tenderness— nothing. Had he lost his mind? I shouted his name with urgency, but again there was no flicker of recognition.

A pounding on the door broke my frenzied, desperate thoughts. The paramedics were here. I ran to the door and let the three men in. One of them moved quickly toward the bathroom where Haywood was now still, but breathing with great difficulty.

"Son! Can you hear me?" The paramedic slipped a blood-pressure cuff around Haywood's upper left bicep as he fired out the questions. Haywood tried to talk, but nothing intelligible came out. I hovered at the doorway, biting my lip to keep from crying again. Looking at his face was tearing me apart. His eyes were absolutely vacant.

"Is he paralyzed?" I asked hoarsely, not really wanting to know the answer.

"No," the paramedic said briskly as he stood up, "but I think we'd better take him to the hospital. He's had a seizure of some sort. Is this the first one he's had?"

Seizure? Haywood? I couldn't think straight. "Uh, I think so. Why would he have a seizure? He's not sick." I said the last sentence pleadingly. Tell me he's not sick, I silently prayed. Tell me this isn't happening. That everything is really okay. That this is all a bad dream.

The two men in the living room went out to get the stretcher from the ambulance. Haywood started to move a bit.

"Son! Can you stand up?" The paramedic looked down at Haywood. Haywood blinked once or twice and tried talking again. What came out was slurred. My God, he sounded drunk! But he couldn't be drunk—it wasn't even six A.M. and we had been sleeping all night. What was going on?

Haywood got unsteadily to his feet. "Who're you?" he slurred, thrusting his finger at the uniformed man.

"Sit down," the paramedic responded, putting a heavy hand on Haywood's shoulder and guiding him to the toilet. Haywood did what he was told but looked confused. I watched him scratch his head absently, then sway like a punch-drunk fighter.

I ran to catch him from falling. "Can he lie down until you're ready to take him?" I asked.

"Sure, if he can walk." The paramedic shrugged his shoulders and started to fill out a form.

"Come on, honey, let's go into the bed for a minute and lie down." I tried to help Haywood up, but he wanted none of it, and he was still unsure of who I was judging from the look on his face. He lurched forward and made his way into the bedroom, holding on to the walls for support. As he crawled under the covers and closed his eyes, the paramedic started to ask me a lot of questions. What was Haywood's social security number? Were we insured? Did he take any medication? I tried to focus on giving the right answers, hoping it would somehow make me calm.

154

As I gave out the necessary facts, my mind started to spin into the future. What if Haywood had had a stroke? Would insurance pay for the costs of rehabilitation, medication, physical therapy? Would we be able to have children? Would he live to be a normal age? Could we be happy with a life like that? Why was this happening to us? We were so young and in love—things like this weren't supposed to happen to people like us! My eyes filled with tears of self-pity.

Before we could leave for the hospital, the paramedic asked Haywood a few more questions to determine his mental condition. "How old are you, son?" He stood over the bed and spoke loudly.

Haywood opened his eyes and shook his head blankly, confused.

"Do you know who this lady here is?" He motioned toward me. Again, Haywood shook his head. That was all it took. I went out into the hallway and started to bawl in earnest. What had happened to my life? My husband had lost his mind! Couldn't we turn the clock back to yesterday and start again?

Stop it, Caroline! My steady internal voice brought me back to the present. Stay in control. You can't afford to collapse now. Someone's got to be strong. I went back into the bedroom, rubbing the arm of my sweatshirt roughly over my eyes to erase any trace of tears.

I bent over Haywood, pushing his perspiration-soaked hair off his forehead. "Honey, we're going to the hospital. You have to get dressed. You're very sick."

Although he didn't respond, Haywood seemed to understand that we had to go. He pushed back the covers and tottered to his dresser. His hands, though, didn't seem to obey his thoughts. I watched him try to open the top drawer, jabbing his closed fist at it repeatedly, not comprehending why it wouldn't open. I hurried to his side to help, getting boxer shorts and a T-shirt out. "Put these on," I commanded. "I'll get your sweat pants and a sweatshirt." I tried not to think about his helpless hands. He got his clothes on and was guided to the stretcher, still bewildered by what was taking place, yet as docile as a child.

"Will you ride with us?" One of the other paramedics looked questioningly at me.

"Where are we going?"

I wanted to call Haywood's parents in Annapolis to let them know what was happening. I needed support. I couldn't go through this alone.

"Union Memorial—it's the closest."

"Okay, I'll be outside in a second. I have to make a call."

Everyone started out of the apartment as I picked up the phone. Haywood's sleepy father picked up on the other end.

"Mr. Miller, Mr. Miller! It's Caroline! Can you come here quick? They're taking Haywood to the hospital! He's had a seizure or a stroke or something!"

"What? Where? What's happening?" His voice was now urgent. I heard Haywood's mother in the background. Haywood had spent so much time over the years in hospitals and emergency rooms from various sports injuries and freak accidents that they were usually prepared for these calls. But this one was different, and they both knew it. They promised to join me at the hospital as soon as possible.

I ran around the apartment grabbing things I thought we'd need: Haywood's wallet, his blood-pressure medication, and some pills he was taking for what his doctor called "panic attacks." Ever since we had gotten married, Haywood had been experiencing frequent and bizarre episodes of hyperventilation when his face drained of color, his voice went up an octave, and his hands got icy cold.

When these came he'd hold on to something—a table, a book, anything—and talk quickly, assuring the surprised people around him that he'd be okay. These "attacks" happened during the day and again at night. Haywood often jolted us both out of a sound sleep with these episodes. At times like this he suddenly sat up, turned on the light, and then walked around for a minute or so, apologizing in a high-pitched voice for the inconvenience.

I felt partly responsible for the attacks, so guilt assailed me every time I watched Haywood go through one. After all, hadn't they started when we had gotten married? Perhaps the stress of having a wife with an eating disorder was too much to deal with, and I never should have confided in him. And,

156

too, the doctor who had diagnosed the "panic attacks" had suggested by way of explanation that Haywood felt uncomfortable with the fact that I was a full-time working woman and he was just a graduate school student. Men couldn't handle that kind of humiliation, you know, he told us.

Although my rational mind told me that times had changed and that society didn't frown upon two-career couples any longer, I still had vague feelings of remorse when I got dressed in the mornings for work. His mother and my mother had stayed home and started families fairly soon after marrying. Was that what I was supposed to do? Is that what Haywood subconsciously wanted and couldn't express? Maybe this morning's episode had been a huge panic attack. I hoped not; I couldn't bear the thought of carrying that kind of guilt around with me.

I glanced around. I hoped I had everything I needed. I grabbed my purse and dashed outside toward the waiting paramedics. I started to climb into the back of the ambulance, but the driver waved me to the front. "You have to ride up here, hon. No room back there." I was too keyed up to argue. I got in front and we sped forward, the siren blaring.

Joggers were outside doing their thing. People were walking their dogs. The paperboys were criss-crossing the streets, tossing the Baltimore *Sun* onto walkways and porches. Their lives were moving ahead as planned. They would all go home to have breakfast and their days would be normal. Yesterday I had been one of them. Today I was in an ambulance with an uncertain future. I turned my face toward the window and let the tears roll down my face.

In just a few minutes we pulled in front of the emergency area of the hospital. I jumped out and ran to the back of the ambulance to watch Haywood get lifted out. His eyes were half open and he looked dazed. "How do you feel?" I asked as he whisked by me. He mumbled something, but it was clear that he didn't know where he was.

As soon as I could, I found a pay phone and called information. I knew the name of his doctor, and directory assistance gave me his home listing. I dialed quickly.

"Hello?" A woman's tired voice answered. People were

still asleep. How could that be? Wasn't everyone up, their nerve endings jangling?

"Mrs. Collins? I'm so sorry to bother you. My name is Caroline Miller, and I'm calling because my husband is a patient of your husband's and he has just been rushed to Union Memorial. Can I talk to him?"

She was instantly attentive. Spouses of doctors were certainly long-suffering, I thought to myself. They must get disturbed and awakened all the time. "He's in the shower. If you'll call back in five minutes, I'll make sure he's here to answer the phone then. Okay?"

I thanked her and hung up. I paced for a few minutes, wishing I was a real cigarette smoker. Then, at least, I would have something to do with my hands. After four and a half minutes I dialed the number again. Dr. Collins was right there to answer.

"Dr. Collins—this is Caroline Miller," I began.

"Yes, yes. What happened to Haywood?" He was all business, wanting the facts. I told him, sparing no detail. As I recounted Haywood's response to the question of whether or not he knew who I was, I started to cry again. "What's wrong with him?" I pleaded tearfully. "Do you think he's had a stroke?"

"No—it sounds like a seizure of some sort. I don't know why, but I can understand your reaction to it. What you witnessed is probably the most frightening thing imaginable. When people have seizures, you can't do anything but stand back and let them go. But at least Haywood won't remember anything about it. He'll probably just come to in a few minutes, totally confused by what has happened and why he's in a hospital."

"Will he remember anything else?" I was still concerned about long-term effects.

"Yes—but I can't be certain until I see him. I'd like him transferred to Johns Hopkins, where I'm affiliated. Can you do that?"

"I think so," I sniffled. "But I have to wait until Haywood's parents get here. They're coming from Annapolis, but it probably won't be much longer."

"Okay. Get him moved and I'll see you at Hopkins. Don't

worry, Mrs. Miller, Hopkins is a top-notch place and he'll receive nothing but the finest care there."

I thanked him and hung up, grateful for the tiniest morsel of hope. I walked back to the room where Haywood was being attended to. His parents were already there, their faces lined with worry. Haywood was now belligerent. "Where have you been, C? Let's get out of here. Why am I here?"

Dr. Collins was right. He remembered nothing about the seizure. I synopsized the morning's events, but he shook his head in bafflement. "I didn't?" he asked in amazement as I told him he hadn't known his age or who I was. "Well, how old are you?" I nervously asked. "Twenty-five" was his confident reply. Well, at least we were on the right track now, I thought with some relief.

Just then the attending physician came into the room. "Your vital signs are fine, so we're going to let you go to Hopkins where Dr. Collins wants to see you. He just called to make sure you could be discharged quickly. Can you all drive there yourselves?" I realized I didn't have a car. Haywood's parents offered to transport all of us, so we gathered our things and left.

Haywood seemed normal, if slightly fatigued. "I don't think we need to go to Hopkins," he complained as we walked to the car. "I feel fine." He *looked* fine, too, which puzzled me. But I hadn't imagined this morning. Something was wrong and we had to find out what it was. His parents tried to be light as we made the ten-minute drive, but it was a forced easiness. We were all nursing private thoughts of doubt and uncertainty.

Because Haywood wasn't in need of immediate care, we had to go through the regular slow admissions process at the hospital while a private room was prepared. Dr. Collins had already called ahead there, too, and by the way people spoke about him and hurried to complete the paperwork, I could tell that he was a highly respected doctor. At least that was a good thing.

I suddenly realized that it was a weekday and that I was expected at work. I looked at my watch. It was nearing eight-thirty, so someone would be in the office. I'd have to let them know I wouldn't be coming in. I fumbled for some change and went to find a pay phone. On my way I passed a bank, a flower shop, a drugstore, a cafeteria, and a bookstore. I paused at the door to the cafeteria. I smelled fresh muffins. Maybe just one. I deserved it. I was under a lot of pressure, after all.

As I wavered, new resolve flooded through me, and the specter of Betsy and other program old-timers hovered overhead. "Breakfast is over, dummy!" my conscience thundered. "Remember? Three meals a day with nothing in between. And no exceptions, unless you have some fabulous medical reason to eat more often." I knew I'd feel lousy and guilty if I ate again. I moved on to the phone. Two points, Caroline.

Walking through the carpeted and cheery hallways of Hopkins abruptly reminded me of my lifelong hospital fantasies. In these frequent reveries, I was deathly ill and confined to a hospital bed where I was taken care of and had no responsibilities. I didn't have to get good grades, play the piano, swim fast, be thin, or act charming. I was just completely helpless and dependent on others to make me feel good.

Once I had mentioned this longing to be taken care of to Betsy, who had laughed and confessed that she had once had a similar urge. "It's so typical of people like us," she said. "Unwilling to take responsibility for anything—always wanting other people to make us better."

Betsy had then told me about her eight months at a hospital eating disorder clinic, where she had naively thought she could be fixed just by being there. Everything had been done for her: prepared meals appeared three times a day, nurses came running at the touch of a buzzer, and her day was completely structured from morning to night. She hadn't even felt the need to take the responsibility for not purging her food because the bathrooms were always locked, nurses standing guard outside.

"It wasn't until I got out and was back into the bulimia within a week, that I realized I had done nothing myself to get well," Betsy told me. "I gained weight to please the doctors, and I didn't vomit because we were watched all the time, but I hadn't accepted the fact that once out in the real world I'd have to do everything myself. So I got sicker than ever, until I found this program and discovered that the key to recovery is admitting and accepting at a gut level that you have a problem, and then taking responsibility for changing everything about your behavior. That whole painful episode cured me of my hospital fantasies for good."

After hearing Betsy's story, I was glad that I hadn't gone into a hospital to recover from bulimia, although I had initially thought that would be the solution, as it was for some people. I was making a lot of progress in this program, I thought to myself as I inserted the proper coins in the pay phone. Several months ago I would have ducked into the hospital's cafeteria and blithely eaten something, then probably gone to purge somewhere out of guilt and frustration. Today I had not done that. "Keep reminding yourself how far you've come every time you don't get into the food," someone had told me after a meeting. "We're so used to beating ourselves up that we've got to learn to pat ourselves on the back once in a while, too." Pat, pat. I had at least one thing to be happy about this morning.

I reached the receptionist at work, who promised to tell the appropriate people about my situation and wished me well. Her kindness made me want to cry again, but I steeled myself and walked back to the waiting area. Haywood's private room was ready, so we gathered our things and went up to the eighth floor of one of the wings. "Dr. Collins ought to be here shortly," one of the nurses said as we were escorted to the right room. "You can just wait here and watch television, if you'd like."

Watching television at least took our minds off our situation. I alternated looking at the "Donahue" show—today Phil was going after child molesters—with staring out the window at the grim scenery. Haywood's room overlooked the parking lot and, beyond that, the depressing housing projects where crime was rampant. Hopkins, while considered one of the foremost teaching hospitals in the world, had somehow found itself smack in the middle of one of the dirtiest and most dangerous parts of Baltimore. Not the kind of atmosphere that was conducive to healing, I thought cynically.

Soon Dr. Collins swept into the room. Short, dark, and intense, he explained to us what he thought had happened and what tests needed to be done to either prove or disprove his hypothesis. Perhaps he had been wrong about the panic attacks, he apologized. Haywood had had a *grand mal* seizure, he believed, which indicated some kind of epilepsy. What needed to be determined was what had caused the seizure: Was there excess electrical activity in his brain? Was there something amiss in his body chemistry? Did he have a brain tumor that had put pressure on something that had manifested in a seizure? He didn't know, but the testing had to start immediately. The country's epilepsy expert was now fortunately at Hopkins, he added, and we would have the benefit of his expertise. He reeled off the tests he had arranged—CAT scans, a spinal tap, extensive bloodwork, and so on.

Nothing registered in my head except for two words: brain tumor. Nothing he said could have upset me more. Someone at the law firm Haywood was going to join in the fall had just died from the effects of a brain tumor. I had once met him at a softball game. The chemotherapy had claimed his hair, and his body had been emaciated. Despite his condition, however, he had seemed cheerful and resigned to his fate. I didn't know what I'd do if Haywood had a brain tumor; I doubted I could accept it gracefully. My mind felt like an unformatted computer diskette. There was absolutely nowhere to put this information in my head. It just didn't fit.

Haywood's parents clearly had the same thoughts I did. They peppered Dr. Collins with questions, for which I was grateful. I couldn't think of anything to ask. I couldn't even think. I just sat numbly in the corner. Haywood asked a few questions but basically just sat on the bed, his lips pressed together with a determined look on his face. If this thing could be beaten, he'd do it, I knew. He had an inner drive that was as tough as nails. Numerous adulatory articles had been written about his sports prowess over the last ten years—especially his lacrosse exploits—emphasizing his ability to take pain and debilitating hits long after others had given up. As captain of Harvard's lacrosse team, he had also played his entire senior year with both legs taped from crotch to toe because of arthritic knees. He had been in tremendous pain every time he had stepped onto the field for years. Pain was something he could endure. *I* just couldn't stand the thought of him being in pain.

Haywood was wheeled out when Dr. Collins left for the

first round of testing. The three of us just looked blankly at each other. Haywood's parents emphasized the positive things he had said, including the fact that some of the country's best doctors and equipment were at Hopkins, so we wouldn't have to worry about poor diagnoses. I kept nodding and saying I thought everything would be fine. I had to keep saying that out loud to reassure myself that everything would be fine. There was a saying in the program about "acting as if" when you just couldn't believe in a Higher Power, or when your day was going poorly and you couldn't find anything to be happy about. If you act "as if" long enough, I was told, the good feelings will follow. So I tried to act "as if" Haywood was going to be fine.

The day passed desultorily. In and out, in and out. Every time Haywood returned to the room after several hours' absence, he was taken out for another test. Finally it was nightfall and there was nothing further we could do but leave. The epilepsy expert—Dr. Seeger—would meet us in the morning to discuss the results of the CAT scan. I kissed Haywood good night and ruffled his thick dark hair. "You'll be out of here soon, love. I'm sure this is nothing serious." I smiled my bravest smile. "See you tomorrow."

When I got home, our apartment looked foreign to me. How many hours ago had we left it so suddenly? The coffee table was on the side of the room. The paramedics must have moved it to get the stretcher out. I dragged it back into place and went into the bathroom. Greeting me was the silent reminder of the morning. Broken glass and other items were still scattered all over. I started to straighten up. At least it would keep me busy for a while.

What could I do tonight? I knew I'd have trouble sleeping, and I couldn't stand the idea of watching television. I didn't think I could concentrate on a book either. A meeting! I'd go to a meeting! At least I'd get out of the apartment and hear tales of hope, I thought with relief. I showered, dressed, and drove up the street to a seminary for an eight P.M. meeting.

I sat at a desk in the corner of the brightly lit classroom and let the words of recovery wash over me. I started to feel peaceful. The warm spring breeze caressed the back of my neck and I felt some of the day's tension melt away.

"Hi, I'm Nancy, a recovering compulsive overeater."

"Hi, Nancy—welcome," we chorused back.

Nancy, a blond, chunky woman with acne scars, started to talk. She told about going to visit her parents over the weekend and having the familiar urge to binge overcome her every time she disagreed with them or felt angry. "Seeing them sets me off," she said, "and my first reaction is always to run to the refrigerator and stuff down my feelings. On top of that, I have PMS and I know that whenever I'm premenstrual the desire to eat—especially sweets—is worse."

Wow. I had never thought about that. Although my period was still very sporadic because of the dieting trauma I had inflicted upon my body, I had noticed that I was really hungry and grouchy right before it occurred and I had always wondered why. Maybe I had PMS, too. I'd have to talk to Nancy after the meeting. She said her doctor had given her a special diet to help quell the cravings and mood swings.

I was contemplating this important fact when I heard my name. "Caroline, do you want to share anything?" The room looked at me. I decided to say a few words.

"Sure. My name is Caroline and I'm a recovering bulimic and compulsive overeater."

"Hi, Caroline."

"Hi. I'm really grateful to be sitting here tonight. My husband was taken to the hospital in an ambulance this morning and I don't know what's wrong with him, but I feel good just being here and listening to you all. It's funny, but when I was at the hospital this morning one of the things that crossed my mind was eating something, even after I had already had breakfast. I didn't give in, but it really reminded me of how out of control I used to be, and how I'd eat whenever the urge struck, or when I felt uncomfortable about something.

"The miracle is that I'm not acting on those urges any-more—at least not today. Another miracle is that I got home tonight and I didn't rush into the kitchen to soothe myself with a nice dinner. I just cleaned up, showered, and came here. I'll eat when I go home after the meeting, and I know it'll be a serene dinner because I came here first. Thanks for calling on me."

When the meeting ended, several people came up to me and hugged me, asking if I needed any support or companionship at the hospital. Although I didn't think I did, I was touched by the offer. One woman chuckled as she warned me about the dangers of people who mistook food for sympathy. "When my mother died, all kinds of people came over with food—tray after tray of it. There I was grieving and the casseroles, cakes, breads, and everything kept coming. I didn't want any of it, but people think it's the right way to express caring. I was pretty new in the program at that point, but I simply called my sponsor every time I felt the urge to eat some of the mounds of stuff, and I got through it abstinently. I know what you mean about wanting to eat when sad and lonely, though. Just keep coming to meetings and calling people, and you'll get through this period just fine. It's always a real turning point when bad things happen to us and our programs don't crumble."

Following the meeting I had dinner and slept soundly. Before I went to sleep, though, I tried to call Betsy to let her know what was happening. But I only got her recording machine—an increasingly common occurrence. Not being able to reach her, however, was not as upsetting as her change in personality during the last few months. Several times she had gotten very angry with me on the phone and insulted me, only to call back a minute or so later and say she was sorry, that I had simply triggered her competitive drive because I was so much like her. She was also unhappy with her job, and once made an off-handed comment that she wanted my job if I decided to leave my company. And one day when I mentioned that I had gone house-hunting for a possible move, she had gone into a tirade about how I had so many gifts that I was unaware of and that she—at ten years older than me—had none of them. I had been taken aback and had started calling her less.

What had thrown me for more of a loss, however, was that she had stopped going to meetings. She was dating a well-known partygoer who was taking her to all kinds of glitzy gatherings, and she had explained to me that she didn't need meetings anymore, that going to church on Sunday mornings had become her meeting. This comment made me uncomfortable. Hadn't she told me sternly time and time again that there was no substitute for meetings, that we had to attend regularly to hear about our food obsession, and that nothing could take its place?

But who was I to question her? She had a number of years of freedom from compulsive overeating and bulimia under her belt, and she had taught me a great deal. Nevertheless, my last thought before falling asleep was that I wanted to switch sponsors. Annie was the person I was thinking of. Everything she said struck home with me, and she had abstained from binging and purging for almost four years while maintaining a sixty-pound weight loss. Once I had even heard her say that she had reached a point of total serenity: she didn't covet anyone's job, boyfriend, body, life, or food. I had been stunned and envious at that revelation. That was the kind of freedom I wanted. I would have to ask her if she could sponsor me when this difficult period was over, however. Too many upheavals at once would surely send me back to the food if I wasn't careful.

When I got to Hopkins the next morning, Haywood's parents had already been there for an hour talking with the doctors. The CAT scan, they told me, had shown a lesion in Haywood's right frontal lobe. Because of that, Haywood was out of the room getting a more detailed scan done of that section of his head. The epilepsy expert, Dr. Seeger, would be up soon with those results to talk to us. We just waited, staring at the television to pass the time.

Haywood and Dr. Seeger appeared within an hour with the CAT scan results, Dr. Collins trailing them. "Nice to meet you all," Dr. Seeger said warmly, nodding his head at each of us. Then he took a seat on the heater by the window and started to talk.

"As you know, we've found a small, but significant lesion in the right frontal lobe of Haywood's brain," he began, holding an X ray up to the light to illustrate. I saw a black knot near the edge of his skull. It looked pretty damn big to me. I didn't like what I saw. I glanced at Haywood; his face displayed nothing.

"I believe Haywood has had a *grand mal* epileptic seizure, and we're lucky he had it when he did. If he had had one just an hour or two later in a car, he undoubtedly would have caused great harm to himself and possibly others, so we can be grateful that he's here today with no major problems." That knot looked like a major problem to me. Just tell us the truth, Dr. Seeger, I thought darkly.

"If this was Haywood's first *grand mal* seizure, which it seems to have been, then I need your help in determining when he might have hit his head—even as a little boy—that might have caused this lesion. Because what probably happened was that he hit his head and the lesion started to form, putting pressure on the brain. The brain then built up electrical activity that it discharged in only the last several years, probably in *petit mal* seizures, and then yesterday's *grand mal* seizure. Dr. Collins and I have conferred and decided that Haywood wasn't having panic attacks and that we're going to cease that medication. Those episodes of hyperventilation and disorientation were all probably just little seizures."

You mean he had been misdiagnosed? That all those panic attack and high blood pressure pills had been unnecessary, and that my guilt had been needless? I glowered at Dr. Collins. A simple CAT scan when the episodes had started would have discovered this problem, and we would have been spared this whole thing.

Haywood's mother furrowed her brow thoughtfully as she searched her memory for head injuries. After a few minutes of suggestions, which Dr. Seeger dismissed as improbable causes, she lit up. "Oh, when he was ten he fell off his bike and his two front teeth were knocked out! Could that be it?"

"Was he knocked unconscious?"

"I think so. I wasn't there, but yes, I think I remember being told that he had been out cold for a minute or two."

"Then that's probably the cause of this," Dr. Seeger said, snapping his fingers. "For about fifteen years that lesion has been gestating, finally putting enough pressure on the brain that the seizures manifested. That would mean that Haywood has secondary epilepsy, which can be safely controlled with medication."

I breathed a sigh of relief. Epilepsy was something I

could live with; a brain tumor was not. But Dr. Seeger cautioned us about finding the proper dosage level and ensuring that the lesion didn't grow into a tumorous mass that would have to be removed.

"We can't be absolutely certain about our diagnosis unless we actually do a biopsy and open Haywood's head up, but that seems unnecessary at this time. We will treat his condition as epilepsy, but I want Haywood to come in for regular CAT scans and bloodwork so that we can keep an eye on that lesion. For now, I'm going to put him on a new medication that has been excellent in controlling seizures. Everyone has different reactions to things, so it would be good if he could just take it easy for a week or two and see how he responds to the dosage."

"We're supposed to go to Florida on Friday," I said, "so that will be at least one week when he doesn't have to do anything. And he just finished exams, so that pressure is off." What a great coincidence that our planned Florida vacation started this week! Higher Power stuff, I'm sure someone in the program would happily tell me later.

"It would also be a good idea if Haywood doesn't drive for a while. We're not bound by law to inform the Department of Motor Vehicles about people who have epileptic seizures, but it is recommended that we do so anyway. In this case we won't. Let's just wait a safe period and see how well he reacts to the medication. If Haywood has no more *petit mal* seizures during the day or at night, then we'll know that this stuff is doing its job."

No more *petit mal* seizures! God, that would be wonderful. We might get a night of uninterrupted sleep for a change. I smiled at Haywood, who had said nothing throughout this exchange. He looked relieved, but something was clearly on his mind.

"I can't drive?" he asked plaintively, looking at Dr. Seeger.

"I wouldn't take that chance, yet. If something happened and you hurt someone else, your savings and all your possessions would be taken from you. You'd be sued for everything."

168

"Well, then, this medication had better work," Haywood grumped. "Caroline's driving leaves something to be desired!"

We all laughed, grateful for the humor. It had been a grim two days and we were ready for levity. Haywood had to stay for another night while a few more tests were run and the medication was arranged for, but at least the crisis was over. I decided to go to work to tie up some loose ends in preparation for our trip, so I kissed Haywood and his parents good-bye and left.

I allowed myself a wry laugh as I pulled out of the hospital parking lot. All those fears I had had about paralysis, children, and insanity the day before had been unnecessary. I had really been projecting into the future, something people in the program warned about constantly. Whenever I mentioned something I feared would occur, someone would say, "Caroline, you're not living in the present. If there's nothing you can do about a problem today, forget it. After all, if tomorrow were so important it would be here right now!"

There was another catchy phrase I had heard at meetings that summarized this attitude: "Yesterday is a canceled check. Tomorrow is a promissory note. Today is cash—spend it."

One day at a time. That really applied to everything in life. So did some of the other program slogans: "First things first," "Let go and let God," and "Easy does it." If I just kept remembering them, I'd be okay in every area, not just my food. And didn't the program counsel to "practice these principles in all our affairs"?

I said a silent prayer of thanks for the program and for Haywood's diagnosis. One day at a time I could deal with anything, even having to chauffeur him around while he tried to tell me how to drive. And I knew just where I'd drive him down in Florida: only this week someone had told me that there were some terrific program meetings in Miami Beach.

TEN

HAYWOOD'S SEIZURE WAS A TURNING POINT for me in many ways. For the first time in my life, I truly felt like an adult. I had not run home for solace nor crumbled in fear at the first sign of trouble. Out of the first major crisis in our marriage, Haywood and I had emerged stronger, happier, and more committed to each other. Each day became more precious as we were suddenly, and painfully, aware that everything that was important to us could be taken away in a flash.

I was also surprised and grateful that I had not turned to food for comfort during the crisis and in the months afterward. After more than a year's worth of meetings, telephone calls, reading literature, and tearful slips, I had my first concrete evidence that I didn't have to binge when difficult times struck. If I had been looking for an excuse to eat, this would have been the perfect opportunity because my anxiety continued for months. Despite the medication's success in eliminating Haywood's seizures, I still had frequent nightmares about finding him thrashing around on the bathroom floor, and every time he was late or out of my sight for very long, I feared he was having a seizure in his car or elsewhere.

I started to look at myself in a new way. Rather than focusing on my flaws and defects, I began to be a bit more generous in evaluating my performance at work, in the program, and at home. No, I wasn't perfect, but I was doing the best I could every day, and that's all that anyone could reasonably ask of me. My self-confidence flowered.

Others noticed the change in me. In the program, more and more people started calling me for advice and asking me to sponsor them. At work I developed a more assertive personality, which put a halt to some of my people-pleasing tactics such as taking on work that wasn't part of my job so that others might like me. Friends who did not know about the bulimia asked about my air of serenity: Are you going to church or something? they queried. You look so peaceful!

As the summer of 1985 wore on, I took several important steps that were instrumental in my recovery. The first was taking an honest look at my career. I assessed the company and my position in it, and decided that I wanted a more active role in management—if not there, then at another place where I could have more of a say in the day-to-day operations.

Within weeks of that decision, I was offered an excellent job out of the blue as vice president at a fledgling communications firm in Baltimore, where I was told I would run my own division and eventually have the chance to buy out the owners. With that promise and a hefty salary increase, I left my secure P.R. niche at the real estate development firm. While part of me quivered in fear that I wouldn't measure up to expectations, I also knew that without change in my life I would just be stagnating.

Another major shift for me was cosmetic: I took eight bags of clothes to Goodwill one afternoon and started my wardrobe over from scratch. I cleared out mountains of skirts, shirts, and dresses that did not fit properly or reflect my new personality. Into the green garbage bags were tossed masculine suits, bowties, ruffled skirts, and drably colored shirts. Many of the items were things I had bought only because my mother thought they were attractive on me. For years, I had totally deferred to her opinions, rarely voicing my own because I thought everything looked dreadful and I wanted her approval. My approach to assembling a wardrobe had been typical of the way I had conducted my life: doing things only because it made someone else happy, never having the courage to state my own needs.

One of the hardest parts of the clothes purging was getting rid of some of my "fat clothes"—things I had carried around with me for years which I considered barometers of my worthiness. If I fit into certain pants or skirts, then I was happy because they reminded me of a thin time in my life. If I didn't—which I almost never did—then I was devastated and convinced that I couldn't show my face in public because I was so obese.

One pair of shorts, in particular, had terrorized me for years. They were cut-off blue jeans from eighth grade, which I hoped I would one day be able to fit into again. On days when I felt slim, I would approach the closet, heart beating crazily, and take the shorts off the shelf, praying that they would slip on easily. They never did, however, and just seeing them was a silent reminder that I was unsuccessful—i.e. a bad, fat, and inferior person.

I had not realized the emotional damage I was doing to myself with this bizarre ritual until I was sitting at a meeting one night and heard a woman talking about her "clothes purging." She said that part of her recovery had meant coming to terms with the fact that her body would never be that of a teenager anymore, and that maturing and having the curves of a thirty-five-year-old woman was normal—not something to repeatedly chastise herself for.

"My sponsor tells me that I am going to be at my right weight if I eat three moderate meals a day and exercise," she emphasized, "and I fought that, thinking that I had to get back into those clothes to be okay. But one day I realized that I wasn't willing to starve myself anymore, or eat Lite Line cheese on Less bread three times a day to get there. That wasn't living. Focusing on an unrealistic goal kept me unhappy, obsessed with food, and unable to be an effective wife or mother."

She said she had finally made peace with her body through prayer and listening to people tell her again and again that she wasn't fat, and that a woman's body was supposed to change with age and childbirth. "So I gathered all the clothes one day when I was feeling good and gave them away. I felt a huge weight lift off my shoulders that very afternoon, and now I wonder why I waited so long," she continued. "It was just one more way of shutting the door on the past, and the peace that came from doing it was indescribable."

After listening to this testimony, I resolved to follow her lead and purge my closet, too. As I loaded the bags and drove to Goodwill, though, I worried that without the clothes I would have no check of my body other than what other people told me I looked like. That would involve a lot of trust. It was also a year and a half since I had set foot on a scale, so I had no idea what I weighed and I still wasn't willing to submit to that process, even at the doctor's office. Some people told me they stepped onto the scale backward for their checkups so that they wouldn't know what the numbers were. I didn't want to do that, though, because I could tell just by listening to the sliding bars what the total was. My doctor had been surprisingly agreeable when I told him, in no uncertain terms, that I refused to be weighed. He said that he could just look at people and estimate their weight, and that I looked fine. Hearing that pronouncement had eliminated ninety-five percent of my fear of visiting him.

Aside from my "clothes purging," another change I made in my appearance was that I started to wear makeup on a regular basis. In college I had experimented with mascara and blush because of a roommate who owned a fascinating collection of powders, rouges, eyeshadows, and lipsticks that transformed her from pretty to beautiful. Watching her I had realized that everyone could afford to enhance their assets and diminish their flaws without looking cheap. But I had resisted investing too much time or money in the effort, alternately telling myself that it was vain to care too much about my looks, with postbinge despair that there wasn't anything good about my features to enhance anyway.

173

People in the program admonished me that it was time to care about my outward appearance, though, and that I had to value myself enough to look well-groomed. I also knew that women in the business world who did not wear makeup were not taken as seriously as women who did wear foundation, blush, lipstick, mascara, and rouge. All of the books and articles I read on the subject warned bare-faced female executives that if they looked like immature high-schoolers, their peers would treat them as such.

Changing my clothes and getting serious about makeup were nothing compared to the painful decision to change my hairstyle, though. One sunny September morning in 1985, one week before I was to start my new job, I looked in the mirror and realized that the long, curly blond locks had to go. Although many people, including Haywood, had told me over the years that it was my best feature, I had also heard it said in meetings that long hair was simply a shield that many compulsive overeaters hid behind. I knew that applied to me; whenever I was feeling particularly bad about my body, I always set my hair in hot rollers and fluffed it up, hoping it would deflect people's eyes from my stomach or swollen face. I also kept it long because I was sure that if my hair was anywhere near or above shoulder length, then it would emphasize what I called my "Great Pumpkin" face.

But I was tired of the hiding. I was wearing bright, peacock-colored clothes, starting a new job, beginning to wear makeup regularly, and I wanted a sophisticated, flattering hairstyle to go with the new me. Gulping hard and fortified with support from program friends, I made an all-day appointment at one of Baltimore's toniest salons.

"I don't know exactly what I want," I said apologetically to Jheani, the stylist who had been recommended to me, after she pumped me skyward in her chair and surveyed me thoughtfully. "I do know that I want less hair and something chic, though. Can you help me?"

Jheani went to fetch Michel, the salon owner. The two conferred in French for a minute or so, unaware that my high school language classes allowed me to eavesdrop on their conversation. "Her hair is too dry, too long, and overpermed,"

Michel commented as he raked his thick fingers through my hair disgustedly. "I don't know if we can salvage it."

The two finally agreed on a strategy, however, and went to work. All day long, I was shunted from the shampoo area, to the smelly perm trays, and back to the stylist's chair, where Jheani finally started to snip insistently. My heart went into my mouth as I watched five- and six-inch chunks of blond hair fall to the floor. But I really became concerned when her scissors began to fashion bangs around my forehead, a look I hadn't had since I was five.

"Whoa!" I said shakily. "I'm not sure bangs are the most mature look for me. Do you really think they are?"

Jheani silenced me with an arrogant look. "You have a wide face, so we need to create some softness around the sides and the top. You will love it when I am done." Then, seeing my fear, she added soothingly, "It's hard to tell what the results will be when your hair is wet. Trust me."

As she started snipping away again, I just gulped hard and took my contact lenses out. At least I didn't have to watch the butchering process. When she was done, my hair was loaded with mousse and coaxed into a soft bob with round brushes and her blowdryer. From what I could see, it was very flattering.

I finally emerged from Michel's at dusk, my arms loaded with a bag of expensive ointments and shampoos. Although I had spent over $150, I felt the day had definitely been worth every penny. My hair had a new, vibrant look about it and was a radical change from the way I had looked before.

I paused when I passed my reflection in a shop window down the street. In years past I had averted my eyes from mirrors and avoided cameras, unable to look at myself without seeing ugliness and fat. Today was different: my clothes fit well, there was a smile on my lips, and my hair was not hanging in long strings around my face. Who would have thought that a self-help group for compulsive overeaters could evoke such a startling transformation? I certainly hadn't. But the bulimia had adversely affected so many areas of my life that a chain reaction of improvement was altering everything about me.

I wanted to rush home and introduce Haywood to his

new wife, but I had to do some grocery shopping and buy our dinner first. We were low on everything and I knew Haywood would not set foot in a grocery store because of the crowds and long lines. I didn't really mind handling the food purchases, though, because he managed the household finances—an area that traumatized me. I was always afraid that money would run out, so I just handed him the bills without opening them. I knew my financial neurosis was connected to my fears of never having enough of anything important to me —food, approval, and attention, for example—and that I would have to learn to face that area eventually. But as they said in the program, first things first. Overcoming the food compulsion was still my top priority, and it merited my undivided attention. The other things would be tackled when I was ready, if they didn't just work themselves out over time.

At the supermarket I took a cart and started to push it through the produce section. I really *did* love to shop for food, especially fresh fruits and vegetables. Everything beckoned: shiny winesap apples, glistening romaine lettuce, and mounds of peppers, cucumbers, and tomatoes. I even loved trying exotic things like jicama, Asian cucumbers, and chayote squash. While I was still passionate about food, at least it wasn't running my life anymore. I could buy and eat it normally, appreciating it for giving me life, a feeling that was new and dear to me.

I was also grateful that my recovery had now enabled me to go to grocery stores without anxiety. When I had been eating off the shelves and stuffing food in my pockets, I had always panicked when I got to the checkout counter, sure that the store manager would descend from his perch near the front, swinging a pair of handcuffs and reading me my Miranda rights. Now that the program had taught me the rigorous honesty of not eating between meals and paying for things I wanted, grocery shopping had become a pleasure.

As I finished getting the things we needed, I passed by the bins of "natural" foods—yogurt-covered raisins, carob maltballs, trail mix, dried fruits, and assorted nuts. My stomach growled as I paused in front of them, eyeing the different choices. I was hungry. I normally didn't shop when I was hungry, but the whole day had been eaten up by the hair appointment and my lunch had been a small sandwich furtively eaten between shampoos.

I started trying to rationalize taking a little piece of something. No one would see me and I could definitely stop with one bite, I told myself. I was also doing extraordinarily well in the program—no sugar, white flour, or other binge foods had passed my lips in months, and my last purge had been around the beginning of the year, several months before Haywood's seizure. Also, maybe if I bought a bag of the raisins and had a few each night I could teach myself to have my binge foods again, but in smaller quantities.

I slowly walked along the row, trying to decide what to do as my mind spun out the delectable possibilities. Carob-coated coconut clusters, peanut butter squares, fig bars, sugar-free mints—there were so many wonderful things to choose from! I started to salivate as I imagined hunkering down in bed with a book when I got home, the food cradled in my lap. The lights would be low, the book mesmerizing: I could just imagine how relaxing and pleasant the scene would be. I reached for the lid of the yogurt-covered raisins bin.

An internal warning voice started to lecture. Hadn't someone recently said at a meeting that these very items had led her into a binge, and that although they were sugar-free they had been so sweet and so reminiscent of all of the carbohydrates she used to eat in vast quantities that she had been unable to stop with just a few bites? I pushed her words to the back of my mind. I was starving and I wanted to reward myself for my months of hard work and perfect abstinence.

The lid of the bin off, I reached up to get a plastic bag to put my goodies in when I saw a young woman several feet to my left scooping some granola into a bag. I took special note of her because as she worked she was cramming handfuls of the crunchy mixture into her mouth, barely pausing to chew. I watched as she filled another bag with carob confections, eating as much as she could while doing it. This bag she stuffed in her pocket. I was astonished at her brazenness; she was stealing!

I stood rooted in place, outrage, disgust, and compassion mingling together. This woman was clearly bulimic. She was well dressed, attractive, and had perfectly applied makeup.

The giveaway was her compulsive behavior and that look on her face that I had come to know so well—an intensity mixed with unsmiling desperation. My heart went out to her as I gazed into her cart. It was filled with ice cream, cookies, crackers, barbecued chicken, and piles of vegetables. Had I been this blatant? Had people looked at me piteously in supermarkets and food stores, wondering if they could say anything to me to stop me from my self-destructive behavior? Had they seen me steal, too?

I stuffed my empty plastic bag between two of the bins and fled for the checkout counter, my heart racing. Looking at the woman had scared me. I didn't want to go back. I didn't want that crazy life again—the lying, stealing, and horrible binges. She was probably going to drive around and eat for hours and throw up in different bathrooms or have a laxative overdose. If I had taken that first compulsive bite of the food in the bins, I probably would have gone on a binge, too.

"You aren't normal, Caroline!" I chastised myself on the way home. "You have a disease, pure and simple, and you can't forget it!" I was shaken that I had been prepared to throw my recovery away so quickly over yogurt-covered raisins. "This addiction to food is cunning, baffling, and powerful like they say at meetings," I thought ruefully to myself. "I've got to remember to take it seriously!"

I decided I had to make a gratitude list soon. People said at meetings that when the food beckoned, a good thing to do was to make a list of things we were grateful for—especially the things that had appeared in our lives as a result of working the program. There was a lot I was grateful for, not the least of which was having the willingness to make such a list.

Haywood wasn't home when I got there. He was probably too frightened of what I would look like and had decided to go out for a few beers with friends to cushion the initial impact of seeing me. He had strenuously argued against my plans to cut my hair and was morose when I had remained steadfast in my desires for a major overhaul. Like most men, he had a fetish about women's hair. The longer, the better—and the sexier.

I put the groceries on the floor and stood in front of the living room mirror. My hair still looked good to me. Now if only I could learn how to recreate the style with my newly purchased round brushes and bottles of mousse, I'd be okay. I tossed my head this way and that, smiling and dipping my head, pretending I was talking to someone. The hair slid back into place perfectly every time. It didn't need those childish barrettes and hairbands I had been chained to for so long to stay out of my face, either. I felt as though the day at the salon had catapulted me from adolescence to adulthood.

I picked up the grocery bags and carried them into the kitchen. As I passed through the dining room, I noticed the red light flashing insistently on the answering machine. Haywood and I had decided to invest in one of these devices after the constant phone calls had started to interrupt our peace at all hours of the day and night. I hoped there weren't too many calls to return. I was tired and wanted to eat.

I grabbed a pad and pen and flopped into the chair next to the phone. I rewound the machine and started to listen to the messages.

"Hi, Caroline, this is Jean. I just wanted to commit today's food to you." She then recited her day's meal plan and added that she would be eating dinner at her boyfriend's house and that she might have some trouble there. "His mother is always trying to fill my plate when I'm done, and she gets offended when I don't try everything," she complained.

Jean said she'd call again once she got to the house and found out what was being served to ask my advice on what to take and what to avoid. "Hope you have a great day!" she chirped at the end.

The next call was from a young girl in the program who had just started calling me. "Hi, Caroline, this is Maggie. I just had a binge and I feel terrible. I think I started to eat because I am worried about my classes, but now I'm so full I can't even sit up to study. When am I ever going to stop doing this? It's just not worth living if my food is going to be out of control!" I heard her start to cry. "Call me if you can, although I'll understand if you don't want to," she concluded.

She always ended her calls like that; Maggie was convinced that no one wanted to be her friend or talk to her, although I tried to explain that talking to her helped me with my program. Often talking to someone else who was not doing well was the only thing that kept me away from the food myself. I'd have to call her back soon.

The next call was from Angie. "Hi, Caroline. I'm feeling shaky and I thought I'd better make a call." Angie relied on me for support and advice, sometimes several times a day, which scared me a bit. She ostensibly had a perfect life: a great husband, three beautiful children, a rewarding job, a lithe body from the twice-weekly aerobics classes she taught, and an unshakable religious faith.

In reality, however, she was leading a miserable double life, eating and purging frequently, often while preparing meals for the family. She said she had hit her last bottom after paying a hefty fee to join a Christian diet club that emphasized group prayer and a rigid meal plan. After trying shots, fasting, Weight Watchers, Diet Workshop, various diets, and psychotherapy, the Christian approach had been her final resort. When that had failed, she had found herself in this program for compulsive overeaters, more desperate than ever.

Angie had heard me share at a meeting and had latched onto me as her lifeline, begging me to be her sponsor and saying she'd do anything I told her to do to recover. "Please help me," she had pleaded. "I just can't go on any longer like this. Twelve years of binging and purging is enough!"

While I had been happy to sponsor her, remembering the admonition that "You can't keep what you don't give away," I was feeling overwhelmed by the enormity of advising her and being her Rock of Gibraltar. I still had difficult times—witness this afternoon—and I worried that I didn't have a big enough reservoir of strength yet to share with her and others.

Tonight Angie was worried about a pot-luck supper she had to attend at her church. She didn't know what to do: should she take her own dinner with her in her purse or just trust that she'd find something acceptable once she got there? "And I'm feeling so fat!" she moaned on the tape. "I tried on some blue jeans today and they were tight and it ruined my day. My arms also look fat. And all the other aerobics instructors are so darn thin!"

I smiled as I listened to Angie. I knew so well that awful feeling of judging happiness by body size and clothes fit. It sounded as if she might be ready for a clothes purging, too. I couldn't imagine that she had ever been thinner, though. A recent fat calipers test at her gym had shown her with seven percent body fat, an astonishingly low level for a woman. Her periods had even ceased, a sure sign that she was too thin or under too much pressure. I sighed, making a note to tell her to throw the jeans out, and listened to the next message.

"Caroline, this is Francine." I could barely hear her voice so I turned the volume up as high as it would go. "I'm so depressed. It was my seventeenth day of abstaining from binging and purging yesterday, but I got an overwhelming urge to binge, so I went to the grocery store and stole some cookie mix. I spent all night baking and throwing up, and I couldn't stop until two in the morning."

At least it didn't sound as though she had been picked up for shoplifting, which was the only hopeful thing about her disturbing message. Once she had been taken down to jail for stealing cookies and had spent the night in detention. Now Francine had a criminal record—all for the love of food.

"When is this shit going to end?" she whimpered. "I gave up drugs, I've been sober for four years, I've spent six weeks in a coma with a head injury, but giving up the food is the hardest fucking thing I've ever done. I just don't know if I can stop!" Her voice was at a peak now; then it dropped off with her final words: "I hope I get to talk to you soon. Bye."

The weight of the calls came crashing down around me. Who would I call first? Everyone sounded so desperate—I almost felt guilty for having a binge-free day. I also felt responsible to each and every one of the women. Hadn't they called and asked for my assistance, my ear? I couldn't possibly eat dinner until I had returned each call, but I didn't know if I had the strength to do it. I was overwhelmed with the pain I had just heard.

I decided to call Annie first. I needed to talk to someone about my near slip in the supermarket before I could start pretending to have wisdom to impart to others. I dialed her number.

"Hello?"

"Hi, Annie. It's Caroline—do you have a minute?"

"Yes, I have about five minutes; then I have to get to the

meeting at Good Samaritan Hospital. It's my fourth anniversary tonight. Are you coming?"

I'd totally forgotten about the important occasion. Annie was celebrating four years of recovery from bulimia, which was sure to be a festive meeting replete with balloons, gifts, and tributes from others in the program about her growth. I looked at my watch. If I ate quickly, I could get there in time.

"Oh, Annie—I forgot. But I think I can get there. I have a few things I need to get off my chest first, though."

"Okay—shoot."

I told her about being in the supermarket and coming within inches of getting back into my binge foods, and then about all the phone calls and my fear of not being able to say the right things to make the people better.

"Okay—first you have to keep reminding yourself where you've come from," she began. "People have told me to keep my last binge 'green,' meaning that I can't ever forget the horrible pain of eating that drove me into the program. You simply can't make the mistake of thinking you're cured, or that you can go back to all that sweet stuff. A diabetic doesn't stop taking insulin to see if he's well, and by the same token you can't go back to your binge foods again, or stop going to meetings and being around other compulsive overeaters.

"You've proved to yourself time and time again that you are a compulsive overeater, and you have no guarantee that you'd be able to stop binging once you took that first bite. Is losing your abstinence worth those odds?"

"No," I admitted ruefully, "but those raisins sure looked tempting. I just get angry sometimes when I realize that I can't eat the way other people eat, and I can't have cake on my birthday, and other things like that."

"Oh, here comes the pity pot," Annie joked. "Listen, you aren't depriving yourself—you're taking care of yourself. And all those people who are eating that stuff aren't all that happy with themselves either. Statistics show that almost everyone in this country is dissatisfied with their weight or is on a diet, or both. And most of them are going to gain back the weight they lose anyway!"

"I needed to hear you say that," I said. "It's easy for me to rationalize eating something I shouldn't because I don't al-

Here are my dad and I at the Ivy League Swimming Championships in 1980. Bloated from binging and built up from weight lifting, I am at one of my lowest points although no one, including my father, knows about my eating disorder.

Haywood and I started dating at Harvard in 1981 during my sophomore year and his senior year. Just several months later we were discussing marriage plans, but, as clearly shown here, my happiness couldn't hide bulimia's telltale signs of a swollen face and chipmunk cheeks.

In November of 1983, Haywood and I put on our letter sweaters to cheer for Harvard at the hundredth anniversary of the Harvard-Yale football game. Although we had been married since June and Haywood knew I was fighting bulimia through willpower and fad diets, he had no idea how sick I was, nor how unsuccessful my attempts to conquer it were. Within three months I would hit my final bottom and seek help from a free, self-help fellowship for compulsive overeaters.

By the fall of 1986, through my program and with the love and support of my husband, I am almost three years into recovery and looking happier and feeling better than I ever could have imagined.

H. Haywood Miller, IV who joined us on May 7, 1989.
His birth has been the biggest change in my life. He is
shown here at one and a half years old.

ways stop to think about the consequences. If that woman hadn't been on a binge in the supermarket, I know I would have gotten back into the food."

"Your Higher Power put her there, I'm sure," Annie laughed. "There are no accidents in this world. Also, just remember that there are a thousand excuses, but not one good reason for a binge."

"Oh, I like that! I'll remember that phrase. But before I let you go, what would you do about these calls? I just feel so overwhelmed!"

"Keep it simple," Annie said. "And remember, some of these people don't want advice—they just want an ear. My sponsor is wonderful. She just says, 'Uh-huh' every now and then while I'm ranting and raving, and then I thank her at the end of the conversation and hang up feeling great. Later I realize that all she's done is listen and offer her own experiences where appropriate.

"You can't counsel these people. You can only share your experience, strength, and hope. Don't try to fix everyone. Just offer what you can. And remember: you can't give away what you don't have."

It was time for Annie to leave, so I hung up, grateful for her words. She was right—I couldn't take on everyone's burdens and feel responsible for their recovery. And I didn't need to call everyone back immediately. I had to take care of myself first and make sure that I wasn't totally drained of my energy. When I was replenished, I would be of most service to others.

There was a wonderful acronym in the program: HALT. I was told that I shouldn't let myself get too hungry, angry, lonely, or tired, and I definitely needed to remedy my hunger before I could leave for the meeting. So I fixed dinner, ate it quickly, and left for the meeting, deciding to put off the calls until I returned home.

Once I got to the hospital, I was glad I had made the effort. I was still thinking about asking Annie to be my new sponsor, and I wanted to hear her whole story before I made that commitment. The large auditorium was crowded, and people were filling the sixty-some chairs that were arranged in a circle. Annie sat facing the group with her husband on her left. That was nice to see; I was always glad when I saw the spouse of someone at a meeting, trying to understand the complexities of the food addiction.

Haywood had gone with me a few times, which had made a huge difference in his attitude toward the many hours I spent going to meetings and talking on the phone. And as at least one concession to my eating disorder, he had promised not to crawl into bed with a pint of ice cream, as was his habit when the sugar urge hit him. He was beginning to understand that to tempt me like that was unkind and self-indulgent, at least at this point in my recovery.

The first meeting Haywood had gone to, he had been self-conscious, afraid that he would be the only man there. He had been relieved to find several others there and had been especially interested in listening to the ones who were bulimic because he had thought only women suffered from it.

The thing that had surprised him the most, however, had been the brutal honesty of the sharing. He heard people talking about sex, abortions, incest, childhood hurts, and other personal things. "Do you talk like that?" he asked incredulously as we left one night. I told him I did because of the healing process of revealing what was on my mind. "You have no idea how wonderful it is to get things out into the open and have people tell you they've done or said the same thing," I explained. "It's not worth it to keep things bottled up inside. You only get sick—or sicker." I also told him a phrase I had heard one night that many thought was true: A problem shared is a problem half solved.

Although Haywood had shaken his head in amazement, I noticed that soon thereafter he began talking about his feelings more openly with me. After being raised in a society that expected men to be tough, macho, and cool, he had shoved his sensitive side under so deeply that it was difficult for him to talk about his fears and hurts. That's why I was thrilled when the program started to rub off on him and he started to tell me things I hadn't suspected he cared about. I had heard that having one person get well in a family positively affected others, but it was exciting to actually see it happen to me.

I took a seat and pulled my needlepoint out. Like so many other people in the program, I had adopted this hobby to keep my hands busy during meetings and while I was spending endless hours on the phone. I was still so compulsive that if I wasn't doing two things at once I felt as though I was wasting time.

"Hi, my name is Annie, and I'm a recovering bulimic and compulsive overeater."

"Hi, Annie!"

"Hi." Framed by balloons and holding several bouquets of flowers that others had given her, Annie began her story.

"Tonight I'm grateful to be celebrating four years of recovery from binging and purging, which is something I never thought I'd be able to do. When I found this program, I was sixty pounds heavier than I am now, I was living in a trailer with a bunch of hippies, I wore long, flowered skirts, and I pulled my hair out from nervousness. I had abandoned my family, I had already been married and divorced once, and I was living to eat and purge, sometimes up to ten times a day. I was a mess."

I chuckled. I was getting used to these stories of transformation, no matter how unbelievable they sounded. To look at Annie today you would never guess that the person she was describing was the person of several years ago. I couldn't wait to get to the part of how she had found her present, clean-cut husband, who was as far from a hippie as one could imagine.

Annie gave a brief overview of her childhood, saying that she was the child always put on a diet, given the smallest helpings at dinner, and who had had the most Spartan lunches packed for school. As her mother had tried harder to keep her caloric intake low, Annie said she had simply begun to sneak food, also becoming addicted to the diet pills her doctor prescribed.

"Somewhere I heard that vomiting was a way to lose weight, so I got hooked on that during my teens, too, and I remember driving around at night to stores in old raincoats, buying candy bars, pizzas, ice cream, and whatever else I could get my hands on to binge with, always ending the evening in some dirty bathroom," Annie said matter-of-factly.

I briefly thought of my own driving escapades in the name of food. How many times had I endangered the safety of other people by binging with one hand and trying to steer with the other? Or had trouble braking suddenly because of a gallon of ice cream between my legs? Once when I was fifteen —before I had gotten my driver's license—I had even taken the family car to the supermarket to buy foods for a binge because I was so desperate. Alcoholics aren't the only menace on the nation's roads, I thought to myself, but because food is legal people can't be stopped for driving while binging.

"Drugs were another area where I got into self-destructive behavior," Annie continued. "I was stoned most every day, all day, for years, and I remember that I didn't even go to my father's funeral because I was so high. I only thought that I was being cool, and that he had never loved me anyway, so it really didn't matter.

"I also got into a lot of alternative religions. I'm from a Jewish family, but I did things like chant to Buddhas, study to become a Christian, live at crystal-gazing ranches, and all kinds of things like that. The one constant in all this was that I was eating all the time, thinking that if I only changed my environment or my clothes, then the binging and purging would disappear. But it only got worse.

"Now I can see that it was the food and my unhappiness with myself that led me down the other crazy roads, although at the time I thought it was the other way around: I thought that all the religions, drugs, and alternative lifestyles caused me to eat because I never found any of them fulfilling.

"When I first found this program—through a reference in 'Dear Abby'—I came to meetings angry, I told people that the program should be changed to suit me and my needs, and I continued to binge for a year and a half between meetings, although it was in smaller and smaller quantities.

"One day my sponsor just told me that I'd better get on my knees and pray for the willingness to get abstinent because she didn't know what else she could say to help me. I was scared of losing her, and I knew that there was nothing else out there to help me, so I did, and I got my abstinence that night.

"I am not perfect, but these last four years have been filled with one twenty-four-hour period after the next of abstaining from compulsive eating and purging. I'm not going to sit up here and tell you that it has been easy, because it hasn't. I still occasionally get crazy food thoughts and cravings, but the difference is that I don't give in to them, and every time I don't, this path gets easier and easier.

"I was told that I would have to have the willingness to do a personal inventory and let go of character defects like judgmentalism, gossiping, self-pity, resentment, and all that, and while I thought I never would, through the help of my sponsor and my Higher Power, I have. I simply am not the person I was several years ago, and sometimes I have to pinch myself to remind me that I have everything I want in my life now, which is a miracle.

"I've heard it said again and again that the only thing you have to change when you get into this program is everything, which has certainly been the case with me. But it happened so gradually that I didn't realize it while it was going on.

"One of the other things I used to do compulsively was sleep with men." My head snapped up to see what her husband's reaction was to this forthright statement. But he looked quite serene, even placid. "What an honest relationship that is!" I marveled to myself. "He must love her an awful lot to not mind her spilling her guts about sleeping around to a room full of people!"

I was about to return my attention to my needlepoint when I noticed an older woman sitting close to Annie on her other side. Was that her mother? It had to be; there were too many similarities in their features. Now I was really astonished. It was one thing to be honest with other compulsive overeaters, but I had to hand it to Annie for letting her family in on the details of her dark past.

My parents knew I was recovering from bulimia because I had driven to their home shortly after entering the program, and told them about the seven years of binging and purging— sometimes under their own roof. They had simply looked at me in shock; they had never even heard the word *bulimia* before.

"Are you blaming us?" my mother asked in surprise, when I mentioned what I felt was an undue emphasis on thinness in our family.

At that point in my recovery, I *did* think it was their fault. I had not yet learned that recovery meant taking responsibility for my actions and not blaming anyone else. I had simply rushed over to confess to them because of the "rigorous honesty" part of the program. Now, as I looked back at that dinner, I could see that I had hoped they would take the blame and admit their culpability, absolving me of responsibility for my past behavior.

The evening had been unsatisfying. I had left angry and resentful that my big confession had not been received like the Second Coming. I had also stayed angry in the following months because my parents never asked me any questions about my recovery; my mom just sent newspaper clippings about anorexia and bulimia and asked in a worried voice if I had been binging and purging every time she couldn't reach me on the phone, or if I sounded tired. And my dad mispronounced *bulimia* every chance he had. Either he was trying to inject levity into the topic, or he was denying that it was a problem in the family. I wasn't sure which, but it annoyed me all the same.

Now, more than a year later, I was reassessing their role in the development of my eating disorder. Perhaps they had brought up my weight and my crazy diets too much, but if I had been a parent observing my behavior, I would have been concerned, too. I had always been trying some new regimen or talking about food, I had constantly been caught sneaking food to my room, and my weight had careened up and down for no apparent reason because I never binged in front of anyone.

One day when I had a little more humility, I was going to apologize for my actions over the years and invite them to a meeting. The program stressed that making amends was necessary for recovery, and I knew that my family deserved a lot of apologies from me for my lies and self-centered behavior. I wasn't ready for that big step yet, though. Perhaps listening to Annie would show me how. I returned my attention to her story.

"I have also had to go back to stores that I stole from and offer to make restitution," Annie continued calmly. Ye gods— that was going to be a tough one for me, too. Apologizing to my parents would be difficult, but I didn't think I'd ever have the courage to return to supermarkets and stores and offer to repay them for all the gum, laxatives, and food I had stolen.

But maybe if I asked Annie to be my sponsor, she could help me with that, too.

"I was terrified half the time I went back to these people and places," Annie said, "but I knew that I'd never be able to shut the door on the old me until I had come clean. My sponsor told me that a guilty conscience was one of the fastest ways to get back into the food, so I did what she told me.

"One of the hardest things I had to do was go back to a friend's house and tell her mother that I had taken a valuable ring from her daughter years before. I offered to pay back what she thought would be fair, but instead she thanked me for having the courage to tell her and that she had suspected me all along.

"That's pretty much the response I've gotten from people; everyone marvels that I have come to make amends, and they usually say that they don't want the payment. Most of all, though, is the freedom it has given me to change into a new, better person. For anyone who is hesitating about taking this step, I can promise you that the self-esteem you will gain is incredible. You will be able to look people in the eye, too, something I had never been truly able to do before.

"In fact," Annie emphasized, "this program has given me more than I could ever hope for. I am a reliable person now and I've been holding the same job for the past three years—getting steady raises and more responsibility—despite the fact that I didn't finish college and I was never together enough before to hold a job for very long. I don't use any mood-altering substances anymore and I don't use men. I have a wonderful husband, we live within our means, and I'm perfectly content with the person I am today.

"My food is not running my life anymore, either, and for that I am most grateful. I have three planned meals every day with nothing in between, and once I finish eating I don't obsess about when my next meal will be, how I'm going to burn off extra calories, and all that silly stuff. I eat simple foods because that is what works best for me. Everyone is different, but I am glad that I have found a food plan that fits my lifestyle.

"Thank you all for being here tonight," she concluded,

"and I'd like to spend the rest of the hour calling on people who have meant a lot to me in my recovery."

The first person Annie called on was her sponsor, who related some humorous stories about how when Annie first came into the program she would binge wildly and then drive to her home and cry about it. "I never would have stopped being your sponsor, but I'm sure glad that you finally got the willingness that night to pray for abstinence!" she laughed.

"And thank you for sharing how long it took for you to get abstinent. It's important that people know that sometimes it takes a while to put the food down, but that recovery is available to anyone who is truly willing to go to any lengths."

A stunning older woman was the next person called on. "Hi, Annie, and thanks for calling on me," she said after identifying herself as a recovering compulsive eater and bulimic who was "powerless over food."

"Congratulations! You really brought back some memories tonight of things I sometimes try to forget about my past. I, too, was hooked on diet pills, which were hell to get off. I used them for twenty years, and only recently one of my daughters said that she used to steal them to get high and diet with. My own obsession with my appearance prevented me from seeing that I was a terrible role model for my own children!

"This program has shown me—as it has shown you—that there are no magic answers out there in pills, shots, or diets. The only way we are going to get well is to work this program, get honest, and help others. I love seeing the transformation in you because I remember when you came into this program in your crazy skirts and tops! Keep coming back and telling everyone your story!"

The next woman Annie called on qualified herself as a compulsive overeater and said, "Congratulations from this corner, too! Not only do I remember the outfits, but I remember how you had no hair and you had to wear turbans around your head to hide it. I totally sympathized with where you were coming from because I was a compulsive nail-biter and for years I had to wear Band-Aids on every finger because they were so bloody from my constant nervous picking. Once I put down the food and started to think and act clearly, though, I was able to look honestly at myself and eliminate those behaviors that were so self-destructive.

"I came here only for a diet, and not only did I lose the weight, but I changed into a person that I like and that people who knew me before still can't believe. I'm happy when I wake up in the morning, instead of always seeing the gray side of life. That is amazing to me. I'm going to keep coming into these rooms until the day I die because this is so much more than a way to eliminate compulsive overeating—it is a way to live a spiritual and fulfilling life. Thanks for calling on me."

The next person Annie called on was a nun with whom I was starting to become friendly. She never wore her habit to meetings, but she always made a reference to her way of life and how it had stifled her for years, leading to enormous weight gain and a distancing from God. Her comments intrigued me.

"Hi, I'm Jill, a compulsive overeater."

"Hi, Jill!"

"Hi. Annie, thanks for calling on me. I loved what you said about wandering from one religion to another because although I never strayed from Catholicism, I kept redefining what God was to me, never once feeling a personal relationship with Him. When I got into this program and people told me to develop a Higher Power that I understood and could turn things over to, I was really resentful because I thought I had a corner on the God market and I knew everything there was to know.

"The truth of the matter was, though, that I had never felt truly close to God, and I certainly didn't feel like he cared about my eating problem. But I did finally develop my own Higher Power that was loving and personal, which enabled me to start getting better. It was a wonderful, humbling process to just let myself be taught about God by other people here, instead of assuming that I had everything figured out. Anyway, thanks for calling on me, and happy anniversary!"

Annie laughed and made a comment before calling on the next person. "I was really averse to this whole God business when I first came in, but people just said that I needed to create a Higher Power that was anything except myself. And that made sense to me. So I made the group my Higher Power for a year or so, and I've gradually moved into the idea that God is the force in my life because I have experienced too many miracles to doubt that there is a God doing for me now what I could not do for myself before.

"But everyone has their own conception of a Higher Power, which is what makes this program so appealing. The hoop we have to go through is so wide that Buddhists, atheists, and Christians can all exist side by side and recover in their own way," she added.

That was certainly true in my case. Betsy had made the definition of a Higher Power so general that I had been able to ease into the whole idea of God at my own speed. Now I was enjoying the peace that prayer and meditation brought me every morning, and I had even started glancing at the Bible for the first time in my life. Somehow things just happened more easily, my words were smoother, and situations worked out better when I made an honest effort to turn the day and my will over to God. It was also amazing to me that prayer worked so efficiently, but I wasn't about to argue with its wonderful outcomes.

Annie spent the balance of the hour calling on others, ending by calling on her mother, who was so overcome with the tributes to her daughter and the joy of the meeting that she couldn't say much except that she was proud of Annie and couldn't imagine ever having a more satisfying and fulfilling relationship with a child. That really moved me. As I listened to Annie's mother, I knew I had to ask Annie to sponsor me. She had everything I wanted: a happy marriage, a close relationship with her mother, and a life totally free of the food obsession.

After joining hands and closing with the Lord's Prayer, I made my way over to Annie to hug her and thank her for her honesty. "You just blow me away!" I marveled. "When I look at you today, I can't believe that you were the person you describe. I mean you dress beautifully, you have gorgeous hair, your husband is wonderful—it's unbelievable!"

"I know." She smiled back at me. "Sometimes I can't believe it myself. But people kept telling me I would be happy, joyous, and free when I put the food down and worked the program, and they seemed so together that I just did what they told me to do. And then all of my dreams came true, too!"

Here was my opening. "Um, are you really busy these days?" I asked, beating around the bush.

"In what way?"

"Well . . . could you sponsor me?" It was a relief to hear the words tumble out.

"Sure, I can take on someone else right now. Call me at work anytime or at home before eight at night. I'd be happy to sponsor you."

I felt the same surge of joy I had felt the first night I had found this program. All of a sudden the possibilities were endless, and I could become whatever I wanted.

"Who's been sponsoring you until now?" Annie asked, puzzled.

"Betsy," I said, adding regretfully, "but I haven't seen her at meetings in months, and when I call her apartment I either get her recording machine, or she talks really fast and says that she's going out on a date. And when I ask her if she'll be at a meeting soon, she says that she's too busy and that other things have to take precedence.

"That really bothers me because she always told me that I had to make the program my top priority, and that I had to get to at least two—and preferably more—meetings a week. Plus, I've seen her running in the mornings and it looks like she's lost a lot of weight, which she couldn't afford to do to begin with."

"It sounds as if she's taking her recovery for granted, or that she's back into her anorexia and bulimia," Annie said thoughtfully. "I know that if I stopped coming to meetings and talking to other compulsive overeaters, then I'd head right back into the food and the toilet, too. I have to put my recovery first, because when the food is messed up, then the rest of my life seems to go badly, too."

"The other thing that has been bothering me," I continued, grateful to finally be putting my gnawing misgivings into words, "is that she seems to be jealous of me. I mean, I don't know why, but she sometimes says things that hurt me. And they hurt me more because I have totally laid myself out to her—flaws and all—hoping that she'll just help me put myself together. And then she turns on me."

Annie chuckled sympathetically before responding. "Well, people in the program are human, and jealousy is a natural emotion. Don't expect people to be perfect or you are always going to be disappointed. And surely you can see why she'd be envious: you're tall, attractive, well educated, well spoken, married, and so on, and she doesn't have a lot of that stuff.

"By the way," she added, cutting off any protests I might have about her observations, "your hair looks great! Is that what you had done today?"

"Yes, do you like it?" I preened, twirling in a circle to let her get the full impact. "I may never be able to recreate it, but I sure like it tonight!"

"Yes," she nodded. "I really do—it just looks more like you than all that hair did before. Another change I've noticed in you is that you seem to be smiling more at meetings and reaching out to others. I can see that this program is really working for you. When I look at you, it's like a flower unfolding."

"Well, it is," I agreed, "but right now I feel stuck. I want to do the personal inventory, but I don't know how. Can you help me with that?"

The personal inventory was the part of the program that I had been dreading, and that Annie had referred to during the meeting when she spoke about having the willingness to let go of her character defects. We were supposed to put all of our shortcomings and character defects down on paper and then read them to someone else. Not only did I not want to see my sins and faults in black and white, but I was darn sure that I didn't want to tell anyone else, either.

It was nagging at me that I hadn't done it yet, however, and that everyone who had completed it said the painful self-scrutiny had improved the quality of their abstinence and life immensely. My competitiveness always flared when I felt someone had something I didn't, so I was willing to at least give the process a shot.

"Sure," Annie answered. "I bought a special notebook and just started to write about the seven deadly sins and my relationship to them. For envy I filled page after page with people and things that I envied, and how inadequate they made me feel. I carried that book around with me everywhere because I got flashbacks of things I wanted to let go of at odd times.

"Finally I was ready to unload all of this stuff, so I called my sponsor, drove to her place, and sat in her living room while I read her the whole book. We talked for hours about all the things I had written. I had been scared that she would think less of me after hearing all my fears, resentments, and defects, but she told me that she had done lots of the things I was so ashamed of, which removed a lot of the stigma from my mind about my own past.

"After the session I went home and burned the book," Annie continued, describing the catharsis. "I didn't want to read it again; I wanted to be free of those destructive traits and behaviors forever. But in addition to the burning, my sponsor told me to pray for the willingness to let go of my defects so that new, more positive attitudes could take their place. She emphasized that the same person was going to binge again, so a personality change was a must.

"There's something somewhere in the Bible that is a perfect analogy for this whole process. It's about not being able to put new wine in an old bottle," she concluded, wagging her finger at me.

I shivered to think that I would have to tell someone about all the terrible things that I had said and done over the years, but I knew deep down that if I didn't, my recovery would be in jeopardy. For alcoholics, I had heard the difference described as one of being a dry drunk or sober. I didn't want to be a dry binger.

I promised Annie I would start on my inventory the next day and headed out into the warm September night after giving her another hug. Red, brown, and gold leaves crunched underfoot as I made my way to the car. September was my favorite month of the year, not just because I was born during it. I always associated new beginnings with the dappled trees, crisp nights, and yellow school buses. No matter how old I got, I would never be able to make New Year's resolutions for

January; the year started for me in September and it always would.

As I drove home I decided to stop at a nearby drugstore to buy a brand-new notebook and some colorful pens. After all, it was the time of new beginnings, and I knew I could become whatever I wanted.

ELEVEN

"CAROLINE, YOU HAVE a call on 31."

The receptionist's announcement through our company's speaker phone startled me. I had been deep in thought while attempting to finish a public relations proposal for a hydraulics company account our company was trying to win. I stretched and yawned as I reached for the phone. No matter who it was, I would only talk for a few minutes; my deadline for the proposal was two hours away.

"Hello—this is Caroline Miller. Can I help you?"

"Um, hello, Caroline," a deep male voice greeted me. "You don't know me, but we have a friend in common—Lisa Santos."

"Oh, sure. Hi." I was a bit puzzled; I didn't know Lisa that well. She was the friend of a friend, and the only time I

197

had ever had a meaningful talk with her was last month at a cocktail party.

"She said you might be able to help me," the unidentified voice continued. "I'm having a little bit of trouble . . ." Here his voice broke off in obvious embarrassment. I intuitively sensed that he was another bulimic, reaching out for help.

"Oh, are you another one of those crazy bingers and purgers like me?" I joked, keeping my voice light.

"Uh, yes, but I can't talk long about it because I'm at work and I don't want anyone to overhear me."

"Where do you work?" I asked, trying to figure out if we could meet for a quick lunch somewhere to talk in privacy.

"Fidelity Savings and Loan—I'm in the management training program in the downtown office."

"Oh, that's not far. Do you want to meet for lunch or something?"

"No, that's part of my problem. I'm afraid to eat in front of anyone now. I know I need help because I starve all day, and go home and binge all night, then stick my finger down my throat to get rid of the food."

This poor guy was pretty isolated—one of the hallmarks of the compulsive overeater in the advanced stages of the disease. "Do you live alone?" I asked.

"Well, my wife just moved out this past summer. We're separated and she has our son."

"Did you just start purging this summer, or is this something you've done for a while?" I was trying to get a handle on his pattern.

"It got bad after my wife left, although I've done it off and on for about ten years as a way to control my weight."

"How old are you?"

"Twenty-nine." I had recently read that most bulimics waited an average of seven years before seeking help and that any time over that made the addiction that much more difficult to break. This guy had some major work to do if he was serious about getting well.

"How did you learn to purge?"

"I was a wrestler in high school—I wrestled at 142 and I'm six-two, which is pretty skinny. My coach and other wrestlers showed me how to do screwy things like take laxatives, sleep in rubber suits, and vomit to make weight," he said, his voice lowering. "I stopped wrestling in college, but I continued to stick my finger down my throat after I drank too much so that I wouldn't have such a bad hangover when I woke up the next morning." His voice broke off again; I heard a cacophony from other people around him.

"So you used purging after college as a way to control your weight," I coaxed, hoping to keep him on the line.

"Uh-huh." His voice was guarded.

"And now you think it's out of control?"

"Uh-huh."

He obviously couldn't share much more at the moment, so I started to babble about my own years of binging—the babysitting nightmares, laxative overdoses, and shoplifting forays. "I was about as down and out as you could imagine," I laughed, telling him how I had finally come to the decision that my binging had gotten totally unmanageable and my life was headed in a downward spiral.

"What did you do? Check into a hospital or something?" His voice sounded a little less cautious. Clearly my story had made him feel less alone in his misery.

"No—I thought about it, but I didn't have the money. I saw an ad in the paper for a free support group of compulsive overeaters that meets every day of the week at all different hours, and I went to my first meeting on a Friday night at a church at Thirty-ninth and Charles Streets almost two years ago."

I stopped in surprise—two years? It seemed like only a few months. I had never dreamed of continuing to attend meetings for this long a period of time when I had first gotten involved. My longest Weight Watchers stint had been about six weeks. Now I hoped to attend meetings for the rest of my life in order to work on myself and my addictive traits.

"Have you gotten better?" he asked hopefully. "Lisa says that you look great."

"Much, much better," I responded enthusiastically. "I was afraid to eat in restaurants or with other people, like you," I said, "but now I can go just about anywhere—not just salad bar places—and not always be looking around for the bathroom, wondering if I will have to purge.

"I also like myself a lot better. I was such a people-pleaser before, trying to make everyone like me. My self-esteem was rock bottom, I hated the way I looked, I wasn't able to get anywhere on time because I was usually binging or recovering from a binge, I wore loose clothes to hide my distended stomach, my face was swollen constantly, and so on.

"I feel like an onion now. I'm constantly peeling off old layers and finding out that there's something underneath that I didn't know about. I'm even beginning to realize that I'm the kind of friend I'd like to have. That's real growth for me."

"You mean that all that good stuff has happened since you stopped binging?" he asked, incredulous.

"You'd be surprised how little you can experience—both good and bad—while you are binging," I laughed. "I was so numb for seven years with the food that I never stopped to grow up and do things. I could kick myself about the opportunities I passed up at Harvard because I was too obsessed with food, or I thought I looked bloated from a recent binge and I didn't want anyone to see me.

"But I'll tell you what," I continued, "I wouldn't take back a minute of those seven years for anything. I don't know if I would have ever had the opportunity to look long and hard at myself, learn how to be honest, or meet the wonderful people I have if I hadn't been bulimic.

"The men and women in my program—and in some of the related programs for alcoholics, drug addicts, and gamblers—are among my favorite people now. These people have taken their addictions and dysfunctional behaviors and used them to do something positive with their lives. They're trying, on a daily basis, to live more spiritual, honest lives, and they are always looking to give another addicted person a hand in recovery."

After hearing Annie share at her anniversary several months earlier that her recovery from bulimia included avoidance of all mood-altering substances, I had taken an honest look at my high school and college use of alcohol and drugs as a method of escaping from tension, fears, and resentments. Although I rarely turned to them now, I knew that my tendency was to run from uncomfortable feelings, so I had decided to completely give up those things as well. My week now included several support-group meetings for abstinence from those substances, too.

"What do you mean, 'spiritual'?" he asked, suddenly suspicious.

"Oh, don't worry about that part," I said blithely. I shouldn't have mentioned spirituality, I chastised myself. I had to get this guy to a meeting first. The Higher Power stuff could come later. Everyone could come to some understanding of a power greater than themselves if they truly wanted to recover, I knew.

"Can you get to a meeting this week?"

"I don't know," he faltered. "I'm awfully busy."

"How badly do you want to give up the binging?" I asked directly.

"I'm not sure. Part of me still enjoys it, but I know I'm damaging my body and my teeth."

I knew all about teeth problems. Just recently I had lost more chunks of my bottom front teeth, leaving me with an uneven jagged row of enamel shells. Although I felt the bulimia was behind me, the damage I had done over the years was so great that it had just taken a few bites of a carrot and some gum to continue the ugly erosion.

"Have you seen a doctor or dentist recently?"

"Last week—I saw both. I didn't say anything about the bulimia, but I was praying that they'd notice something or ask me so that I could have an excuse to admit it. Frankly, I'm too embarrassed to say anything first. I can't imagine that there are many men with this thing, are there?"

"You'd be really surprised," I replied, thinking about the bulimic men I knew in the program. While the vast majority of people at the meetings were diet- and weight-obsessed women of all ages, more and more men were showing up every week. From listening to them I had learned a great deal about the special pressures men felt to be slim and attractive.

I had also met men outside the program who had broadened my knowledge of the prevalence of male eating disorders. In fact, during the past summer Haywood and I had struck up a conversation in a saloon in Lexington, Kentucky, with a handsome bartender and model about this very issue. He had confided in us that he was bulimic and that many other male and female models he knew were, too. His reason for developing the disorder, he told us, was that when he modeled bathing suits the photographers wanted to see a certain definition in their buttocks—something they could not achieve through weight lifting, only through extreme weight loss.

So in an effort to continue to earn the very lucrative fees, he had learned how to vomit from another male model, and now he wasn't sure he could give it up, or that he even wanted to. The money from modeling was too good, he said, showing us hunks of gold on his wrists that he had bought with some of his astronomical salary. I had looked at the bracelets with pity. They could just as well have been a pair of golden handcuffs.

"So I wouldn't be the only man in the meetings?" the unidentified voice on the phone asked hopefully.

"Not at all. In fact, if you can get to the Friday night meeting, I'll make sure to introduce you to at least two bulimic men I know who go there regularly. One of them is quite heavy, and the other is thin and muscular. You see—we come in all different packages!" I tried to sound bright and cheerful.

"By the way," I said suddenly, "what is your name? How will I know you if I see you?" He described himself, saying his name was Bob.

"Okay, Bob," I responded. "My name is Caroline and I'm tall and blond. I'll look for you Friday night. I'll hang around the literature table before the meeting, so if you can get there early we can talk more and I'll introduce you to some people."

"Okay," he agreed doubtfully. "I'll do my best to get there. Thanks for spending all this time with me. I feel better already."

We exchanged good-byes and hung up. I wasn't hopeful about seeing him on Friday night. He hadn't sounded as though he was ready to give up the food. You really had to be sick and tired of the lifestyle to have the willingness to trust in the program and give up the food crutch. Someone had said to me just the other day that if ready, a baby could get someone abstinent, and if not ready, God couldn't help the person. "We can only plant the seeds of recovery," she had said. "We aren't responsible for whether or not people follow through with the program."

I leaned back in my chair and stared out the huge window in front of my desk. From my second-floor vantage point I could see the faces of the men and women below hurrying on their appointed rounds through the gray slush. It was lunchtime, so the streets were crowded with people striding purposely to the various restaurants, fast-food spots, and delis nearby. What a freedom it is to go to a restaurant and eat normally, I thought thankfully, wondering how many of the passersby were worrying about their imminent food intake, obsessing about calories and slenderness.

One sight that always gave me some perspective on my eating disorder was the one I passed every morning on my way into work. A fountain in front of our historic office building served as one of the bathing spots for some of the local homeless men and women who wandered the streets. They obviously had no money with which to buy food, and I often saw compassionate people handing them sandwiches and hot coffee as they went by. I always felt ashamed of my own past extravagances when I saw them, guiltily thinking of how I had never thought twice about eating the equivalent of five lunches in the space of a few minutes, knowing full well that it would all come back up immediately.

My thoughts returned to Bob. I knew that he was not unusual in having used vomiting as a "hangover cure" because Haywood had told me about the prevalence of the practice one day while we were watching a sports show. The subject had been horse racing, with a major segment devoted to the diminutive jockeys and what they did to maintain their low weights. We were both incredulous about what we saw.

"This is how many of them cope with the weight limits," the TV reporter said as the camera wheeled into the locker room. There he interviewed a smiling teenage boy who got on the scale as the film rolled. We watched as the quivering needle had settled at 106 pounds.

"I have to be 100 for my next race," the boy laughed, "and I just pigged out at lunch, so this is what I do."

Then the camera and reporter dutifully followed the

jockey as he walked into the bathroom where a huge sign proclaimed over some of the stalls, "Flippers Only."

Flipping, it turned out, was vomiting, which the camera mercifully did not film. Viewers of the show, however, were left with no doubt that this was an accepted and common practice among jockeys for making weight. The reporter didn't even add a sentence or two saying that it was an addictive and dangerous practice that could result in long-term medical complications.

"I can't believe that they are irresponsible enough to run that piece!" I fumed to Haywood. "I'll bet that hundreds of people are going to get addicted to bulimia as a result of it!"

It was then that Haywood told me that he and a number of his college buddies had resorted to purging, especially after parties and other occasions when drinking was obligatory. Although Harvard didn't have fraternities, Haywood had been a member of a "finals club," which had often hosted initiations and parties where drinking was a major ingredient of the evening and the male camaraderie.

Haywood had not continued purging for weight control or any other reason, but Bob clearly had. And I figured that there were probably hundreds, even thousands more like him in the country who were too embarrassed to seek help. Men, my male program friends had informed me, found it much more difficult to admit weaknesses, especially about something as fundamental as eating. I could understand that; I had been unable to confide in my doctor, but I was sure that some macho complications entered into a man confessing powerlessness over food to another man or woman.

"Caroline—guess how much I weigh today?" The man who worked in the office next to mine suddenly appeared in the doorway, standing tall and proud.

"I can't," I responded, although I knew precisely how much he weighed. As I had passed the art department that morning, I had seen a big sign he had posted with his morning's tally. This man was incredibly obsessed with his diet, and he never passed up an opportunity to let people know he had lost 100 pounds during the last six months. I was sick of hearing about it and his new weight-lifting regimen.

204

"I weigh 157!" he said happily, sucking in his stomach and turning sideways for my benefit.

"That's terrific," I responded half-heartedly. "Do you want to go to lunch to celebrate?"

"Lunch? Absolutely not!" he thundered vehemently. "Tomorrow I plan to be 156, so I had a protein shake this morning and that is all I'm going to have. By the way," he said, returning to his desk and coming back into my office, "have you seen the article in *Flex* this month about this supplement?"

He pushed the article in front of my face. I had made the mistake of telling him that I used to do Nautilus weight work as part of my swimming training, and now I was supposed to be up on, and interested in, power lifting and what special supplements enhanced musculature.

"This substance converts fat to muscle, it says," he added excitedly. "If you are going to the health food store for lunch, will you look for it in the vitamin section? I'll pay you back when you return."

"Sure," I said, standing up to end the conversation. Too much talk along these lines made me uncomfortable. I was trying to move away from the obsession with weight and body size, and this man spent almost all day within earshot talking about both issues with messianic fervor, lecturing others on how to change their diets and lifestyles to achieve the same weight loss. Many days I just had to shut my door to avoid hearing him, although I knew that it made me look unfriendly. My nickname at the company, he had informed me, was "the Nordic Princess."

I couldn't completely shut out all weight and diet talk from my life, though. So many people were always dieting, talking about their latest fad regimen, convinced that it would be the one that would finally make them thin and happy. Just last week, I had dropped in at my former company to visit the office manager and, after asking what was new, had heard all about her latest plans to lose weight. She even had the instructions pasted on the wall right next to her typewriter. Ten minutes later, the same question to another person had elicited the news that she had rejoined Diet Workshop for the umpteenth time. I had groaned inwardly both times, knowing that unless they made fundamental changes in their personalities and responses to stress, they would be on the diet merry-go-round for a long, long time.

I put my coat on and grabbed my personal inventory notebook to flip through while I ate lunch. Annie was going to listen to me read it tonight, and I wanted to look at it in its entirety first. I had been scribbling phrases and specific occurrences for almost three months, and now I felt ready to let go of the bad memories.

"Is there anything else I can get for you?" I politely asked my weight-obsessed colleague.

"Nope. I'm picking up some pants and jackets that have been taken in for me, and I don't want to ruin the fit with food. Do you know how many inches my pants have been taken in since July?" he asked, eyes gleaming.

"Oh, ten, maybe?" I called over my shoulder as I went out the other door. One more minute of this kind of talk and I was going to go crazy.

At the health food store I settled into one of the knotted pine booths and looked at my tray. I had been good today. This store featured a buffet line that always tempted me to take huge helpings—probably reminiscent of the years of binging at all-you-can-eat cafeterias—but today I had only allowed myself moderate helpings of the vegetarian main course, a hot vegetable and a salad. My eyes always begged for more, but I had had it drummed into me by people like Annie that one moderate helping was enough for anyone. I didn't even allow myself two trips to the salad bar because Annie continually cautioned that second helpings of anything set a bad precedent.

I closed my eyes for a brief second and said a quick prayer to my Higher Power for giving me an abstinent meal. This was new for me. Once I had noticed Annie having a moment of silence before eating at a restaurant and I had decided to try it, but only when by myself. I still was private about my spiritual side.

I opened my notebook and started to read and eat at the same time. As Annie had suggested, I had concentrated on the seven deadly sins and my experiences with them in doing my inventory. I started with the "sloth" page. I certainly had been slothful over the years, I noted as I scanned the entries. Many times my appearance had been unkempt only because I had been so worn out from the binging and purging to do anything with myself, and more often than not I had let my surroundings go to pot when I had been unhappy. Someone at a meeting had said the cleanliness of her apartment was in direct proportion to her feelings about herself. I could relate to that—our apartment had improved dramatically over the last two years since I had started cleaning up my emotional house.

Envy: that deadly sin took up the next several pages. There were few people I had encountered over the years whom I hadn't envied in one way or another. One girl had a body I wanted, another had a job I coveted, another had looks that would launch ships; the grass had been greener in everyone else's yard for years. Would I truly be free of envy if I followed through with reading this to Annie? It seemed impossible. Envy was as natural to me as drinking water. But people swore it had changed them. I read on.

After envy was greed. Boy, had I been greedy. Not just about food, but about all kinds of things: money, friends, presents for myself—the list was endless. I winced as I reread my jottings. I was so ashamed of my lavish spending on clothes that I starred it in the margin. Annie had said that she and her husband lived within their means. Would she think I was awful if I told her exactly how much I had doled out on myself? The numbers were so high that it was painful to look at. Between the hair appointments, shoe bills, jewelry purchases, and new dresses, I had spent a fortune. Maybe I would skip that part tonight. Annie didn't have to know everything!

Lust. Well, President Carter, you aren't alone, I thought to myself as I looked at my lustful musings. I, too, have committed adultery in my heart. If Jimmy Carter could admit that to *Playboy*, then I could tell Annie my secrets. And she would certainly be understanding; after all, hadn't she said that she had written entire notebooks about her lust and promiscuity?

I flipped on. Pride—lots here. This section had been torturous to write. I had loads of egotistical vanity and I really hated admitting it to myself. Over the years I had done more than my share of boasting to cover up for my low self-esteem. One memory that had come back to me while working on this part was of carrying my New York *Times*es and *Wall Street Journal*s around at Harvard so that the headlines would be prominently displayed, thus letting everyone know what an educated soul I was. Ugh. I shuddered to think of it.

My false pride had also made me unable to take any criticism well. My skin was extraordinarily thin, so I had tried over the years to place myself in positions where I would shine, thus eliminating the need for self-correction. This trait, which I euphemistically called "sensitivity," had kept me from taking truly challenging courses in school, as well as from trying any new sports or activities. My reasoning was: If I can't win or be the best, why even try?

I remained riveted on this section. There was an awful lot I would have to let go of. Another result of my pride had been the inability to hear other people praised. No one could possibly be better than I in anything without inviting my criticism. So whenever my parents had praised one of my friends in the past, I had immediately rejoined with something negative about that person, secretly wondering if they wanted that person as a son or daughter instead of me. I had even gone on an adoption kick when I was younger, insisting that I was not their natural child and that they had picked me up somewhere. This attitude had affected me at work, too. If someone I perceived as incompetent made more than me or got a raise, I went on a verbal rampage, decimating him or her to whomever would listen.

I took a break to look around the cafe. I loved coming here; people seemed quieter and gentler than the average restaurant goers. Maybe that was because no meat was served. I had read somewhere that people's personalities mimicked what they ate, and that that was why vegetarians were so docile and even-handed. Plants were nice; animals were fierce. It was an interesting theory.

The middle-aged Korean woman who ran the cafe bustled up to my booth. "Carrot juice today?" she queried in her broken English, her face split into a broad grin. "It take oxygen to brain. Good!"

Some days I ordered a huge glass of carrot and celery

juice to wash down the entrees, but today I was going to have to pass.

"My palms are turning yellow again," I responded, turning my hands up to show her.

I had had this problem once before. When I was a senior in high school, my father had solemnly entered my room one evening and sat down, saying he had something serious he needed to discuss. My heart had started to beat fast. Had they found the food under my bed? Their money missing? Heard that I was shoplifting at the supermarket?

"Caroline, let me see your hands," he had said. "Your mother says your palms are yellow."

Surprised and relieved, I had turned my hands up for him to see. I had peered at them too. They *were* yellow!

"We think you might have jaundice," my father had said. "You must go to the doctor."

A trip to the doctor had enlightened us tremendously. I had been eating so many carrots in my vegetable mania that my palms and skin had taken on a definite yellowish cast from the carotene. Although it wasn't toxic, only complete abstinence from them would relieve what he called "carotenemia."

Now my carrot juice fetish had done it again. In a way it wasn't so bad because I looked slightly tan year-round, but I was trying to be moderate in all things, so I was going to have to cut back a bit.

"Beet juice then," my Korean friend continued, undaunted. "Good for body. We use beet leaves in it too."

I smiled and shook my head again. I didn't want to run the risk of turning red, either. "No, I'm done now. Maybe tomorrow."

As she leaned over to remove my tray, I noticed that I had left several forkfuls of both my entree and the salad. I briefly thought of telling her I wanted to finish them, but I kept my mouth shut. I didn't have to eat every single thing on my plate anymore, but it was a tough habit to break.

The first time I had left a restaurant with some of my uneaten dinner wrapped in a foil peacock, I had danced a jig of happiness when I got home. "Don't you know what a big step it is to not eat everything at a restaurant?" I said to Haywood as I tripped around the bedroom, annoyed that he wasn't thrilled to pieces for me.

"So? Doesn't everyone leave food if they're full?" he had responded, puzzled and unimpressed.

I had turned away. He couldn't possibly understand my ebullience, and it really wasn't fair of me to expect him to. At least my program friends would be happy for me.

I looked back down at my notebook. Only two sections remained—anger and dishonesty. Anger was a major bugaboo. I was angry about a lot of things. I got angry in traffic when I didn't go as fast as I wanted; I was angry when I didn't get my way; I was angry when I couldn't eat what I wanted, when I wanted; I was angry when I was around friends who were still bulimic and who practiced their disease unknown to others; I was angry that Haywood could eat ice cream and I couldn't; I was angry that I couldn't get well overnight; and on and on and on.

My anger had bred a lot of resentments. Someone had said in the program that resentments and fear were two of the main things that would return someone to binging if they weren't honestly confronted and dealt with. Just about everyone and everything that I resented, I feared. And it was usually because they made me feel stupid, powerless, and immature. Sometimes I even resented Annie because she seemed to have her life together. I wondered if I would have the courage to tell her that.

I moved on to dishonesty. Well, that word seemed to have defined my life. Seven years of duplicity, of covering up my behavior and lying about it, had left a firm imprint on my mind. My dishonesty had even spilled over into my driving; sometimes I parked in "No Parking" zones and took right turns at red lights when signs prohibited it. Didn't everyone? I justified it to myself. Who doesn't stretch certain truths on income tax returns, pad expense accounts, and tell someone they look great in a certain outfit when they look dreadful? I was really confused on this issue. Where did harmless white lies end and hurtful ones begin?

I slapped my book shut and got up to leave. As I passed the food again, I looked longingly at the baked apples in the dessert area. I knew they didn't have sugar in them, but I also knew honey was just as dangerous to me as the white granular stuff. Oh well, a regular apple would have to do.

I picked out a crisp green Granny Smith apple and went to pay my bill at the cash register. My attention strayed to the "natural" sweets crowding the counter before me. I chomped ferociously on my apple. Those carob-coated things still sang like sirens to me.

As the cashier dropped my change into my hand, I glanced at the total on the register. He had undercharged me by two dollars. Should I take the money or tell him? Despite two years of "rigorous honesty" being pounded into my brain, I still hesitated. Abe Lincoln came into my head. Hadn't he walked several miles through the snow to return a few measly pennies to a shopkeeper who had made a mistake? He had become President; maybe there was a direct correlation.

I took the Honest Abe approach. "I had an entree today, not just a salad," I said to the cashier. "I owe you two dollars."

"Oh, thanks," he said gratefully. "I personally have to make up any shortfalls at the end of the day. I'd better be more careful." On the way back to the office, I felt so happy that I fed two expired parking meters. Honesty felt pretty good!

Later that evening, my goodwill had given way to worry. As I sat silently in my car in front of Annie's quaint apartment building, I began to feel foolish. What was I doing here with this silly notebook on the seat next to me, filled with my innermost secrets and fears? Wasn't it enough that I had done the footwork and written the painful things down? Did I really have to read them to someone?

I looked down the deserted street, trying to build a credible case for leaving. Maybe I could say I had gotten sick, or that I had lost the notebook and I'd have to start again from scratch.

Despite my best efforts to summon up the courage to leave and lie, however, I couldn't follow through with my negative thoughts—otherwise known in the program as "stinking thinking." I reluctantly got out of the car and walked up the stone path to the front porch. "God, you'd better give me the strength to go through with this," I sternly commanded my unseen Higher Power, "because I sure don't think I have it."

The neatness of Annie's apartment took me aback. Everything was in its place. I didn't even think that there was any dust lying around. Bill, her husband, jumped up to greet me when I walked in. "I hope you don't mind," I joked nervously. "I've come to dump my sins in your back room." He just smiled. He was used to having Annie's "pigeons," as we were sometimes called, come over to spill their secrets.

Annie shut the door on the back room, and I settled onto one of the thick, cushioned couches. I immediately put a pillow over my stomach. That was one of the ways I still tried to hide my body, especially when I was feeling fat and vulnerable.

"I'm a little scared," I said with a thin smile.

"I know how you feel. When I did my first inventory, I drove around my sponsor's block five times before I could bring myself to walk up to her door. After it was over, though, I wondered what I had been so frightened of!"

"What do you mean by 'first' inventory?" I asked, alarmed. "Do I have to do this more than once?" I didn't want to go through this kind of soul-searching on a regular basis.

"No, no," Annie laughed. "I've just done a few because my first one was so incomplete. I didn't read my sponsor everything, and I kind of glossed over my weak points. She caught me on it, though. She told me to go back and be more thorough, and to also make a point of listing things I liked about myself. After all that tearing down, it's important to remember that you have good points too."

I didn't think I had glossed over anything in my inventory. One thing I was good at was beating on myself and finding fault. But I sure didn't want to go through it again, so I'd have to read Annie everything now, including the shopping sprees, so I wouldn't have to come back. As for my positive traits—well, maybe I'd do that when I really had some solid self-confidence.

"Okay, how do I start?" I was eager to get the ball rolling.

"Just read," Annie said, leaning back in her chair with a cup of herbal tea warming her hands. "Stop and elaborate if you think it's necessary at any time. Or I'll ask you about something if I'm not clear about it."

I opened my notebook, lowered my head, and began. At first my voice quivered apologetically on every point, but soon I was picking up speed and calmness, feeling a tremendous sense of peace descending upon me. The accumulated weight of almost ten years of guilt, sadness, and anger began to lift. I suddenly understood why Catholics went to confession. What a catharsis it was to admit your weaknesses and shame, and to have someone tell you that all was forgiven!

Every now and then I paused to explain certain situations and people to Annie. She didn't say much, and her face never displayed a moment's worth of horror, pity, or surprise. I could have been reading her my grocery list. Occasionally she permitted herself a laugh, accompanied by "I did that too!"

When I got into my resentments an hour later, I put the book down and looked directly at Annie. "I have tremendous hatred for someone right now, and I don't think that I'll ever get over it. It's especially bad because I see her so frequently, and I feel smoke coming out of my ears whenever she's around."

"Whoever this woman is, you are giving her a lot of power to let her affect you this way," Annie remarked. "What does she hook into in you?"

"I have known her and her husband for a while, and although they don't see Haywood much, they have met him. One morning I noticed that this woman was actively avoiding me and being incredibly rude whenever I did speak to her. Initially my feelings were really hurt, but I wrote it off to her having a bad day or something.

"Then her husband started to avoid me, so I got suspicious and made some discreet inquiries about what was going on. I found out that she is convinced I'm after her husband, and that they have been arguing about it for some time. She has also said things about me to other people, and now I hear my nickname is 'Jezebel.' This stupid town is so small that it's going to get around no matter what, and I'm going to have a nasty reputation at the age of twenty-four!" I finished angrily.

"Well, *are* you after her husband?" Annie asked evenly.

"Annie!" I sputtered, "he is in his sixties! He's more than forty years older than I am!"

"So? Haven't you ever heard of May-December romances? All kinds of men ditch their wives for cute young things when they hit menopause. Maybe this woman isn't really worried so much about you as she is about him. Maybe he's had a bunch of affairs in the past with younger women, and she senses he is interested in you. Put yourself in her shoes: you've got to feel sorry for someone like that. Think of the shame and hurt she must feel every time he flirts with someone. If you hate her, you'll just make yourself sick."

Hmm—I hadn't thought of any of that. Annie's observations made sense. Maybe I was just a lightning rod for all of this woman's frustrations and fears. I was still angry, though, at the way she was treating me.

"Okay, I see your point," I said, "but she has no right to snub me day after day as if I've done something wrong. I don't even find her husband mildly attractive! It totally ruins my day to see her. I have knots in my stomach that won't go away for hours."

"You have to pray for people like that. My sponsor told me to do that for everyone I resented. She said that I had to get on my knees and pray for their health, wealth, and happiness, and to wish that they had all the good things that I wanted for myself."

"There's no way I'm ever going to do that!" I said forcefully. "That woman ought to be praying for me!"

"Caroline, what is the point in getting so exercised over this silly person?" Annie asked calmly. "You're obsessed with her, and I can promise you that that kind of resentment is a quick way to stay in your disease and your sick thinking. If you pray for her, you will find yourself feeling better about yourself and her, and soon you will be able to detach from the situation without feeling all this anger."

"I don't believe you," I said flatly.

"How will you ever know unless you try it?" Annie smiled reasonably. "Plus I thought you told me you were willing to go to any lengths now to get well."

I grumbled a little to myself and started to read again. I

didn't want to admit that she might be right. A few minutes later I stopped again to clarify another resentment.

"Okay," I said, "this is a tough one. I've found myself actually getting angry and a little envious toward people I know who have eating disorders and who continue to practice their disease around me. For example, I had lunch with someone recently, and she ate like a truckdriver and then disappeared to the bathroom. Her gag reflex is instantaneous, so she purges within seconds and is back at the table before anyone can suspect anything. She is constantly drinking diet soda so that the food will come up easily, and she clears her throat all the time, saying that she has a cold—even in July!

"I want to shake her and tell her that she is killing herself, but on the flip side I'm angry that she can eat all those foods and stay so slim. Purging was never easy for me, and I always put on weight!"

"Do you really want to go back to that life?" Annie asked. "You saw that woman binging in the supermarket several months ago—didn't that terrify you and remind you of how painful and desperate binging is?"

"Yes, but every now and then I have brief thoughts about wanting to eat an entire cake, or have some ice cream or something else really fattening. And when I see someone doing that and getting away with it, I get angry."

"Caroline, you have to just pray for that person and be available if they reach out for help. Have you confided in this person about your bulimia?"

"God, yes. I took her to several meetings with me last year. She opened up a little bit, and her stories scared the pants off me. She went to a tiny college in the boonies and had to borrow a friend's bicycle to ride to a supermarket and buy her binge foods. Then she would ride to a park and sit behind a tree and eat everything, then throw up into the grocery bag and leave it there.

"Now she's into total denial. She swears she's fine and that she has a fast metabolism, but I know for a fact that she never exercises, which could have explained how she can eat so much. I should feel sorry for her, but sometimes I don't," I concluded.

"You've done everything you can, Caroline. Let go of it.

Sometimes people have to really hit a low bottom before they have the willingness to give up the food. It's either that or they die. Don't take on that burden. Just try to pray for her and remember that that kind of life made you suicidal and unhappy. Would you want to give up being able to go to restaurants, refraining from shoplifting, driving calmly, being reliable, telling the truth—all that stuff—for food?"

"No, I guess not." I hadn't stopped to think about any of these things before. I could see how healing this inventory process was; it was giving me a new awareness and understanding of issues that had baffled and upset me for years.

I finished reading my notebook a few minutes later, omitting nothing. Annie and I talked for another hour, discussing the shopping binges, lust, envy, and other sins in detail. Annie offered a lot of her own experiences as constructive examples of how to go forward and change my behavior so that the same things wouldn't happen again.

"You have to be willing to let go of some of the character defects and shortcomings you mentioned tonight," she counseled. "It sounds like gossiping, jealousy, resentment, false pride, and lying are just a few of the things you have to say good-bye to. But you have to really want to be free of them, because lots of people aren't. They can't imagine life without constantly gossiping or being envious of someone else. And many people hang on to negative attitudes and behaviors because they think that if they become 'too perfect' no one will like them."

"Hmm, I guess I am willing to surrender most of them," I said thoughtfully. "Gossiping is hard, though. I've always thought that knowing what is going on and talking about it is a way to appear really on top of things. I also wonder how you can possibly carry on an interesting conversation with someone if you aren't gossiping or talking about someone else. That's human nature! What does that leave as possible topics? Religion and the weather?"

"Look, don't worry about that now. If you honestly pray for your character defects to be removed one by one, the right behaviors will just appear. Some of the more stubborn ones might pop up from time to time, but you have to keep praying that they'll be lifted from you. For the most part, though, you'll find that identifying defects, admitting them to some-one else, and then honestly praying for their removal will completely change you.

"After that you'll have to do your amends. Judging from your notebook there are a lot of people you have hurt, lied to, or stolen from, and you'll have to go back in person and apologize or make restitution."

I gulped hard. I really dreaded that part of the program. "When do I have to start that?"

"Soon. And if you appear to be procrastinating, I'll push you. But amends are delicate. You can't go rushing back to everyone in a burst of remorse, because in some cases it hurts others to bring up the past—for example, extramarital affairs. It would only make you feel better to admit something like that. We can discuss your amends before you do them to make sure that you're proceeding the right way."

"Okay, that sounds good," I said, relieved. Christmas was next week, and I just wanted to relax and give myself a break for getting through the inventory process. I'd tackle the amends as part of a New Year's project. "What should I do with this in the meantime?" I asked, pointing at the notebook. "I never want to look through it again."

"Burn it," Annie said simply. "Burn it and tell yourself that all of those negative things are now in your past and that you are now free to move forward into a new and better life. And if you can't burn it, bury it or throw it out. You'll feel great later."

I stood up. "I'll burn it tonight. I'll make a pile of the pages and put them in the bathtub. Haywood will think I'm crazy, but he's getting used to this stuff now, I think," I laughed.

"Thanks so much," I said, hugging Annie warmly. "I'm so glad I finally did this and I'm grateful to you for listening. You're a real friend."

Bill jumped up again when we came out of the back room. "How'd it go?" he smiled.

"Don't go back there for a while," I joked. "Too many old demons lurking around that I just unloaded on your wife."

Outside, the inky sky was studded with stars. The frosty air couldn't even begin to pierce the warmth and love I felt. A

Christmas carol suddenly popped into my head that summed up my sentiments. Not only did it say that it was the season to be jolly, but that it was time to don gay apparel. Gay apparel was just one of the things I was planning to don this holiday season. How about a new personality? I giggled as I drove home humming.

TWELVE

ONE OF THE FIRST THINGS I heard upon entering the program in February 1984 was that with diligence and a qualified sponsor, the program's recommended steps of recovery could be as effective in changing behavior as any kind of psychiatry. For some reason the group's honest sharing, counseling by peers, restitution for past wrongs, emphasis on a complete spiritual change, and helping others in a similar bind worked miracles in transforming formerly desperate people into sane, happy, nonaddicted men and women. For some, in fact, the program had worked where years of expensive and time-consuming therapy had failed and, in fact, worsened their relationship with food.

Despite the fact that I could see the program transforming me daily into a new and different person, and I had heard all the horror stories about ineffective psychiatric counseling, I decided to enter therapy in early 1985 for several reasons. One major area I needed to work on was my relationships with men, a subject I had difficulty discussing honestly at meetings and with my sponsor. My dateless, unhappy teenage years had left permanent scars on my memory, and I had to fight continual feelings of worthlessness and unattractiveness, especially at work. I knew that paying someone would force me to delve into this painful topic.

Another reason I entered therapy was because of a frightening outburst on my part. One night Haywood and I had been arguing about something trivial while I was preparing my dinner, and I had simply snapped in anger and frustration and started to scream at the top of my lungs. In the midst of my hysteria, I had menacingly raised the knife I was chopping vegetables with and pointed it at him. His face had gone from anger, to shock, to horror, and within seconds I had begun to sob, instantly sorry for my emotional overreaction.

The incident, isolated and unusual, had nevertheless left a mark on both of us. I was shaken that I could have acted as if I wanted to hurt the person who perhaps loved me more and knew me better than anyone in the world. Clearly the rage and frustration that I had kept inside over the years and just stuffed down with food was starting to spill out and, unchecked, I knew it could be harmful to myself and others. The episode also made me worry about my mothering abilities: What if a cascade of white-hot fury came on when I was with a defenseless child? Would I strike the child? The thought had chilled me to the bone.

Together these two reasons prodded me to supplement my group meetings and telephone calls with twice-weekly visits to a therapist. The woman I selected to work with saw several people I knew who raved about her tremendous compassion and ability to help her clients confront and solve thorny issues. Deirdre Jennings was the kind of woman I admired, too. She was bright, no-nonsense, and had raised several children by herself while pursuing her own graduate studies. She also worked out of her home, just two minutes from my job, so I could see her during my lunch hour. She and I liked each other immediately, so we went to work.

The first thing we tackled was the whole issue of men. Deirdre walked me through my adolescence and teen years, forcing me to confront the fact that despite my bitterness at never dating, I had also done my best to deflect any passing male interest. By wearing baggy clothes, isolating myself with binges, never doing much to make myself pretty, and concentrating on dieting, I had denied my femininity and halted the process of maturing—both emotionally and physically.

Much of this was due to my overwhelming fear of the opposite sex, I began to see. I didn't know what it stemmed from, but I knew that its roots went back many years. I had vivid memories of walking miles out of my way to avoid construction sites as a young girl so that I would not have to endure whistles and stares. I was also furious if I was out jogging and a male driver honked his horn. I never thought that either occurrence was a friendly acknowledgment of prettiness; I was sure it meant that the person had rape on his mind. Given this attitude, it's no surprise that I viewed men with a mixture of fear and hatred.

We discussed my reasons for marrying Haywood. While I knew that I loved him dearly and had been captivated by his personality and inner strength, Deirdre made me recognize that marrying so young had also been a way of taking myself off the market so that I wouldn't have to deal with dating or further rejection. Haywood was also about as nonthreatening as I could get: gentle, kind to a fault, thoughtful, and devoted to me. The world was not filled with men like him, however, and Deirdre helped me accept that I would have to deal with people who were nasty, indifferent, and crude. I couldn't shelter myself forever.

Another thing we focused on were the sexual overtures I began to experience at work and in social settings. Because I had missed out on dating and didn't know what flirting was all about, it took me longer than most people to see when a man's friendship had crossed the boundaries from good-natured teasing to extramarital interest. When I finally did realize what was going on in those types of situations, I usually became scared and angry, convinced that men and women could not be friends, and I vowed to cut off all contacts with the person in question. I also lost all my naivete about the sanctity of marriage: from what I observed, wedding bands simply heightened the excitement of going after someone.

Not only did I have to learn, then, that there were all varieties of marriages, and that some men were simply inappropriate choices as friends or mentors, but I also had to address my tendency to defer all authority to them. At work this had become a problem because I found myself accepting cramped offices, smaller raises, and fewer perks than I deserved because I didn't have the confidence to confront the men responsible for the oversights. Later I would castigate myself for my lack of assertiveness, vowing to be stronger the next time—much in the same way that I had repeatedly promised myself over the years that every binge would be my last and that "next time" I would be better.

This submissive attitude was decisively addressed one day when, with Deirdre's coaching and the support of people in my program, I confronted a top executive at my company about a sexist remark he had made to me in a meeting. I had been the only woman in a room full of men one night, strategizing about an upcoming presentation, when the man had suddenly interrupted the discussion to ask me if I had to go home to make dinner for Haywood. I had been speechless —especially considering that almost every other man in the room had wives *and* children to get home to—but I had assured him that I did not need to leave. I had fumed for a week, though, until I found the courage and the voice to state my objections.

"Tom," I began one afternoon, "I'd like to talk about something you said last week that is still bothering me."

As I had calmly stated my objections despite the nervous thumping of my heart, Tom had been genuinely apologetic and surprised that his comment could have been interpreted as anything but solicitous of my welfare.

"You know, I didn't go to Harvard to work for pin money," I explained. "I'm putting my husband through law and business school, and I intend to work for many more years. With that one sentence, you cast aspersions on my commitment to my job, and who knows what those other men thought of my attitude toward my work afterward?"

Like getting through Haywood's seizure without binging, confronting Tom was a turning point for me in my dealings with men. Almost overnight I stopped giving them the power to shape how I felt about myself, and I began to form friendships with men that were equal: no flirting and no dominance on either side. My performance at work had improved and my self-esteem had continued to rise.

Deirdre and I also spent a lot of time on my anger and how I needed to learn appropriate ways of expressing emotions. I had absorbed the lesson from my parents early on that winners did not cry and anger was unfeminine. As a result of this, I had tried to maintain an even-tempered, placid exterior at all times; perfect self-control was my goal. Because of this unrealistic attitude, I still behaved in ways that were inappropriate to certain situations. I laughed during sad movies and funerals, cried when I should have gotten angry, and found it impossible to have fun during light-hearted occasions. In fact, when Deirdre once asked me what I did for fun, she drew a blank stare from me. Fun? I didn't even know where to start. Life was a serious matter, I thought.

Just as I had to relearn how to eat, I had to relearn how to behave. Without food as my anaesthetic and punching bag, the feelings—fear, rage, sadness, bewilderment, and hurt—all kept bubbling up, and I didn't know what to do with them. Deirdre and people in the program coached me assiduously. "It's okay to be angry or scared," they told me. "Just don't eat over your emotions—feel them." I began to cry when hurt, confront people when angry, and laugh when the situations called for it. The ancient Greeks held the maxim "Know thyself" as one of the highest ideals a man could aspire to. Now I tried to know myself after years of being someone else, but it was hard and took daily self-scrutiny of my actions.

My relationship with Deirdre became very close. She encouraged me to call her between sessions, and at times we talked on the phone every day. Other people who were in therapy marveled at this; their counselors discouraged dependence and never allowed phone calls. Deirdre also did something unusual in that she confided in me about her own past and illustrated points with her personal experiences and struggles. I felt this was the proper approach for me because I had isolated myself from people for so long, and a distant relationship with a therapist might have simply perpetuated that pattern.

Because of her unconditional love and support, as well as her unfailing accuracy in analyzing troublesome situations, I trusted Deirdre implicitly and usually followed her advice. One day, however, about one year after starting therapy, she made a suggestion that I didn't like at the close of our hour.

"I think that it is time you reduced your dependence on your eating disorder group," she said, watching closely for my reaction.

For a moment I said nothing. The group had saved my life, and the people in the rooms had become my friends and confidants. But was it possible that I had indeed invested too much trust and time in them? Was Deirdre right about this too? I couldn't think clearly; I was confused.

"Why do you say that?" I asked, putting my mug on the arm of the small bottle-green sofa I was curled up on. "Do you think I've made it too important or powerful, like I did with men?"

"Perhaps," she said carefully. "But more to the point, you have made great progress both toward overcoming your eating disorder and improving your relationships with other people, and I think it is time you focused on the idea that you are well—not diseased."

I pondered her statement as I stared out the window at the cold February landscape. Was she right? Was I completely recovered from the bulimia? Should I stop thinking in terms of a lifetime disease that is arrested one day at a time, and instead focus on the idea that I was totally healed, that my bulimia was a thing of the past?

The idea of stopping attending meetings definitely had its appeal. By the time I got home at night from a hard day at work, the last thing I wanted to do some days was drag myself to a meeting or get on the phone. And I knew Haywood would be pleased if I had more time for us. As it was, we were able to snatch only two hours a day together—usually at night—and often these brief periods were interrupted by people from the program phoning to talk.

As I sat looking out the window, I also thought about how I had satisfied most of the program's suggestions for recovery. Although I had not made the bulk of my amends, I had completed the personal inventory, sponsored several people and watched them improve with my help, ceased binging and purging with the exception of a few, very minor slips, and my personality and appearance had changed dramatically for the better.

"Maybe you're right," I said slowly, returning her gaze. "It has always bothered me that I have to call myself a compulsive overeater and bulimic when I speak at meetings. It seems as if we're always reminding each other how sick we are. I'd prefer to say something like, 'Hi, my name is Caroline and I'm totally recovered from bulimia.'"

"Well, just think about it," Deirdre said as she stood up. "I'm not telling you to do anything. I just think that you spend a lot of time at meetings and on the phone that you could be spending doing other productive things. Also, I feel that when you are helping other people and listening to their miseries, you are unconsciously taking on their burdens, which could drag you down and jeopardize your own recovery."

I promised I would think about it as we hugged good-bye. Deirdre had an ample figure which she said had once been slender and shapely. She had started to put on weight about ten years earlier, though, when she had become a supervisor at an all-male institution. It had been her way of being taken seriously and not as a sex object, she thought, but she had been unable to lose the weight in the intervening years and still struggled with her diet. I had suggested my program several times as a possible source of help, but she had insisted she wasn't compulsive and I had dropped the subject. Who was I, after all, to advise my therapist?

After leaving Deirdre's house, I spent the rest of the day at work thinking about what I would do with my free time if I didn't go to so many meetings. Movies, museums, and long walks with Haywood were possibilities I considered. We might even go to lectures about archaeology, investigate some cute restaurants in different corners of the city, and have intimate dinner parties. I didn't stop to think about the fact that neither one of us liked to do some of these things; I just let my mind spin out some romantic ideas of marital bliss.

By the end of the day my mind was made up. I'd take a respite from the program—perhaps brief—to see if I was cured. I'd continue to talk to Annie and some of my other friends occasionally, but I'd focus instead on developing a life that revolved around new activities that kept me out of the kitchen and out of myself.

When I got home, I immediately went to the phone to call Annie.

"Hi, Annie—it's Caroline. Do you have a sec?"

"Sure, I'm just cleaning up from dinner and getting ready to go to the meeting."

"Well, actually, that's why I'm calling."

"What? About dinner?" She sounded puzzled.

"No—about meetings. I was talking to my therapist today and she suggested that I not go to meetings for a while because I've been doing so well. She said, and I agree, that going to meetings can sometimes perpetuate the idea that we're sick for life."

"Well, we are!" Annie said emphatically.

"I don't really understand that," I rejoined. "How if we abstain from binging and purging, are we still sick? What's the point of reminding yourself again and again that you have a lifetime disease?"

"Caroline, I thought we had gone through this before," Annie said wearily, reminding me of the diabetes analogy. "Compulsive overeating is cunning, baffling, and powerful. It's like a snake—it will turn on you and bite you when you least expect it. I've never known anyone who has been able to stop going to meetings and maintain their weight loss or recovery from an eating disorder like bulimia.

"You told me yourself that watching Betsy drop out of the program had scared you," Annie continued. "She was cocky enough about her recovery to stop going to meetings and look what happened to her! Someone saw her last week at the supermarket with her arms loaded with cookies and things. She's obviously back into her disease and has too much pride to come back to meetings. And she had five years of abstaining from binging and purging when she dropped out!"

Having Betsy slip back into her bulimia and anorexia had indeed shattered me. Watching my mentor resume lengthy

226

running bouts, get back into binging, and then deny that anything was the matter had been a great lesson to me. Not only would I never put anyone on a pedestal again, but I swore to myself that I would never allow myself to return to the bulimia.

Annie's words made me uncomfortable. Would not attending meetings lead me down the same path as Betsy? I hoped not because I was resolved to give my experiment a try. "I'll have more time for Haywood if I don't go to meetings," I argued, telling Annie about all the things I'd do to fill the time formerly spent on program activities. "And the phone has been driving him crazy. He refuses to answer it anymore, or listen to the messages on the recording machine, because he says that they are never for him. I don't blame him, really.

"Besides," I continued, "I've got a lot of spiritual books and program literature that I can read to keep me on the straight and narrow." This part was certainly true. Ever since I had met someone in the program who had had a near-death experience and had left his body and gone to a place of warm, brilliant light and love, I had been intrigued by the notion of the indestructibility of the soul. I had gotten scores of books that discussed spiritual truths and religious phenomena, and I had found that many of the tenets of the books paralleled the program's outline. With these books and the program materials, I felt I could continue to grow and learn.

"You're getting yourself into trouble," Annie warned. "I've never met anyone who could maintain abstinence with a pile of books either. There is something very important about meetings, about seeing and talking to other recovering compulsive overeaters, and about helping others that is indispensable to remaining abstinent. How are you going to be able to stay out of the food and give service without sponsoring anyone or going to meetings?"

"I was thinking about going to work in a soup kitchen," I responded. "Haywood goes every Monday morning."

"Caroline, I can't stop you from doing what you're doing, but none of those things will keep you out of the food necessarily. You almost killed yourself with bulimia. You have to remember that. You know—keep your last binge 'green'?"

"Look, it's not as if I'm saying good-bye forever," I assured Annie. "I'll still call you occasionally and talk to the people who call me. It's just that I feel the need to get a little distance from the program right now."

"Okay," Annie sighed, "but remember that you can call me any time you want. And if you decide you need a meeting, you know where to go. In fact," she said, "I'd better run now or I'll be late to the one at eight o'clock. I'll talk to you soon, I hope. Bye."

As I replaced the receiver in the cradle, I felt relief mixed with a tinge of worry. Annie had over four years of abstinence from binging and purging, and I only had about a year. Had she ever felt this way? Why wasn't she out doing more things with her husband after four years of no slips? She was more involved in the program than I was; she sponsored four people, ran retreats, chaired meetings frequently, and helped attend to the business side of the program, too. I pushed my doubts aside. I was just busier than she was. I was a rising executive woman, and I had more important matters to attend to. A little break from the program couldn't possibly hurt me, I told myself.

For the next month or so I filled my new free time with different activities and my food was manageable. I found myself staying at work longer, but not really accomplishing a whole lot more than I had before. Some nights I just stayed because I knew I didn't have a meeting to attend, and I figured that all corporate executives proved their worth to their companies by putting in fifty- and sixty-hour weeks.

Haywood was happy that I was around more and on the phone less, but we never did any of the various things I had plotted to fill our spare hours. And on top of that, because of my formerly frequent attendance at meetings, he had gotten involved in a number of charitable activities, including the soup kitchen, and was not at home as much as I had expected. In fact, a few nights I caught myself wondering if I should go to a meeting when I returned home to find a message on our machine saying that he would be having dinner at a local home for the mentally retarded where he was a volunteer.

But I never acted on those thoughts. The longer I stayed away from the meetings, the firmer I was about recovering on my own. I was fine, wasn't I? I was buying food, fixing meals, going to restaurants, and attending social gatherings, and I was not binging or purging. I was even losing more weight, I thought. My skirts were getting looser, and formerly snug pants weren't so snug anymore.

One day I mentioned this to Deirdre. "I think I'm losing weight," I said happily. "And I'm not purging either. But I'm still not used to my body being thin," I continued, perplexed. "I keep looking in the mirror expecting to see my formerly bloated body, and when I don't sometimes I feel uneasy."

"That's because you were addicted to pain and feeling bad about yourself for so long," Deirdre explained. "You have to get used to feeling good about yourself, accepting compliments gracefully, and not always expecting something bad to happen when something good comes along.

"In fact, I think you're doing extraordinarily well and can do all those things by yourself now," she continued. "We have addressed your issues with men and your mixed emotions about being a woman, your food has stabilized, you like the way you look most of the time, you are happier, and your reactions to stress are much healthier. I think it might be time to end therapy."

End therapy? I felt as if I had been kicked in the stomach. Without my meetings and program calls, my reliance on Deirdre had increased even more, and some days I phoned her answering machine to commit that day's food plan. I couldn't imagine not seeing her anymore and asking her advice, and I didn't think I had enough self-confidence to make it in the real world without therapy as a crutch. I felt like a baby bird being rudely shoved out of its comfortable nest.

I started to mumble a feeble protest, but Deirdre was firm. "Caroline, you are a strong individual with about as much willpower and drive as I've ever seen. You are very special and have been very dear to me, but it's time that you realized that all the answers you will ever need are inside of you. You need to rely on yourself more and trust your instincts. Your heart will never lead you astray if you truly listen to what it tells you, and I think you are mature and well enough to hear it now."

As we hugged good-bye for the last time, I cried. I felt alone and scared. Where was all the trust I had so blithely counseled other people they needed to have in their Higher Powers when things were tough and they felt abandoned? Clearly I had been "talking the talk, not walking the walk," as they said in the program, because at that moment, I didn't feel as if there was any force out there taking care of me. I knew I could rely on Haywood for support in some areas, but it was difficult for him to understand my still-occasional mood swings and self-deprecating thoughts. He had a natural, sunny outlook on life that I was trying to learn. He had also never had a compulsive day in his life.

As I drove home from work that night, I thought again about the possibility of returning to the program. But that would mean that I had failed at my "experiment." The people who had called me during the last month had been put off by my statement that I was going it alone because I was "recovered." I had too much pride to go back to a meeting now, even just for friendship; I'd just tough this time out alone. God was clearly putting me through a big test of sorts, and I was determined to pass with flying colors.

In the succeeding weeks, I poured my energies into my job. But the harder I worked, the emptier I felt. Outside of my program friends, I hadn't met many people in Baltimore in the three years I had lived there, so I didn't know who to call when I had time to relax. I missed the camaraderie and support of the meetings, but I soothed myself with the fact that I looked thin, my food was "clean," and I was delving into different spiritual areas. My life also seemed to be on the right track; my career was advancing, and together with Haywood's law firm salary, we were living quite comfortably and making grand plans for the future. To outside appearances, we had it all. Then disaster struck.

"Caroline, could you come down to my office, please?" The co-owner of the communications company barked his order through my speaker phone. He sounded angry, but that wasn't unusual. He was always upset about something, yelling at someone about their performance.

"Sure," I responded to the instrument, standing up. I had a grim feeling of foreboding. For several weeks I had had premonitions of a confrontation with him. And last night I had had a very disturbing dream about my job suddenly being terminated.

I walked into his darkened office. John had his feet on the desk and he was already halfway through his first of three packs of cigarettes for the day. His partner, Alan, sat across the desk in a chair next to the one I now slipped into. Neither man looked at me.

Before I knew what had happened, I had been fired with three weeks of notice. "You don't fit in here," I heard them saying, alternating between looking at their hands and looking at me through the cigarette haze. "You've done a very good job, but we don't feel that we need a public relations component at this time, and our budget can't cover your salary and expenses."

I was shocked. I had been lured away from my other, very secure job four months previously with such complimentary phrases as, "We hear you are excellent at what you do," "We're looking for someone dynamic like you to learn to run the business and buy us out in a few years," and "Public relations is the growth area for our company and we'd like you to start and head up that division."

Heady stuff for a twenty-three-year-old. I had leaped at the chance to join this small, innovative company with a shot at running it one day. I had also jumped at the large salary and vice president's title they had bestowed upon me. Things had seemed too good to be true.

But they were right. I didn't fit in. Much as I had tried, in my own way, to fraternize with some of the designers and writers who had worked together for years, I had never seemed to earn their trust or friendship. The "Nordic Princess" title had also rankled. Almost from the start I had been put into a pigeonhole and observed as a curiosity.

Being a pretty woman there had also turned into a tremendous liability. Once John had returned from a visit with the president of one of the company's major accounts and loudly informed me that the man had seen a picture of me in the paper and wanted to deal with me only on the next visit. I couldn't help but notice that our company's main link to that organization had also heard the comment and not found it amusing. Another time I had pleaded to have more work to do involving a plastics company client, only to be told that their female liaison was jealous and wouldn't work with me.

"You know how silly women can be!" Alan had explained to me with mock exasperation, rolling his eyes for effect about female idiocy.

No matter what I had tried to do to rectify these situations, I had not been able to come to a happy solution in my few months there. As I heard my future at the company being dashed in the funereal office, I tried to explain my position, and my strong feelings that the time I had been there was not long enough to judge a "fit."

Nothing I said mattered, though, so I politely thanked the two men for their time and went back to my office to try to fathom what had just happened to me. I closed the doors and sank heavily into my chair. I had just gotten fired. I had never once permitted myself to think that this would ever happen to me. I had simply assumed that Harvard graduates with *magna cum laude* credentials were protected from this kind of thing.

As the shock wore off, the tears started. Life was so unfair! How was this going to look on my employment history? John and Alan had said they would give me good recommendations, but I knew it wasn't great to have brief job stints listed on a résumé. Often attitude problems, embezzlement, and other unsatisfactory dealings were suspected when jobs terminated quickly.

And our debt. God, did Haywood and I have our share of debt! We had just bought a pricey condominium in a nice section of Baltimore, we had car payments, I had thousands of dollars worth of loans to pay back for college, and on and on. The financial obligations were fine with our combined salaries. With just one, however, things were going to be difficult.

Suddenly I got very, very angry. I did not deserve this kind of treatment. So many of the problems they had stated simply stemmed from the fact that I was a woman and a pretty one at that. All my life I had tried to emulate the ideal female—intelligent, thin, witty, and attractive—and now that these things were starting to come together for me, I had convincingly found out that they weren't always assets in the business world.

232

I had had my first clue about this kind of corporate pettiness while working at my previous job. Several months after beginning there, I had heard two women discussing me with brutal candor in the bathroom. It had been an instant replay of the time I had heard myself being discussed after being admitted early to Yale and Harvard in high school.

"But what does she *do?*" I heard one low-level accounting person say with puzzlement. "I know what her salary is and she couldn't be worth that much!"

"I don't know—what is public relations?" the other one snickered.

"Frankly, I just think she was hired as a trinket—you know, someone to take company visitors to lunch and dinner," the accounting clerk giggled maliciously. "She probably thinks that her blond hair and smile can get her whatever she wants in this world."

Angrily remembering that scene, I pulled an empty box over to my desk and starting throwing some of my books and knickknacks into it. "I am not going to let this get me down," I vowed to myself. "Just like I'm beating this bulimia thing on my own, I'm going to make it. I'm a survivor!"

The next few weeks were filled with emotional ups and downs, doubt, and a lot of financial fears. Although Haywood was very supportive, I still felt alone when he left for work every morning, and I stared at the phone, summoning up the courage to call my contacts to let them know that I was out of work. I felt humiliated and embarrassed, but I did my best not to show it.

Fortunately, however, I had made enough friends at different companies that I was offered several intriguing jobs in a relatively short period of time. I wavered on what I wanted to do, though. I couldn't imagine myself ever getting caught up in a stifling office job again where I would have to deal with the petty politics and back stabbings that were so common. Although I knew that just about everyone else in the working world put up with that sort of thing, I felt strongly that it would debilitate me severely and would probably send me back into the food if I didn't find a more supportive atmosphere for at least a year.

As luck—or my Higher Power—would have it, I was presented with a spectacular opportunity to help plan the retirement gala for a retiring United States senator that would pay me handsomely enough for several months to forestall having to make any immediate decisions about my future career plans. To celebrate my new position, I decided to shop for a colorful spring and summer wardrobe. So after running and showering one April morning in 1986, I headed downtown to a unique women's clothing store where I knew I'd find one-of-a-kind outfits, bold jewelry, and friendly salespeople.

Several things caught my eye right away: a two-piece dress with huge flowers dancing all over it, a slim white cotton skirt with unusual pleats, and a fitted knit dress. I took my size twelves into the dressing room and started to try things on.

As I slipped the flowered skirt on, though, I realized that it was too big—I'd need a size 10. But I knew I wasn't that slim; nothing I owned was that small. The skirt was mismarked, surely. I tried on the white skirt next. It, too, was too big. I stared at myself in the mirror. As much as I had sensed I was losing weight and people had said as much, I still hadn't let it sink in. Was I now a size I had only dreamed of for years? I turned sideways and looked carefully at my body. Gosh, I did look thin!

Eagerly I tossed the flowered ensemble and the skirt over the dressing room door and asked the saleswoman to get me smaller sizes in both. When she brought them, I found that they did, indeed, fit. I was elated. I decided to buy both and to wear the flowered ensemble home. I even bought a perky straw hat with a pink band around it to complement my new outfit. I felt like kicking my heels up and shouting in glee.

On the way home I decided to stop at the natural food store to buy some much-needed groceries. Feeling thin and attractive gave me loads of energy; as I mounted the stairs of the Golden Temple Emporium, I made plans to pick up the dry cleaning, shop for some overdue wedding gifts, and take some shoes to get repaired.

My cart filled quickly with brown rice, pesticide-free produce, and water-process decaffeinated coffee beans. As I made my way to the checkout counter, I noticed a big sign over some bins of snacks: "Sugar-Free! Natural Food Treats! Try some on us!" In front of the bins were samples of the items—carob-coated rice cakes, whole wheat fig bars, honey-preserved papaya sticks, and much more. My eyes greedily devoured the scene.

No—I couldn't taste them, I told myself. I might not be able to stop, and I had gotten in trouble with these kinds of foods many, many times before. I started to push my cart on when a devilish little voice inside me took over.

"Caroline! Stop! Those things are sugar-free! Did you see that? Sugar-free! They won't hurt you. After all, you are cured. You are normal now. Normal people eat things like that. They taste a little bit and stop. Come on—that program of yours is a thing of the past. Don't be so damn rigid with yourself!"

The cunning voice taunted me as I stared at the treats. "Okay," I silenced my mind, "I'll buy some carob-coated rice cakes and some fig bars. I've never had them and they can't hurt me unless I let them."

As I filled a plastic bag with these two items, I sampled both. Mmmm . . . they were delicious! Maybe I would just make these things my lunch. I sampled some more, eating the other things on the tray, too.

Within a minute, I knew I was out of control. That sickening feeling of powerlessness surged through my body. I was on a binge, and I knew deep in my bones that nothing short of a miracle would stop me. Something evil slipped into my body and the rational Caroline left. I filled three other bags with food, eating as I stuffed the food in. I wanted to cry, but my remote-control personality had its grip on me.

I got to the counter and made a huge frozen yogurt sundae, loading on the toppings, as my purchases were totaled. I ate half of it before the clerk could weigh it. He glared at me, but I didn't care. I wanted to get to the car fast to eat more.

Outside I shoved my bags on the front passenger seat, taking out the biggest bag of cookies and tearing into it. I grabbed a handful and shoved them in my mouth, dipping them into the yogurt. Faster and faster I ate. The cookies were gone within two minutes.

Better drive home now, I decided, or I won't be able to purge. As I pulled out of my spot, I put another bag of food in my lap. Steering with one hand and eating with the other, I sped up the street, barely noticing other cars or traffic lights. My mind was on the food. Nothing else mattered.

I decided not to stop to get our mail in the front office. I not only didn't want to lose any valuable time, but I didn't want to run the risk of having to talk to anyone. I parked and got out of the car, leaving crumbs and sticky fingerprints on the steering wheel and door handles as I strode toward our building, keeping my head down.

I got inside our place without incident and closed the door, double-locking and chaining it. I carried the bags into the kitchen and set them down. What would I eat next? I ignored the produce and concentrated on the carbohydrates, quickly demolishing everything I had bought.

But I still wasn't satisfied—what could I eat next? I felt like a jungle animal hunting down its prey. My hands shook as I opened the refrigerator door. Nothing much here—just yogurt and cottage cheese. But it would have to do. I grabbed the cartons and a spoon, shoveling the contents in as quickly as I could, spilling the cottage cheese on my coat and new dress. Already the dress was too tight for comfort.

Next I went to the cupboards. Crackers and spaghetti sauce. I greedily dipped fistfuls of crackers into the sauce and ate them quickly, my eyes scanning the shelves for other things: I settled on Shredded Wheat and Grape-Nuts. I got a big bowl out and filled it with the cereals, dumping the contents of both boxes in. I would have to replace the Grape-Nuts later because Haywood would notice that if it were missing. I poured on his whole milk—ignoring my own container of skim milk—and slurped everything in.

I felt caught in a time warp. I had forgotten how mechanical my actions and feelings were when I was on a binge. I was focused only on sating the monster within that demanded as much food as I could possibly get inside me. I was totally numb as my hands moved back and forth, putting things in my mouth that I didn't even like.

"Who were you to think you could wear a size 10?" the devil taunted me again. "You'll never be that size again. You don't deserve it. You're worthless! Nyah-nyah!"

I started to cry. I *was* worthless. I was sick and out of

control. What had happened to me? Everything was just beginning to go well and here I was binging! It didn't make any sense.

The phone started to ring. I stared at it mid-bite, frozen, my heart pounding. I couldn't pick it up. I had to purge. I waited for the answering machine to click on so that the dreadful ringing would stop.

I quickly stripped in the living room, throwing my clothes and coat on the couch. My stomach bulged out with a vengeance. I looked as if I was about to give birth to a basketball. As I headed into the bathroom I heard Haywood's voice. My blood ran cold. Was he home? No, no, I calmed myself, it was only him leaving a message on the answering machine. I crept to the door of the den, crazily thinking I had to be quiet so he wouldn't hear me.

"Just wanted to see how you were doing, and tell you how much I love you," I heard him say. "Talk to you later!"

If only he could see me now, I cried with new despair. Somehow the thought that he did care, but that he couldn't even begin to help me, made me feel that much more desperate.

I stumbled into the bathroom and leaned over the toilet, suddenly realizing that I hadn't purged in so long that I didn't know if I still could. Maybe I should drink hot water with mustard powder to make me gag, or syrup of ipecac, I thought. What if I couldn't get the food up? The thought was so horrible that I dismissed it. I'd stay here until I did—that was all there was to it.

I had, indeed, lost my proficiency with vomiting. It took about five minutes of probing the back of my throat with my fingers, and then a toothbrush, before anything came up, and another twenty of painful vomiting until I was satisfied enough to stop. My body was totally ravaged. I was perspiring profusely, my eyes were bloodshot, and my heart was beating erratically. The corners of my mouth were stretched and cracked, and blood dribbled out the side from my raked throat. The last thing I thought of as I lay down on the floor was that the room was getting very, very dark. Maybe I was dying. The thought was not unwelcome.

Twenty or so minutes later, I came to. I had fainted,

237

probably from an electrolyte imbalance. As I dizzily sat up, I noticed that I had never flushed the toilet. I did so and got unsteadily to my feet. I felt pains shooting through my legs. I looked at them—they were totally white and drained of blood. What had I done to myself?

I tottered into the living room, where I stared vacantly at the mute signs of my binging frenzy. My clothes were scattered about, crumbs dotted the floor, and discarded plastic bags led me back into the kitchen. I was too tired to clean anything right now, though. I had to get help first. I knew I was going to die if I didn't.

I went to the bedroom and lay down wearily, wondering if I had the strength or the voice to call anyone. But I knew I had to. I cleared my throat and dialed a friend from the program with whom I had been very close. I couldn't possibly call Annie yet. She had warned me about the dangerous course of my actions and she had been right.

Cynthia answered on the first ring. "Hello?"

"Cynthia—it's Caroline. Do you have a minute or two to talk?"

"Sure, stranger! I've missed you at meetings. How have you been? Busy?"

I poured out my heart and Cynthia listened quietly, saying little. "You know, I tried to drop out, too," she finally offered when I was done, "thinking that I could do everything myself. This is a program of humility. We need other people to help us get well. We need a Higher Power and we need each other. We can't isolate or be too proud to reach out—it's deadly."

"I guess I thought that it would be good to have more time with Haywood and that I was well enough not to need the program," I said lamely. "But maybe I was also running away from making some of my amends. I'm afraid of going back to some of the stores I stole from. I think I still have too much false pride."

"Maybe so," Cynthia said. "But I know that amends are crucial if you want to stop binging and purging for good. I just sent off a check last week to a jewelry store I took a ring from fifteen years ago. I tacked on some money as interest.

Just that little action has made my life and food easier in the last week.

"Caroline," Cynthia continued, "we have a lifetime, deadly disorder. You have to put your recovery ahead of everything else. And it doesn't sound like your therapist understood the importance of the meetings. A lot of them don't, or they feel threatened by the idea that their patients can get well without them in a free, self-help fellowship.

"Another thing you have to remember," she added, "is that it takes a very strong marriage to survive this program. I'm sponsoring a woman right now who's getting a divorce because her husband can't stand the idea of her getting thin and changing. He did things like buy her cookies and chocolates to sabotage her efforts, and he threw a tantrum every time she went to a meeting. Finally, he admitted that he was jealous of her—that he didn't want her to get so attractive that other men liked her."

"Wow," I breathed. "Well, Haywood isn't like that because I know he likes me better when I'm not binging and depressed, but I don't think he fully accepts, either, the idea that recovery is a long-term project that requires lots of meetings, phone calls, and sponsorship.

"But to be fair," I continued, "it was my idea to leave the program, not his. I just thought he'd be happy if I did. I also was getting into a guilt trip about whether or not it was vain to worry about my body so much."

"Caroline—the last thing this is, is vain! How would you like to be dead like Karen Carpenter or some of the other people who have died from this disease? I read in the paper recently about a British model who—after starving herself for a photo shoot—went on a binge and ate ten pounds of food, only to die of a ruptured stomach. It was vanity that *killed* her!"

"Yeah, you're right," I admitted. "What really scares me, though, is that I thought I was doing well and taking my recovery seriously. How could I have fooled myself so easily?"

"It's easy to get cocky," Cynthia responded. "But the program talks about how that time is going to come when you aren't going to have the mental defense against that first bite, and that's when you have to have a lot of meetings under your belt, and a lot of solid abstinence. You're a baby in the program! One year is a lot of time to not binge and purge, but you have a long, long way to go, too.

"Now," Cynthia said abruptly, "when will you get to your next meeting?"

"I'll be there tonight," I promised. "I'm never going to make the mistake of dropping out again. I want to live."

"Okay—see you then," Cynthia said. "*Ciao!*"

I stared at the mauve ceiling of our bedroom after I hung up. Thank God for this program, I thought gratefully. And thank God for people like Cynthia who don't judge me or make me feel inferior when I've fallen away and had a slip.

Streaks of sunlight fell across the bed, warming my face and hands. I pulled the heavy patterned comforter over my legs and closed my eyes to rest for a few minutes, thinking about Cynthia's words and my arrogance at thinking I could do recovery my way. The program had a phrase about how "half measures availed us nothing." I couldn't afford to be half-assed anymore about my recovery from bulimia. I had to make a total, lifetime commitment to the program, and follow through with the last few steps of the program—particularly the amends.

As I drifted off to sleep, names of people I'd have to write to and make financial restitution to floated through my head. My apprehension was gone—I'd do them no matter what. If that's what it took to stay out of the food, I was game. Never did I want to descend into the pits of hell again as I had this afternoon.

THIRTEEN

FOR THE NEXT SEVERAL MONTHS, meetings, phone calls, and working the program to the best of my ability became my top priority. There was no meeting too big or too small for me to attend. I made a lot of calls to people who were into solid recovery, and I badgered them relentlessly about what they did to keep themselves healthy, happy, and free from compulsive overeating.

"What do you eat? When do you eat? Do you ever eat fruit between meals? Do you eat *hors d'oeuvres?* Have you ever had a slip? Why did you slip? How did you get back on track? What do you say when you pray? Do you tell other people about the program? How many meetings do you attend every week?" And so on. I went after recovery with a vengeance, as I never had before.

I also made a point of reaching out to people who were just entering the program and struggling with the idea of surrendering to a power greater than themselves and the wisdom of the group. I found that my slips and misplaced cockiness about my own recovery had given me a valuable perspective that I could not have had otherwise. Time and time again I counseled people, "Stay here. Work this program. There is nothing else out there that works. I know."

I truly became "teachable" in the best sense of the word. If there was a problem on my mind, if I was upset with someone, or if I just felt out of sorts, I got on the phone or went to a meeting and talked about it. My experience had shown me that even if my big toe hurt, I'd better tell someone because otherwise it might spread up my leg and really cause problems. "Name it, claim it, and get rid of it" was a program phrase that I embraced.

I began to really live the program slogans in a consistent way—not just give lip service to them. "Let go and let God," "Easy does it, but do it," "One day at a time," "First things first," "Keep it simple," and other phrases became my *raison d'être*. I also established an unchanging daily routine to foster my spiritual growth. The first thing I did upon awakening was spend some time in prayer and reflection, using the program's daily guides for inspiration. And at the end of the day I spent a few minutes analyzing how I had passed that day, asking myself: Is there anyone I hurt today whom I need to apologize to? Did I reach out my hand to someone who needed a sympathetic ear or a friend? Was I selfish in any way? If I die in my sleep, will I have left the world a better place in some small way?

The more I sought to scrutinize my behavior, the more of a conscience I seemed to develop. Things I used to do without thinking twice, like criticizing people or parking in illegal spots, became intolerable. On two separate occasions I called people I had run with that morning to apologize for saying something about someone else that in hindsight seemed spiteful. I had quivered in fear before calling both men—who were quite prominent in the city—but their surprised responses to my apologies had ushered in a change in their attitudes toward me. As they and others began to respect me more, I began to like myself more, too.

I had to completely humble myself to the program. Much as I wanted people to think I was strong and self-reliant, I made myself talk at meetings and on the phone about my total failure after trying to stay abstinent on my own, and my lingering worries about food, my weight, and the arrogance of thinking I had been completely cured. I tried to listen with every fiber in my body to people who were in long-term recovery, absorbing their wisdom and strength.

In addition to attending as many meetings as possible for my compulsive overeating, I also made a point of getting to as many meetings for recovering alcoholics as I could. I wanted to live a life free from all mood-altering substances, and I found that listening to the inspiring tales of recovery from alcoholism bolstered my resolve to stay out of the food, too.

I heard men and women discuss the lying, hiding, stealing, and manipulating that had accompanied their obsession with drinking, which closely paralleled my experiences with food. When they talked about hiding their bottles in clothes hampers and under car seats, I thought of the food and laxatives I had concealed in the same places. When they told tales of lying and being unable to keep promises and appointments, I thought of my own broken engagements and bizarre stories to cover up my binges. And when I heard about blackouts and waking up without remembering anything that had happened the previous evening, I thought of my seven years of memory lapses and nocturnal binges when I couldn't remember whether or not I had gotten up in the middle of the night and eaten, or whether it had all been a bad dream.

At first when I was called on at the meetings, I hesitated in identifying myself as an alcoholic or drug addict. Although I had abused both substances at times, I hadn't lost as much or gone as low as some of the men and women there. The more I listened, though, the more I realized that my own episodes with spree drinking and marijuana had been addictive and degrading. I had had a blackout the first time I had gotten drunk when I was fourteen, and whenever I had had alcohol in college, I had loaded up on sugary drinks like margaritas and later regretted my actions. I had also, during college, made a drug buy in New York City, a depth to which I had never thought I'd sink.

It took a conversation with a woman after a meeting one day, though, for me to admit that the labels "alcoholic" and "drug addict" might apply to me. Tara was a woman in her forties, recovering from addictions to Valium and alcohol. She asked me a very direct question.

"If you had to live without drugs or booze for the rest of your life, would you miss them?"

I looked away. It bothered me that I could not say "no" immediately. In the back of my mind I still harbored the faint idea that I could occasionally handle both things if I chose to.

"Caroline, it's not enough to just say you don't want to drink or use drugs again," Tara continued, sensing my discomfort. "There has to be a gut-level acceptance that you abused those substances, and that your body cannot handle them correctly. Part of that acceptance is identifying yourself as an alcoholic and drug addict."

"But I didn't drink in the mornings, I didn't squander a lot of money, and I didn't get arrested," I protested. "I can't relate to a lot of the stories I hear here. Don't you have to do all those things to admit you are addicted to alcohol or drugs?"

"The only requirement for membership is a desire to stop using those things," she responded. "I know of some people who try to compare themselves out of the program because, like you, they don't think they are 'that bad.' They decide to go find out if they really can't handle drugs and liquor, and then they spiral downward. Some are never lucky enough to find their way back into the program. I guess you can go find out whether or not you are really addicted, too."

No way. My experimenting with food had ended in abject failure. I didn't doubt that alcohol and drugs would be the same. From that day forward, I identified myself as an alcoholic and drug addict whenever called on at a meeting, and felt that complete commitment to recovery that had previously eluded me. I had reached a new level of surrender, and my sense of peace increased. Whenever I spoke at a meeting of recovering alcoholics, though, I made sure I said that I was also powerless over food, and that I was a recovering bulimic.

244

This always triggered queries from people after the meetings who wanted to talk about their own struggles with multiple addictions.

Typical of these exchanges was one I had one afternoon with an older woman who took me aside to talk privately after the meeting ended.

"I've never told anyone this, but I think I'm becoming a compulsive overeater," she confided, her voice low.

"What makes you think that? Have you transferred your obsession from alcohol to food?"

"Well, I'm not sure. It just seems that ever since I got off the booze three years ago, I've been drawn to eat sugar in huge quantities. I used to be very thin, and now, look at this!" With embarrassment and anger she pointed to her stomach, which was beginning to protrude from her loose wraparound skirt. "I hate it, but I can't stop eating!"

"I don't know a lot about the mechanics of alcohol in the body," I began, "but I know it's pretty sugary. Perhaps your body is crying out for sweets. Can you substitute fruit or something like that instead when the cravings hit?"

"I guess so," she said resignedly, "but then I'd really feel like I had given up all of my pleasures. I've stopped drinking and smoking, and now it seems like all I've got as a vice is pies, ice cream, and chocolate, and I don't want to give them up yet!"

"Well, when it gets unmanageable and you are really uncomfortable with your eating habits, I'd be happy to take you to a meeting for compulsive overeaters with me. But you really have to want to get well, and you have to accept that you have a life-long disease that requires constant vigilance and attendance at meetings with other recovering compulsive overeaters, just like you do here for your alcoholism. I originally fought the idea of being sick for life, but now I accept it wholeheartedly. It wasn't easy, and it took a lot of humility, but it's been worth it."

"I guess that's the problem," she sighed. "I'm not willing to get into another program yet; I'm still at the point where sobriety is my top priority. Maybe later down the road I'll do something about this weight thing. Right now I'm not happy about it, but I'm not unhappy enough to do anything about it, either."

Conversations like this one helped me recognize the big differences between recovering from alcoholism and recovering from a food addiction. Many times I heard people at meetings for recovering alcoholics describe themselves as "first-nighters"—people who had not had a drink since the night of their first meeting. I had never met anyone like that in the program for compulsive overeaters. You simply could not put down food for the rest of your life and move on; it had to be dealt with on a daily basis, and a "slip" was not as clear-cut with the food.

Taking a drink or snorting a line of cocaine was a clear break of abstinence from those substances. But because everyone's meal plan was different, a slip with food to one person was not a slip to another. Some people who were hypoglycemic ate five small meals each day—to rigid three-meal-a-day'ers, this might be considered a slip. Some people in the program could handle small amounts of sugar without binging; others—like me—could not. Some people ate very small meals and considered an occasional generous portion a slip— to someone else that just might be a large, but abstinent, serving .

Abstinence from compulsive overeating involved a lot of trial and error with different foods, and sometimes painful tumbles from the wagon. But I found that everyone gradually settled into regimens that worked for them. For me, this meant three committed meals each day, abstinence from sugar and most refined flour products, and no purging. As long as I adhered to those guidelines, I felt I was in recovery from bulimia. Some people were stricter with themselves, others were looser. But just as we all had our own conceptions of Higher Powers that worked for us, we all had individually tailored food plans. It was tolerance for people's differences that kept the program strong and effective.

One of the things I had to confront in designing a food plan that worked for me was that I had equated a number of soft, sweet foods with love—a difficult association to break. Many of these things were substances I had been given when sick because my mother thought they would make me feel better. Had my later binges on pudding, ice cream, and yogurt been desperate, unfulfilling searches for that kind of maternal affection when I was depressed? And if so, what were some of the things I could do to nurture myself in a healthier way?

One set of people who especially seemed to equate food with love were grandparents, which my grandmother, Donny, demonstrated many times over the years. Usually she was happily ensconced in our kitchen when I came home from school and swimming workouts, whipping up her secret butterscotch sauce or something comparable. Our conversations usually went something like this:

Donny: "Hi, sweetums! What can I make for you?"

Me: "Nothing, thanks. I'm not hungry."

Donny (opening the refrigerator): "We have tuna fish, quiche, squash casserole, and I made some pecan pie. Let me cut you a nice slice of pecan pie. I'll warm it in the microwave oven and put some ice cream on it."

Me: "No—really. I ate lunch just a little while ago. I'm not hungry."

Donny: "Eggs are good for you. Your sister loves egg salad. Can I make you a little egg-salad sandwich?"

Me: "Eggs make me sick."

Donny: "Caroline! Don't say the word 'sick'! There is no sickness in this world! God is all! Would God make you sick?"

Then we'd be off on a theological discussion about God, nature, mind over matter, and Christian Science, which at least got us off the food topic.

Haywood's maternal grandparents were the same way. Whenever we went to Kentucky to visit them, I knew we were in for culinary feasts, Southern style. From the moment we'd arrive, his grandmother would talk about the foods she had worked on for days, especially the annual gigantic angel food birthday cake for Haywood and the dozens of chocolate chip cookies, which we always were given stacks of to take home with us.

The first few times I had visited, I had fallen into an abyss of biscuits, fried chicken, pork roast, cookies, and cinnamon kites, not knowing how to turn them down without hurting someone's feelings. Through the program, though, I learned that I didn't have to eat to show someone I cared about them, and that it was okay to say "no" when I knew I'd be uncomfortable eating a certain food.

Another association I had to break was that it was somehow my moral duty to eat. Once when I was young I had been having dinner at a friend's house when her father had thundered, "People in this house clean their plates at meals! There are millions who are starving in India!" I had looked down at the disgusting plate of meatloaf and lima beans, and had cowered in fear, but I had obediently eaten every single morsel, eager to please and placate him. For years afterward, though, I had carried around the absurd idea that the more I ate, the happier the world would be.

Food had had another important purpose in my life; eating the right foods, most athletes believed, guaranteed superior athletic performance. Therefore preparing for big swimming meets had always involved buying and eating special foods, which changed over the years, depending on the prevailing medical theories. One year it was commonly believed that steak and Jell-O was the way to go because of the high protein content. Soon, however, the carbohydrate revolution had swept that notion away, and we had replaced the protein extravaganzas with lasagna, toast, and waffles. Because most of my binges were on these kinds of foods anyway, it just gave me license to eat even more. The more I eat, the faster I'll swim, I told myself.

In my new commitment to the program, I decided to make my meal plan as simple as possible. All foods that had any remote connection to what I had formerly binged on were eliminated. Tofu, brown rice, and vegetables became my staples. With so little emphasis on food, my program became more and more focused on the increasing emotional and spiritual changes that were taking place. More and more people commented on the big difference in my attitude and my appearance, too, which opened the door for me to finally talk openly about my bulimia with people who were not connected with my program.

The more I lifted the shroud of secrecy from my past, the farther I felt I was distancing myself from it. I also learned that many more people than I had ever expected were grappling with the very same issues with food, and were eager to find out how I had been able to stop binging. I began to receive phone calls from all over the country—from friends and friends of friends who had heard about my frankness in discussing my struggles and were eager to help themselves or someone close to them.

For example, one evening I received a call from a high school friend I hadn't seen or heard from in five years. Through our high school's alumnae magazine, she had noticed that I was in the same career field that she was interested in, and she wanted to hear more about opportunities for women in the job market. Gradually our conversation had steered toward our common writing background: her father and my mother had both pursued journalism careers, and we had worked together on our high school newspaper. I mentioned that I was working on a book about my recovery from bulimia and the phone line had momentarily gone dead.

"You had bulimia?" she said with obvious disbelief a few seconds later. "I thought you had everything going for you. You never looked sick!"

"Well, it's easy to get away with it," I laughed. "I never got very thin and I became really skillful at lying and stealing to cover up for my binges. Do you know much about bulimia?"

"Oh yeah," she said. "I've been bulimic for twelve years —I taught myself how to purge when I was ten, and I thought I was the only one who knew how to do it back then. I thought it was the greatest diet trick in the world."

Now it was my turn to be shocked. This young woman had had a very distinguished academic career, both in high school and at one of the country's top universities, and I had always envied her petite size and dynamism.

"I really shouldn't be surprised," I said after regaining my composure, "but I wouldn't have guessed you. I mean, you were thin and all, but I certainly didn't think there was anything unusual about your eating patterns."

"It's been a long struggle for me," she responded. "When I was fourteen, my parents found out about my bulimia because I went into the bathroom to try to purge dinner at a resort where we were staying and I used a little cocktail fork to scrape the back of my throat to make myself gag. I swallowed the fork, though, and I was terrified that it would puncture something in my intestines or stomach, so I had to tell them about it. Then I was rushed to the hospital and operated on to get it out. It was awful."

"And you didn't stop purging after that?"

"No—I'm still bulimic. I just can't stop. I've even been hospitalized in a treatment program for it, but nothing seems to work. Just when I think I've got the behavior under control, something will happen and the first thing I know I'm binging again."

"Have you heard of this program?" Then I told her about my group and the fact that it had branches all over the world. "I know that there are lots of meetings in the Washington, D.C. area. Look in the phone book and call the hotline number. I think you'd really like the meetings. I was pretty desperate several years ago, and now I really feel like I'm going to be okay."

Two weeks later I got a call from the same girl who told me that she had attended her first meeting of the program in Washington and that she hadn't ever felt as much hope about recovering from bulimia in her life. She also said that she had had her first uninterrupted ten days of abstaining from purging on her own in twelve years.

Another time I received a call from a friend of my older sister's, who had heard through the grapevine about my bulimia. Jan had graduated from a women's college several years previously and had been employed since then in the garment district of New York and at several of the country's top fashion magazines. I had known her only slightly and was therefore puzzled when I heard her voice.

"Caroline," she said shyly, "I hope you don't think I'm being forward or anything, but I'm calling because I know you had bulimia and I really need help."

"You're bulimic, too?" I was getting used to the frequency of these calls.

"Yes, but I think I'm probably really different from most bulimics."

I had to laugh when Jan said that; every bulimic I knew was convinced that she or he was the most unusual, the most unique or the worst bulimic ever to walk the face of the earth. People like us were always trying to stand out in some way. I asked her how long she had been purging.

"Years—longer than I can remember. I did it off and on throughout high school because everyone else did, too, but when I went to college it really got bad. I will never, ever send a daughter of mine to an all-women's college after what I went through. Girls were purging left and right, locking the bathroom doors, being competitive even about their skill at vomiting. And the administration was really unsympathetic. Most of the time they just made the girls live off campus— they wanted the problem off their manicured grounds and didn't want to have to confront the issue."

We then talked about the huge quantities of food available at college, comparing notes on the "All You Can Eat" ice cream fests that prevailed at Harvard and her college to help students get through exam periods.

"The more emphasis they tried to take off drinking parties, the more they played up the food get-togethers," I remembered, laughing. "Going to the ice cream things was awful, but it was almost as if you were expected to go—you know, the support-your-House-and-be-enthusiastic kind of thing. If the administration had any idea how much of that ice cream went straight into the toilet afterward, they'd be horrified!"

"Well, I thought that once I got out of college I'd be free of the food and all," Jan continued, "but it only got worse. It seems like everyone in New York is thin and beautiful and you feel that if you're not, you're a loser. And in the fashion industry, I swear, everyone has an eating disorder! I don't know many models who aren't bulimic, anorexic, or sick with some other eating problem. Being around people like that all day long only made me worse, so I quit my job last week and I really want to concentrate on getting well. So that's why I'm calling," she concluded. "How did you recover?"

"Well, the first thing I have to emphasize is that I know I have a disease that is arrested one day at a time. I wouldn't call myself 'recovered' yet. But if I keep going to meetings, talking on the phone, and giving service to the program, then there's a good chance I'll stay clear of the food," I began.

"There are no guarantees, however. I've had my slips—mostly when I got really arrogant about my progress. You've got to develop a healthy sense of humility for this thing. It's cunning, baffling, and powerful, and it will grab you when you least expect it if you aren't constantly aware of slippery places and people."

Jan and I talked for another hour, and she promised to attend a meeting in New York City as soon as she could, but I didn't hear from her again. I hoped she was getting involved in the program, but I knew that it wasn't my responsibility to see that she got well. I was only responsible for planting the seed and helping more if asked; beyond that, it was her individual responsibility to begin the task of honesty, amends, and change. I had had to learn this lesson when Bob, the man who had called me at work, had never showed up at a meeting after I had talked to him, but someone had reassured me that I had said all the right things, and that he would come into the program when he was truly ready.

Once I received a plea for help from the president of a sorority at a big Southern university, who asked me how she could deal with the large number of bulimics in her house. Although group meetings had been held at their sorority about the problems of disappearing food and locked bathrooms, a number of the "sisters" could still be heard in the bathrooms late at night, purging after their binges. The campus had no personnel trained to deal with bulimia, and this young woman was at her wits' end trying to figure out how to be helpful.

Her story didn't surprise me much. I had been at a party several weeks earlier, where a recent graduate of a large university had told me that purging in some of her school's sororities was a badge of honor, and that the more proficient one was at eating huge quantities of food and getting rid of it, the more popular she was. As jaded as I thought I had become to the disease, I had been surprised at the openness of the practice there. I had been terribly secretive and would have been mortified if I had been caught purging, or if anyone had known about it.

Another time Haywood came home one night and told me that one of the young retarded women he had met through his volunteer work was bulimic, and that the attendants where she lived had to constantly watch her after eating to see if she was heading for the bathroom to purge. The fascinating twist was that she was mentally impaired enough that she hadn't read the same fashion magazines other bulimics had read, and really hadn't had any pressure put on her to be thin. Was there a physiological basis for her behavior? I wondered.

There were several intriguing studies theorizing a physiological basis for bulimia that I had heard of, but no hard evidence. One man I spoke with who ran a treatment center for alcoholics, drug addicts, and eating disorder sufferers, said that a high percentage of bulimics came from alcoholic homes and that perhaps the inability to metabolize ethyl alcohol correctly—the x-factor, it was called—was related to the inability to process sugar properly and the addiction process. I had also read that some doctors were having success in treating bulimics with antidepressants, the idea being that some critical neuro-transmitters, like serotonin, weren't properly circulating in binge eaters' bodies.

Although nothing was conclusive, I hoped that there would be something discovered soon that would prove that bulimia had a physiological basis and was not simply a matter of sheer willpower in staying away from food. People had once believed that alcoholism was a character weakness which could be controlled through willpower, but studies had conclusively shown in the 1950s that it was physiological in nature. The result had been that a lot of the stigma associated with the behavior had been removed, enabling huge numbers of people to admit they were licked and get help.

After all, I heard time and time again at meetings for recovering alcoholics that when you have diseases like cancer, diabetes, and epilepsy, no one tries to tell you to get well through willpower. Alcoholism was no different, they stressed, and, I hoped, neither was bulimia. All the willpower in the world had gotten me nowhere, and I had never been able to understand how a single bite of sugar could lead to such terrible consequences despite my best efforts to stop. The only thing that made sense to me was that I had been born with—or had developed through years of binging and purging—a chemical makeup that left me powerless over sugar and other highly processed foods the minute they hit my bloodstream.

The medical complications of bulimia also interested me. I had personally experienced the ravages of the disease: heartbeat irregularities, crumbling teeth, memory loss, dry skin, and hormonal dysfunctions, among other things, but I was curious to know what other problems arose from it. I had heard reports about people who developed goiters from a lack of iodine, experienced cardiac arrest from syrup of ipecac poisoning, and had severe potassium deficiencies. But I was still surprised when I met a young woman in Kentucky who told me that her bulimic sister had been in a car accident and that subsequent X-rays had shown that she had the bones of an eighty-year-old woman. Apparently her nutritional intake had been so poor that her skeleton was sixty years older than she was!

As I had listened to this woman describe her sister's tribulations, I wondered why the numerous destructive effects of bulimia hadn't been more written about or hadn't received more publicity. A voracious reader, I had combed the bookstores and libraries during my seven years of purging, looking for anything that would explain what I was going through and offer solutions to the problem. The books and articles I had found, though, had bored me and left me confused. Every doctor and psychiatrist had a different approach to the problem, most of which didn't ring true with me. When I finally found one highly regarded work by a doctor who said that bulimics had fears of being pregnant, and that therapy should involve strapping a pillow to their stomachs to get them used to the bulge, I had given up in disgust. Pregnancy, or a fear of it, had definitely not been on my mind when I had become bulimic at fifteen.

Knowing about my eating disorder, the editor of a women's magazine asked me to do a comprehensive article on the disease, which led me to New York to interview the head of a prestigious hospital's eating disorder unit. I had hoped I would come away with answers to my many questions, but my two hours with this older man had instead disturbed me. Very bluntly he told me that treatment for bulimia was uncertain—that the medical profession was about as advanced in discovering a workable cure as they had been in 1850 in learning to treat tuberculosis.

"We just don't know what works," he said. "We give our in-patients and our out-patients a smattering of everything, hoping that something will take with them. So we employ a variety of techniques: behavioral therapy, assertiveness training, psychotherapy, family therapy, nutritional awareness, gentle exercise, antidepressants, and so on. But it's total guesswork, at best. I think it's healthy, however, that the medical profession is now admitting that it is stymied. Perhaps some of our arrogance about being able to treat anything will disappear."

I thought about the dozens of men and women he said were being treated at his center and who were on the waiting list, desperate to be well and willing to spend whatever it took to get there. Although most insurance companies now covered the cost of eating disorder treatment, the majority of the men and women treated at places like this would probably come away much poorer, still angry, still desperate, and still binging if what this doctor was telling me was true.

Most, he said, would return to binging—perhaps in smaller quantities or with lesser frequency—but they would return nevertheless. It was a depressing interview, and on the way home I thanked my Higher Power for letting me stumble into my free support group, which the doctor had known little about and was unwilling to consider employing as part of the center's treatment program.

When I arrived home that afternoon, I called Annie to tell her about my trip. "I'm not surprised" was her only response to my account of the meeting. "Do you know how many people are in our program who have gone through hospital treatment programs and gone right back to the food? A lot of them don't get any better until they encounter the simple principles of our program. And I think that a lot of hospitals underestimate the importance of continuing contact with other recovering compulsive overeaters, making amends, and being honest in every area of our lives as part of getting well."

I knew she was right. I was currently sponsoring two women who had both been through several treatment programs apiece at some of the finest medical centers in the country. I thought that some of the methods employed had been inane and barbaric. For example, one woman said that when she had refused to eat one evening she had been locked in a room with pads on the walls and given a sedative. Later, also as part of her treatment, she had been forced to vomit into a trash bag and carry it around with her wherever she went in the hopes that she would become disgusted with her behavior and not do it again. It hadn't worked.

"Speaking of amends," Annie changed the subject, "how are yours going?"

I had promised Annie that my renewed commitment to the program would include being thorough in making my amends. So I had set to work calling and writing people to apologize for things I had said or done that might have hurt them in some way. Among the people I had written to were high school friends whose friendships I had neglected, college roommates whom I had stolen from, and a swimming coach whose sweatshirt I had taken and whom I had hated for wanting to weigh me periodically.

I had been gratified by everyone's responses. Old friends were eager to pick up where we had left off and said they had all wondered why I had begun to isolate myself so much and rebuff all social gatherings and friends. My college roommates were similarly understanding, and my swimming coach returned my check uncashed, telling me to give the money instead to a favorite charity. Although no one had turned away from me, several people had not known how to respond to my confessions and openness, so they had said nothing. Annie helped me learn not to expect anything from anyone; the amends were for my peace of mind, not public acclaim or candidacy for sainthood, she said.

I had felt better and better as I had worked through my long list of restitution, checking with her every time to see if my amend was an action that would not harm myself or others. I still had a major one to make, though, and I dreaded it.

"Annie, I'm going to have dinner with my sister in Washington next week, and there's something I know I ought to do, but I'm scared."

"Nothing could be that bad. What is it?"

"For years I went to a certain supermarket near our home

256

and ate food out of the bins, shoplifted laxatives and gum, and opened packages, ate out of them, and stuck them back on the shelves. I know I have to make an amend there and offer to repay the store, but I'm frightened and I don't have the money to do it."

"Just pray for the strength," Annie counseled. "You'll find a way to get through it somehow."

The next week I was driving down the interstate to Washington when my conscience started its familiar dialogue with me. Conscience perched himself on my right shoulder; fear on the left.

Conscience: "You really have to go there, Caroline. This amend has been on your mind for a while, so you know it's something you must act on. You won't rest easy until you have taken some action."

Fear: "Oh, shut up! You're carrying this rigorous honesty business too far, dummy. No one in their right mind would go back to a supermarket and offer to repay money for food stolen years earlier when they don't even have the necessary funds."

Conscience: "You're just scared."

Fear: "Damn right I'm scared! What if I'm fingerprinted and locked up? What if one of my parents' friends overhears me making the amend? What if they make me write a check on the spot? What if? What if? What if?"

Conscience: "Caroline, just stop struggling so much. You can't try to tailor-make everything in your life to suit you— especially not this program. What you are supposed to do has worked for thousands of others. You're no different, no better and no worse. Give it up. Or do you want to go back into the food?"

Fear: "Stop trying to scare her. Besides, she's going to be late for dinner if she doesn't hurry. She doesn't have time to stop at the store."

Did I have time? I looked at my watch. Traffic had been so light that I had glided into Washington a full half hour before I was due for dinner. The message was pretty clear to me. I had time to make the amend, so I turned my car and headed in the direction of the familiar supermarket, praying for strength.

"God," I sternly rebuked Him, "there had better be a good reason why you are making me do this. I am scared and I don't know what to say, so you had better give me the right words and the right attitude to get through this." I also tacked on a little prayer for courage.

I parked and entered the supermarket. It was easily one of the biggest ones I had ever been inside. On the right of the cavernous building was the produce and dairy section where one could get every kind of fruit or vegetable known to man. I walked through the area, smelling the fresh fruits and pausing to test the ripeness of the beachball-size cantaloupes.

Everything looked so inviting that I decided to do some shopping while I was there. "You're procrastinating," Conscience bleated. "Just go find the store manager and get it over with!"

"In my own time. I'm in here, aren't I?" I shot back silently, getting a shopping cart and beginning to wind through the store.

I felt pain and nostalgia as I traversed up and down the familiar aisles. Here I had bought some Cocoa Puffs cereal for a binge, and here I had eaten the multicolored marshmallows out of the Lucky Charms cereal. Oh, and over there I had slipped gum in my pocket countless times, and salivated in front of the candy display.

On the other side of the store, which featured a bakery and a bookstand, I stood in front of the spot where I used to sit and read magazines, gobbling Mylanta pills and laxatives, interspersed with handfuls of food. Who was that sad little girl who had eaten, shoplifted, and lied for her food addiction? As I walked around mentally reliving the years of turmoil and desperation, I knew there was no turning back on making the amend. I had to shut the door on the past once and for all. I headed for the checkout counter with my few purchases.

"Where is your store manager?" I said to the young man ringing up my items. "I'd like to have a word with him or her."

"I'll get him for you—he has to okay your check anyway because you don't live around here." The cashier pressed a button next to him that sounded throughout the store. Far down the checkout aisles I saw a man who looked to be in his thirties step out of an enclosed booth and walk toward us. I thought I had never seen a meaner-looking man in my entire life.

"Jesus God, help me," I implored as the manager got closer. My loose cotton shirt was beginning to stick to my back. Maybe if I fainted I wouldn't have to go through with this.

"Could I have a word with you?" I stammered as the moustached, somber-looking man glanced at my check and scribbled his initials on the back.

"Sure," he said brusquely, looking at me. "What is it?"

By now the cashier was staring at me, wondering what in the world was going through my head. I felt like a sideshow freak.

"Could I talk to you privately?" I asked the manager. My voice was beginning to squeak and I felt light-headed.

The manager looked piqued and waved his arm five feet to the left. "How about over there?"

Here goes, I thought, as I picked up my bag and moved to the appointed spot. I looked at the floor and then up at him and started to speak.

"I've come here to make an amend for some things I stole here in your store starting about ten years ago," I said, gathering strength as I pressed on. "I'm a recovering bulimic, and I'm in a program that suggests that we go back to people and institutions we have stolen from and offer to make amends. I'd like to repay the store for the food, laxatives, and other things I took." Relieved at my confession I looked at the man for his reaction.

Now it was his turn to look at the floor. He was probably mentally totaling what I owed, I thought fearfully. At least a few hundred dollars would be in order. Haywood would kill me for doing this.

When the manager finally looked up at me, he had tears in his eyes. What was going on? I was the one who was supposed to be crying—not him! This amend wasn't going as planned. I decided to elaborate a little to fill the awkwardness of the moment. I told the manager the name of the program I was in and waved my arm over at the bins of natural foods. "I was one of the people who stand around and help themselves to the food," I babbled. "I believe I have a disease that is arrested one day at a time, and I know I will get back into that behavior unless I offer to make restitution for past wrongs."

"I just can't believe you have the courage to come here," the manager finally said. "I'm familiar with what you are doing because I had to do the same thing for my alcoholism. We must be in the same kind of program."

My mouth dropped open. I could have been knocked over with a feather. The manager continued to talk.

"Consider restitution made. I know how difficult it is to make amends like this, and I'm impressed with your commitment to the program."

He wasn't going to take my money! That relieved me tremendously, but I was still amazed at the coincidence that we both attended the same kinds of meetings. "Well, you must get people coming in here all the time to make amends," I rushed on. "I don't know many compulsive overeaters or bulimics who haven't eaten in supermarkets."

"No—you're the first one who's ever approached me," he said. "I didn't realize it was so easy to eat in here. We're probably losing lots of money through that channel. I'll have to alert our store detectives to be on the lookout for people with that sort of behavior."

We talked for another minute or so as he walked me to the door, shaking my hand warmly when we got there and congratulating me on my courage in approaching him.

"I've learned something today," he said, "and you've given me the strength to finish making my amends, too. There are a few I haven't been able to face, but I think my Higher Power must have put you into my life today to spur me on to finish them."

Both of our Higher Powers had been at work, I thought wonderingly and gratefully as I got into my car. What had astonished me the most about the whole episode, however, had been that the little prayer I had uttered to myself before I had entered the store had had three simple points: Please give me the courage to go through with this, give me the words to make the amend come out right, and finally please make the manager be in a similar program.

It had been a far-fetched prayer, but it had happened.

Never, ever again will I doubt the existence of a loving God that is looking out for me, I vowed to myself as I drove to meet my sister. And never again would I doubt the efficacy of prayers. Now that I was earnestly asking for help and trying to stay well, God was making miracles happen daily in my life and my bulimia was finally becoming a thing of the past.

I was truly, as the program suggested, becoming "Higher-Powered."

FOURTEEN

AS DIFFICULT AS IT WAS to make my supermarket amend, the most daunting task on my list of restitutions was an apology to my parents for my behavior during the seven years of my bulimia. I could see now that I had put them through a lot of pain, but I couldn't bring myself to say the simple words, "I'm sorry." Every time I thought about writing a letter to them, I became paralyzed with fear. Maybe they wouldn't accept my apology and forgive me for the stealing and duplicity I had practiced in their own home, unknown to them. Maybe they would never be able to forget my hateful words and sullen silences that I had let them think were their fault, when in fact they had been the results of postbinge depressions and intense self-hatred. And maybe all the times I had stayed at college during vacations instead of coming home because I hated the way I looked had driven too large a wedge between us. I continued to cower and avoid the amend as 1986 ended and 1987 began.

But the more time that went by, the more I knew it had to be done. Whenever I talked to my parents, my recovery was rarely spoken of. They didn't ask about my meetings and I didn't offer any explanations. We always talked around the subject, leaving a great hole between us that I knew only I could fill. Several times I sat down to write letters to them, only to start crying and be unable to finish. Some of the letters were maudlin and self-pitying; I didn't have the true humility an honest amend requires. Some were even angry. "If you hadn't emphasized my weight or put me under so much pressure, I never would have become this way," I wrote in one. That letter was thrown out unsent, too. It wasn't true, and it would have put them on the defensive.

I turned to Annie for guidance. She and her mother had patched up a disastrous relationship because of Annie's involvement in the program. Annie told me to try my hand at another letter and to only emphasize all the things I felt sorry for, and to be matter-of-fact. "Don't allow yourself a moment's thought about what they could have done differently. All parents do the best they can, and the past simply can't be changed. Your sole responsibility is to apologize for your actions and to change yourself."

Finally, in February, I was able to put together a long letter to my mother and father that I was proud of. I recalled specific instances that I was ashamed of and that I knew had hurt them. I included some program literature in the envelope and explained that making amends was a necessary part of ensuring that I would never go back to the food. I ended by saying that I didn't think they would ever understand the forces that had driven me to abuse myself with food for so many years, but that I hoped they could forgive me and move on. Then I told them that I loved them very much, something I had never done before. When I left the letter on their dining room table one afternoon, I knew that I had taken the most important step toward leaving my bulimia behind.

Their reaction was sudden and gratifying. They called me to thank me for my candor and said they wished they had

263

been aware of my pain so that they could have helped me. And again they asked how they could have been blind enough not to notice the bulimia. Their guilt at not putting the obvious clues together—the obsession with weight, missing food, mood swings, hours in the bathroom, and trips to the doctor —was sharp. But I reassured them that a bulimic can hide the disease for years, and will not seek help or recover unless she or he really wants to. It had taken all the secrecy and pain to bring me to the point where I could seek help on my own, and I wasn't sure if a confrontation with them or anyone else would have been as effective, although I knew that approach had worked for others.

My parents were fascinated with the program. They liked the emphasis on turning one's will over to a Higher Power and making amends. For the first time, they began to ask me a lot of questions about the bulimia, and I honestly shared my experiences with them. And then my mother asked me a question that made my blood run cold.

"Your father and I would like to come to a meeting with you," she said one afternoon. "Washington's Birthday is on Monday, and we both have that day off. Can we come to Baltimore that night and take you to dinner after your meeting?"

My hand froze on the phone. Going to a meeting with them would be one of the most intimate things we could do. It was one thing to talk to them in person, but the gut-level sharing of the meetings brooked no dishonesty. If I was called on, I would have to share, and I didn't know if I could open up with them there. I also suddenly worried that they would hate the meetings or find them too spiritual. I was about to make an excuse for why we couldn't go to a meeting when my mother continued on with enthusiasm.

"Caroline, you have no idea how proud we are of your recovery. Your father and I have nothing but admiration for your strength and courage, and we just want to see what this program is all about."

I crumbled. "Sure. Be at my place at about five P.M. The meeting starts at five-thirty, and then we can go out afterward." I decided to just let go and let God. Whatever was going to happen at the meeting was obviously out of my hands.

On Monday afternoon, my parents pulled up in front of my building all smiles. They were excited about this new venture, and they knew that I was taking a big step by letting them in on this part of my life. We drove to the meeting at a local store where I put them in two chairs on the side of the room. I was in charge of opening the meeting that night, so I busied myself with the preparations as the room filled. Putting out the literature kept my hands from shaking in nervousness.

At five-thirty I started the meeting. Annie was the speaker that evening, and as I listened to her powerful story of recovery again, I lost my uneasiness about having my parents there. Annie was a miracle and so was I. It really didn't matter whether or not my parents liked the meeting or found it interesting. I was grateful to be alive and into recovery, and I owed my life to the group. No matter what anyone else thought, I was proud of being a part of this program.

When Annie finished, she called on people to share. I was one of the first people she asked. Without thinking twice, I started to talk about points of her story that had paralleled my own life. I heard myself saying things about my former loneliness and self-hatred, things I never would have confessed to before in front of my parents. I felt my cover being stripped away. "This is me, Mom and Dad," I seemed to be saying. "I'm not perfect, and I have these kinds of feelings. And I hope you can accept me the same way I have accepted myself."

When I was finished, I looked back down at my needlepoint as other people talked. Every few minutes I snuck a look at my parents to see what their reactions were. They seemed fascinated as person after person talked about bulimia and compulsive overeating, and shared honestly about relationships, family problems, and work. Then I saw my dad's hand shoot up.

"Oh, dear God, what in the world does he want to say?" I thought, panic-stricken. "Oh, Annie, please don't call on him!" I silently implored her.

Too late. Annie pointed at my dad and asked him to speak.

"Hi, my name is Bill and I'm Caroline's father." I forced myself to look at my dad.

"I'm here tonight for the first time with Caroline's mother," he said. I saw that my mother had tears in her eyes; I felt tears welling up in mine, too. "We're here because we love our daughter very much and we're trying to understand her disease. It helps us very much to be here and to listen to you all, and we are grateful that you let us come.

"Caroline and I haven't always gotten along over the years," he continued, "but she has apologized to us for things she has done, and I know it is because of this program that she has the courage to do that. So I'd like to ask her to forgive me for any pain I've ever caused her. Will you forgive me, dear?" My father looked directly at me. I had never loved him or my mother more than I did at that moment.

"Of course," I said, smiling broadly, trying not to cry. Too many other people in the room were crying for me to start, too.

After the meeting ended, I made my way across the room to hug my parents, another thing that I had recently started doing. I thanked my father for opening up in front of a room of strangers, and told him how lucky I felt to have them as parents. We all cried. I felt as if the turmoil of the past had completely fallen away and that all was forgiven.

Since that night, my recovery has steadily continued a day at a time. As my life and my relationships with other people have continued to improve, my gratitude toward my program has deepened. By finally facing my bulimia, I have been given the tools to repair my damaged relationship with my family, raise my self-esteem, change my outlook on life, and put food in its proper place. Some days, in fact, food and my weight is the last thing on my mind. That alone is a miracle.

This program has also given me back my honesty. When I was young, I prided myself on my truthfulness. As the bulimia took over my life, though, I lost the ability to be honest, least of all to myself. Lying became a way of continuing to practice and hide my disease and, although it started because of my food obsession, it spread to other areas of my life. By making amends and coming clean, I have returned to the honesty I possessed as a child and can now look people in the eye again.

I have developed a healthy sense of humility, too. No longer do I think that my willpower is capable of controlling my surroundings or behavior. I believe that there is a Divine Plan of which I am an infinitesimal part, and I know that when I put God's will before my will, things will work out the way they are supposed to.

One of the most interesting things that has happened to me during my years of recovery is that people, places, and situations that threaten my serenity and abstinence have fallen away or been forcibly removed from my life. Although I initially mourned the death of certain friendships, in hindsight I saw that their personalities and mine no longer meshed. The saying that "like attracts like" definitely holds true in this regard. The people I now have attracted as friends and colleagues are people who mirror the values and attitudes I am striving to emulate.

Every now and then, I am suddenly aware of the changes my personality has undergone. This happened once at a high school reunion, where an old classmate approached me and said enthusiastically, "What's the dirt on people? Let's be nasty and talk about who's fat and who's seeing whom. It's so much fun that way." My noncommittal reply had thrown her, especially because I used to be known as the class's Rona Barrett. No one had been more surprised than I, though, because for years I had used gossiping as a way to bolster my low self-esteem. Now I know of healthier ways to feel good about myself.

One of the things the program promises will happen as a result of finding a Higher Power, getting honest, and helping other people is that feelings of uselessness and self-pity will slip away. Although I didn't think I would ever be free of either attitude, that promise has come true for me. Whenever I am feeling low and mired down in selfish concerns, I force myself to call someone who is struggling with the food. It isn't long before I have forgotten about myself, and I always feel ebullient when I hang up the phone. By turning my painful years of bulimia into lessons for other people, I have found a calling that is truly satisfying.

One of the questions I am frequently asked—whether I am addressing a school audience or standing at a cocktail party—is whether or not I intend to continue attending meetings for compulsive overeaters now that I am doing so well. I always reply that I plan to, God willing. I know through agonizing experience that my food addiction is out there waiting for me to get cocky and complacent again, and that it will gobble me up if I give it half a chance to come back into my life. I also know that my former "stinking thinking" could return if I am not careful, regardless of whether or not I get back into the food. By attending meetings I continue to work on the positive character traits I am nurturing daily.

I am not perfect, but I have come a long way from the pathetic, scared, and angry young woman who went to her first meeting in 1984. Just as I have grown, changed, stumbled, and learned patience in the last four years, I know that the future holds nothing but more transformations and more joy for me. I am grateful that I have been given the opportunity to recover, and I pray that I will continue to show up for life, one day at a time, and not run away from it ever again.

BULIMIA SELF-TEST

1. Do you spend a lot of time worrying about your weight and wishing you were thinner?
2. Does your weight frequently fluctuate by anywhere from five to fifty or more pounds?
3. Have you ever tried to make yourself vomit after eating too much?
4. Have you ever used diuretics or laxatives as a weight-control method?
5. Have you purchased a number of diet books, tried different weight loss fads, or joined and dropped out of several weight loss organizations because you couldn't stop eating compulsively for a significant period of time?
6. Have you ever used syrup of ipecac as a vomiting aid?
7. Have you ever shoplifted food, laxatives, diuretics, diet

pills, or syrup of ipecac because you didn't want anyone to suspect that you were getting them for yourself?

8. Do you have frequent feelings of remorse and guilt after eating what might be called a "forbidden" food?

9. Do you spend a lot of time reading recipe books, shopping for food, and cooking?

10. Have you avoided social gatherings because of your obsession with your size, the fit of your clothes, or because you have just binged and don't want anyone to see you?

11. Do you find yourself using food as a way to escape from confronting uncomfortable situations and feelings?

12. Are you convinced that you are too heavy, despite comments from others that you are not, and do you believe that losing weight will solve all your problems?

13. Do you exercise compulsively to make up for extra calories?

14. Have you ever had to buy food to cover up for a binge, or lied about your eating?

15. Do you have eating habits that others consider strange, like picking the raisins out of raisin bread, or only eating certain amounts of foods at certain times?

16. Do you eat in secrecy and hoard food because you don't want anyone to see the amounts you consume, and then eat either lightly or normally in front of others?

17. Are you addicted to the scale and do you measure your feelings of self-worth by what your weight is?

18. Have you found yourself neglecting hobbies and other formerly pleasurable activities because binging occupies your time and thoughts?

If you answered "yes" to any four of the above questions, then you are abnormally preoccupied with your weight and either you are a candidate for developing bulimia, or you have it already.

Denial is one of the main hallmarks of a bulimic. The disease is progressive, however, and does not often go away through determination or willpower. Face your problem honestly and seek help early before the addiction is an ingrained part of your life and your coping mechanisms, because the longer you wait, the more difficult it will be to recover.

TEST FOR FAMILY AND FRIENDS
OF A SUSPECTED BULIMIC

1. Does this person spend a lot of time talking and worrying about his/her weight, and seem preoccupied with having a flat stomach?
2. Does his/her weight fluctuate frequently by anywhere from five to fifty or more pounds?
3. Does he/she spend a lot of time in the bathroom with the water running, especially after eating a meal?
4. Does he/she go on eating binges, then follow them with compulsive exercising, fasting, or known laxative/diuretic and syrup of ipecac use, or vomiting?
5. Has he/she ever been caught for shoplifting, especially with food or other diet aids?
6. Does he/she have unexplained health problems like tooth erosion, heartbeat irregularities, swollen salivary glands, persistent hoarseness, broken blood vessels around eyes and cheeks, distended stomach, amenorrhea, potassium deficiencies, or an electrolyte imbalance?
7. Does he/she spend a lot of time alone (baby-sitting, driving around, living alone, etc.) during which you suspect he/she is eating secretly?
8. Does he/she wear a lot of baggy clothing to hide a distended stomach?
9. Does he/she express remorse after eating what might be called a "forbidden" food, or after eating a normal-sized meal?
10. Does he/she display an abnormal interest in eating disorders, yet deny ever having suffered from one?
11. Does he/she have few or no close friends and poor social interaction skills?
12. Does he/she have strange eating habits, such as picking raisins out of raisin bread or eating parts of certain foods at certain times?
13. Has he/she neglected friends and hobbies for no good reason?
14. Does he/she eat abnormally large meals for a slim figure and do little or no exercise?

Answering "yes" to any three or more questions above indicates that the person in question has bulimic tendencies or is suffering from it already. Before confronting someone in a nonjudgmental way, it is important to learn as much as possible about bulimia and to have phone numbers of helpful organizations ready to share with the person if he/she is amenable to seeking help. Offering to attend a free self-help group with the person, such as Overeaters Anonymous, could also be beneficial in removing some of the fear and shame about seeking assistance.

Don't allow the bulimic to manipulate you with denial, tears, or promises to stop by him/herself. Bulimia can cause irreversible medical problems and, in some cases, death. To avoid the problem or hope it will disappear by itself is to enable the disease to progress and perhaps to be a party to someone else's death.

EATING DISORDER ORGANIZATIONS

There are as many different ways to recover from bulimia as there are different kinds of people. What worked for me may not work well for you, so here is a list of organizations and resources to help you make your choice. It is always helpful to enclose a self-addressed stamped envelope when requesting information.

American Anorexia/Bulimia Association, Inc. (ABBA)
418 East 76th Street
New York, NY   10021
(212)734-1114

Anorexia Bulimia Care, Inc. (ABC)
P.O. Box 213
Lincoln Center, MA   01773
(617)259-9767

Anorexia Nervosa & Related Disorders, Inc. (ANRED)
P.O. Box 5102
Eugene, OR   97405
(503)686-7372 (for information and referrals)
(503)344-1144 (to request publications list)

Anorexics Bulimics Anonymous
P.O. Box 47573
Phoenix, AZ   85068

Center for the Study of Anorexia and Bulimia
1 West 91st Street
New York, NY 10024
(212)595-3449

Foundation for Education about Eating Disorders
P.O. Box 799
Middletown, MD   21769

International Association for Eating Disorder
Professionals (IAEDP)
34213 Coast Highway, Suite E
Dana Point, CA   92629
(714)248-1150

National Anorexic Aid Society, Inc. (NAAS)
1925 East Dublin Granville Rd.
Columbus, OH   43229-3517
(614)848-9900

National Association of Anorexia Nervosa and
Associated Disorders (ANAD)
P.O. Box 7
Highland Park, IL   60035
(708)831-3438

Overeaters Anonymous
World Service Office
4025 Spencer Street, Suite 203
Torrance, CA   90503
(213)542-8363

Rational Recovery Service
Box 800
Lotus, CA   95651
(916)621-4374
(916)621-2667

Photocopy this order form!

My Name is Caroline $12.95 5 or more copies $10.50 each		
Feeding the Soul $8.00 5 or more copies $6.95 each		
BULIMIA: A Guide to Recovery $11.95 5 or more copies $9.95 each		
Eating Disorders Bookshelf Catalogue *(Do not add shipping below.)*	**FREE**	
Subtotal - - - - - - - - - - - - - - - -		
Tax (7% Calif. residents only)		
Shipping - - - - - - - - - - - - - - - - 1 item: $1.95 / 2-4 $.95 each / 5+ $.75 each		
TOTAL * * * * * * * * * * *		

Unconditional guarantee!

NAME _____

ADDRESS _____

CITY/ST/ZIP _____

PHONE _____

Phone orders to: (619)434-7533 -or-
Enclose payment (or institutional PO#) to:

**Gürze Books
P.O. Box 2238
Carlsbad, CA 92018**